Machu Picchu

Machu Picchu   Unveiling the Mystery of the Incas

Edited by Richard L. Burger and Lucy C. Salazar

Yale University Press   New Haven & London

Set in Electra type by The Composing Room of Michigan, Inc.

Printed in Italy by Grafiche SiZ

The Library of Congress has cataloged the hardcover edition as follows:

Machu Picchu : unveiling the mystery of the Incas / edited by Richard L. Burger and Lucy C. Salazar.

p.   cm.

Includes bibliographical references and index.

ISBN 0-300-09763-8 (cloth : alk. paper)

1. Machu Picchu Site (Peru)   2. Santuario Histâorico de Machu Picchu (Peru).   3. Incas—Antiquities.   4. Yale Peruvian Expedition (1911)   5. Peruvian Expeditions (1912–1915)   6. Bingham, Hiram, 1875–1956—Archaeological collections.   7. Peabody Museum of Natural History—Archaeological collections.   8. Peru—Antiquities.   I. Burger, Richard L.   II. Salazar, Lucy C.

F3429.1.M3M33   2004

985′.37—dc22

2003017366

ISBN 978-0-300-13645-6 (pbk. : alk. paper)

A catalogue record for this book is available from the British Library.

The paper in this book meets the guidelines for permanence and durability of the Committee on Production Guidelines for Book Longevity of the Council on Library Resources.

10 9 8 7 6 5 4 3 2 1

Contents

Acknowledgments

We are deeply grateful to the many people who have made possible the creation of the exhibit Machu Picchu: Unveiling the Mystery of the Incas and this catalogue, which has been designed to complement it. Primary funding for the catalogue comes from the National Endowment for the Humanities and the Provostial Research Fund of Yale University. Essential funding for the exhibit was provided by the National Science Foundation, Connecticut Council for the Humanities, National Endowment for the Humanities, the Heritage Mark Foundation, Yale University, the Bingham Foundation, Annie Hurlbutt and the Peruvian Connection, members of the Peabody Museum's O. C. Marsh Fellows, Susan Foote, and other individuals in New Haven and beyond.

The enthusiastic support of our colleagues at other museums has been essential in assembling the remarkable set of Inca and colonial objects that supplement the Bingham collection. We would like to thank Andrés Alvarez-Calderón at the Museo Arqueológico Rafael Larco Herrera, Gabriela Schwoerbel, Benjamin Guerrero, and Hilda Vidal at the Museo Nacional de Antropología, Arqueología e Historia del Peru, Marie Fauvet at the Musée de l'Homme, Craig Morris and Sumru Arankali at the American Museum of Natural History, Julie Jones at The Metropolitan Museum of Art, Diana Fane and Nancy Rossoff at the Brooklyn Museum of Art, Jock Reynolds and Susan Matheson at the Yale Art Gallery, Jeffrey Quilter at Dumbarton Oaks, Richard Townsend at the Chicago Art Institute, Jonathan Haas at the Field Museum of Natural History, Patrick Kirch, Madeline Fang, and Leslie Freundt at the Hearst Museum of Anthropology, and Michael Whittington at the Mint Museum. We also thank Mike Hanke and Ann Marshall of Design Division Inc., for helping us to envision and produce the exhibition.

The photographs of the pieces from the Yale Peabody Museum, which constitute over 80 percent of the catalogue objects, were taken by Yale Peabody Museum staff photographer William Sacco. Vladimir Gil, Ben Diebold, George Lau, Antonio Murro, and Neil Norman provided assistance in our lab. The conservation and restoration of the objects in the Bingham collection proved to be a major undertaking in its own right and involved many individuals over several years. We would like to acknowledge the contributions of David Diestra, Ellen Howe, Linda Merck, Sarah Nunberg, Alison Salazar, and Catherine Sease. Sharon J.

M. Rodriguez and Sandy Ruggiero assisted in the preparation of the catalogue manuscript. At the Yale Peabody we received broad support from the museum staff, including Michael Anderson, Lucas Barton, Richard Boardman, Walter Brenckle, Melanie Brigockas, Maureen DaRos, Maishe Dickman, Larry Gall, David Heiser, Eric Hoag, Tony Kobylanski, Marge Kuhlman, Barbara Narendra, Sally Pallatto, Jeannie Pappas, Jane Pickering, Ray Pupedis, Yahya Abdul Shakur, Rosemary Volpe, Ken Yellis, Kim Zolvik, and Kristof Zykowski. Eliza Cleveland, Joe Jolly, Patty Pedersen, and Britt Wheeler helped make it possible to raise the necessary funding.

Others at Yale whose aid we would like to acknowledge are Michael Coc, Michael Donoghue, Frank Hole, Laura Leonhart, Linda Lorimer, Bill Massa, Alison Richard, Dorothy Robinson, Cesar Rodriguez, and Sally Tremaine.

Among the many of our friends and colleagues who provided intellectual stimulation and support during this endeavor, we thank Fernando Astete, Alfredo Bracamonte, Enrique Gonzales Carré, Victor Chang, Karen Mohr Chavez, Sergio Chavez, Brendan Cohen, David Noble Cook, John Alfred Davis, David Dearborn, Marilyn Fox, Heather Lechtman, Kristof Makowski, Ramiro Matos, Enrique Mayer, George Miller, Daniel Morales, Anita Mujica, Susan Niles, Maria Luisa Rizo Patrón, Brent Porter, Jeffrey Quilter, Charles Remington, Jim Richardson, Carolina Salquero, Daniel Sandweiss, Kathy Schreiber, Elliot Schwartz, Chip Stanish, Ann Underhill, Gary Urton, Berta Vargas, John Verano, Ruth and Ken Wright. Finally, we thank Harry Haskell and Nancy Moore at Yale University Press for their patience, diligence, and unflagging interest in this project.

Essays

I   Introduction

Richard L. Burger and Lucy C. Salazar

Machu Picchu is one of the best known archaeological sites in the world. Its distinctive image pervades the public imagination, thanks to its depiction in everything from television documentaries to car commercials. In terms of general recognition, it has eclipsed the much larger and historically more important Inca capital of Cuzco. No other archaeological site in the Americas has captured the public imagination so effectively, and consequently, it is difficult to imagine that only a century ago, Machu Picchu was unknown to all but a tiny group of farmers and traders living in the isolated lower Urubamba region of southern Peru. By 1875, rumors of the Inca ruins had reached Charles Wiener, the Austrian explorer. In 1902 Augustín Lizarraga, a local muleteer, visited the site and engraved his name on one of the temples. Nonetheless, until 1911, Machu Picchu had escaped the attention of the world of scholars and travelers, much as it had the Spanish chroniclers of the sixteenth and seventeenth centuries. It remained hidden by dense vegetation, familiar in detail only to the farmers who grew corn, sweet potatoes, yucca, and other subsistence crops on the grounds of the ancient site and its terraces.

The renown that Machu Picchu has achieved following its "scientific discovery" on July 24, 1911, by Hiram Bingham III and the subsequent visits by millions of travelers have not made it the best-understood archaeological site in the Americas or even in the Central Andes. On the contrary, Machu Picchu's construction and abandonment have remained shrouded in mystery, the subject of numerous and often contradictory theories. Fortunately, over the past two decades, significant progress has been made to achieve a better understanding of Machu Picchu and its context within *Tahuantinsuyu*, the Inca Empire.

The present volume offers a broad vision of this emerging understanding, along with a catalogue of representative objects recovered by the 1912 Yale Peruvian Expedition from Machu Picchu, supplemented by some of the finest examples of Inca artistic production. This book is being published in conjunction with the opening of an exhibition, *Machu Picchu: Unveiling the Mystery of the Incas*, at Yale University's Peabody Museum of Natural History. The exhibit will subsequently travel to other museums in the United States before returning to the Yale Peabody Museum.

The origins of the exhibition, *Machu Picchu: Unveiling the Mystery of the Incas*, and of this book, go back to the early 1980s. As specialists in Andean archaeology, trained in the United States and Peru, respectively, we thought it logical to begin working on Hiram Bingham's archaeological collections when we joined the Yale University community in 1981. These collections had been cared for at the Yale Peabody Museum, but only rarely studied or exhibited since their arrival in New Haven some seven decades before. Perhaps Bingham's sudden departure from archaeology — first to serve in World War I as a trainer of fighter pilots, and subsequently to pursue a political career (lieutenant governor and governor of Connecticut, U.S. senator) — discouraged further research on his archaeological collections.

In the intervening decades, exciting discoveries in Peru pushed back the origins of Andean civilization to over three millennia before the Inca, and provided evidence of a cultural richness and technological sophistication not even hinted at in the historical records left by the colonial Spaniards. As a consequence, for much of the twentieth century, Inca archaeology remained underdeveloped and Machu Picchu was largely ignored by investigators. Even after interest in the Incas began to increase in the archaeological community in the 1970s, Machu Picchu was often treated as an anomaly of more interest to tourists than to serious scholars. The numerous unlikely theories proposed by Bingham, as well as some new ones added by guides and mystics, continue to be disseminated. In contrast to these proposals, we concluded in 1982 that the site could be best understood as an example of an Inca royal estate that would have been used by members of the Inca court as a country palace, a place to which they could go in order to escape from the capital for rest, relaxation, and other elite activities.

Our research on the collections excavated by the Yale Peruvian Expedition in 1912 reinforced our belief that Machu Picchu had been an Inca royal estate, comparable to better-known sites such as Pisac and Ollantaytambo. In order to fill out this picture, we involved Yale undergraduate and graduate students in laboratory analysis and engaged colleagues, such as geologist Robert Gordon, from other departments at Yale to help us. We also brought specialists from other universities to carry out research on poorly understood portions of the collections, such as the animal and human bone re-

mains. At the same time, Peruvian colleagues, such as Alfredo Valencia and Arminda Jibaja, intensified fieldwork at Machu Picchu as part of larger projects to conserve and restore the site. Historical research on Inca Cuzco was also proceeding apace, with attention turning to land records and other legal documents that had been previously ignored. In 1987, one of the preeminent scholars of Inca history and archaeology, John Howland Rowe, published his analysis of colonial documents in Cuzco archives demonstrating that the site of Machu Picchu had been part of a royal estate established by Inca emperor Pachacuti following his conquest of the lower Urubamba in the mid-fifteenth century AD.

The combination of the new historical, laboratory, and field research on Machu Picchu created a firm foundation upon which a Machu Picchu exhibition could be based. By producing such an exhibition, it is our goal to provide a clear picture of Machu Picchu and the people who lived there, as well as giving the public an opportunity to see the materials excavated at this famous site. It is our hope that this book and the exhibition it complements will serve to raise public awareness of the remarkable political, cultural, and scientific accomplishments of the Inca before the arrival of Europeans to the South American continent. It should also provide an instructive case study of the way in which contemporary scientific and historical scholarship allows archaeologists to develop a compelling understanding of the forgotten past.

The chapters that follow seek to provide a new vision of Machu Picchu. The contributions by the editors offer syntheses of the current interpretations of Machu Picchu that have emerged from the studies of the Bingham collections over the past two decades. Susan Niles draws upon her own original fieldwork in the Urubamba drainage, providing the book with an overview of the phenomenon of Inca royal estates in order to place Machu Picchu in broader cultural context. University of Cuzco archaeologist Alfredo Valencia Zegarra, the individual who has done the most fieldwork at Machu Picchu since Bingham's expeditions, has contributed a summary of his recent investigations at the site. This book would not be complete without a consideration of the role that Machu Picchu has come to play in contemporary Peruvian culture and society, and anthropologist Jorge Flores Ochoa, director of the Museo Inka at the University of Cuzco, has provided us with a fascinating account of the multiple meanings and uses of this unique site in contemporary Peruvian politics, the world of nonprofit organizations, and the global tourist industry.

To set the scene for these chapters and the ensuing catalogue, we present Bingham's first detailed magazine account of his find, entitled "The Discovery of Machu Picchu." The article originally appeared in *Harper's Monthly* magazine in 1913. We have not modified Bingham's narrative, but we have taken the liberty of adding historic photographs to those in the original article. Although some of Bingham's assumptions have been superseded by subsequent research (for example, the "megalithic" walls at Sacsahuaman are now known to be coeval with, rather than antecedent to, the Inca occupation of the site), his account of encountering Machu Picchu remains a vivid retelling of the events on this unique and historic day. Readers should note Bingham's frankness about the role played by Peruvian residents in bringing him to Machu Picchu, as well as his acknowledgment that he was not the first outsider to hear of or visit Machu Picchu.

Readers of this book should be aware that the term *Inca* has multiple meanings, reflected in its use in this catalogue. Inca is the term which typically applies to the small ethnic group centered in the valley of Cuzco, often broadened to apply to the entire empire that this group built and governed, although Tahuantinsuyu was the native name for this polity. The term *Inca* is likewise applied to the cultural patterns that characterized this group and is sometimes used, somewhat imprecisely, to refer to general characteristics of the material culture of this period in the Central Andes. Finally, the king or primary ruler of Tahuantinsuyu, technically known as the Sapa Inca (or Unique Inca), also has been called the Inca. Specialists have become accustomed to this profusion of related, but distinct, uses of the word *Inca*, but they can be confusing to the uninitiated. Another potential source of confusion is that the Urubamba River and the Vilcanota River refer to the same river that wends its way around Machu Picchu.

Between July and November of 1912, the Yale Peruvian Expedition under the direction of Yale history professor Hiram Bingham III excavated in the central architectural core of Machu Picchu as well as in the cave tombs on the eastern slopes. These investigations yielded a varied collection of ceramic, stone, and metal objects utilized by the site's inhabitants. The archaeological materials recovered reflect the varied activities and social identities of the people at Machu Picchu. Owing to the multiethnic character of Machu Picchu's servants and artisans, drawn from throughout the vast empire, there is more variability among the artifacts recovered than in a typical Inca site. These objects from Machu Picchu form the core of the exhibition and the catalogue section of this book.

As a country palace, Machu Picchu was a center of elite activity, including numerous religious rituals, and many of the portable items the royalty used were of sufficient value to be removed from the site before it was abandoned. In order to show the range of items that would have been used by the Inca elite, we have supplemented the objects excavated at Machu Picchu with exceptional Inca specimens purchased by Bingham in Cuzco during his visits, as well as pieces from museums in France and the United States. When combined with the objects excavated at Machu Picchu, the selection in the catalogue provides a broad sense of Inca artistic and technical accomplishments. Finally, the exhibition includes an epilogue component that addresses the question of Machu Picchu's abandonment and the emergence of a distinctive Peruvian culture that melds elements of its Inca and European antecedents. The colonial and more recent objects in the catalogue section of this book illustrate the complex and fascinating processes of cultural transformation.

This book and the exhibit it accompanies, as well as the three historic Yale Peruvian expeditions that inspired them, are the result of close and prolonged collaboration between the citizens of Peru and the United States. The location of Machu Picchu was first signaled to Bingham by Peruvian colleagues in Cuzco, and he was later guided to the site by local Peruvian farmers. Bingham's explorations would not have been possible were it not for the support provided by the Peruvian government, particularly its president, Augusto Bernadino Leguía, and the success of the 1912 excavations depended both on the local knowledge of Peruvian participants such as Toribio Richarte and Anacleto Alvarez, as well as the expertise of American staff such as George Eaton and Ellwood Erdis. In the subsequent decades, Peruvian scholars such as Manuel Chavez Ballon and Alfredo Valencia Zegarra have worked jointly with American scholars such as John Rowe to further our understanding of Machu Picchu and the archaeology of Cuzco, and their contributions are reflected throughout this book. The objects from Machu Picchu that appear in this catalogue and in the exhibit were conserved and restored by both Peruvian and American conservators. As the editors of this book and the curators of this exhibit, we view this historic collaboration between Peru and the United States as mutually beneficial and suggest that these associations continue in order to enrich both nations.

2.1 Plowing in the Urubamba Valley. A halt for breakfast.

II The Discovery of Machu Picchu

Hiram Bingham III

One of the chief problems that faced the Yale Peruvian Expedition of 1911 was the question as to whether the young Inca Manco, fleeing from Pizarro's armies and establishing himself in the wilds of Vilcabamba, had left any traces in the shape of ruined palaces and temples. So we went about asking every one if they knew of any such.

It was known to a few people in Cuzco, chiefly residents of the province of Convencion, that there were ruins, still undescribed, in the valley of the Urubamba (Figure 2.1). One friend told us that a muleteer had told him of some ruins near the bridge of San Miguel. Knowing the propensity of his countrymen to exaggerate, he placed little confidence in the report, and had passed by the place a score of times without taking the trouble to look into the matter. Another friend, who owned a sugar plantation on the river Vilcabamba, said he also had heard vague rumors of ruins. He was quite sure there were some near Pucyura, although he had been there and had never seen any. At length a talkative old peddler said there were ruins "finer than Choqque-

quirau" down the valley somewhere. But as he had never been to Choqquequirau, and no one placed any confidence in his word anyhow, we could only hope there was some cause for his enthusiasm. Finally, there was the story in Wiener's picturesque but unreliable *Pérou et Bolivie* that when he was in Ollantaytambo in 1875, or thereabouts, he was told there were interesting ruins down the Urubamba Valley at "Huaina-Picchu, or Matcho Picchu" (sic). Wiener decided to go down the valley and look for them, but, owing to one reason or another, he failed to find them. Should we be any more successful?

We left Cuzco about the middle of July. The second day out brought us to the romantic valley of Ollantaytambo (Figure 2.2). Squier described it in glowing terms years ago, and it has lost none of its charm. The wonderful megaliths of the ancient fortress, the curious gabled buildings perched here and there on almost inaccessible crags, the magnificent *andenes* (terraces), where abundant crops are still harvested, will stand for ages to come as monuments to the energy and skill of a bygone race (Figure 2.3). It is now quite generally believed that the smaller buildings, crowded with niches, and made of small stones laid in clay and covered with a kind of

Note: This article originally appeared in *Harper's Monthly* magazine, vol. 127, 1913, pp. 709–19.

2.2 View across the wheat fields to the mountains north of Yucay.

stucco, were the work of the Incas and their subjects. On the other hand, the gigantic rocks so carefully fitted together to form the defenses of the fortress itself probably antedated the Incas, and, like the cyclopean walls of the Sacsahuaman fortress near Cuzco, were put in position by a pre-Inca or megalithic folk who may have built Tiahuanaco in Bolivia.

At all events, both Cuzco and Ollantaytambo have the advantage of being the sites of a very ancient civilization, now shrouded in romance and mystery. The climate and altitude (11,000 feet) of Cuzco deprive it of lovely surroundings, but here at Tambo, as the natives call it, there is everything to please the eye, from lightly cultivated green fields, flower-gardens, and brooks shaded by willows and poplars, to magnificent precipices, crowned by glaciers and snowcapped peaks. Surely this deserves to be a place of pilgrimage.

After a day or two of rest and hard scrambles over the cliffs to the various groups of ruins, we went down the Urubamba Valley to the northwest. A league from the fortress the road forks. The right branch ascends a steep valley and crosses a snow-covered pass near the little-known and relatively unimportant ruins of Havaspampa and Panticalla. Two leagues beyond the fork, the Urubamba River has cut its way through precipitous cliffs. This is the natural gateway to the ancient province of Vilcabamba. For centuries it was virtually closed by the combined efforts of Nature and man. The dangerous rapids of the river were impassable, but the precipices on the north side might with considerable effort be scaled. In fact, the old road into the province apparently lay over their dizzy heights. Accordingly man had built at the foot of the precipices a small but powerful fortress, Salapunco, fashioned after Sacsahuaman, but with only five salients and re-entrant angles. The cliff itself was strengthened defensively by walls, skillfully built on narrow ledges.

Salapunco has long been unoccupied. My first impression was that it was placed here to defend the Ollantaytambo Valley from enemies coming up from the Amazon valleys. Later I came to the conclusion that it was intended to defend against enemies coming down the valley from Ollantaytambo. As a monolithic work of this kind could not in the nature of things have been built by the Inca Manco when fleeing from the Spaniards, and as its whole style and character seem to place it alongside the well-known monolithic structures of the region about Cuzco and Ollantaytambo, it seemed all the more extraordinary that it should have been placed as a defense against that very region. Could it be that it was built by the megalithic folk in order to defend a possible retreat in Vilcabamba? Hitherto no one had found or reported any megalithic remains farther down the valley than this spot. In fact, Squier, whose *Peru* has for a generation been the standard work on Inca architecture, does not appear to have heard even of Salapunco, and Markham makes no mention of it. It never occurred to us that in hunting for the remains of such palaces as Manco Inca had the strength

and time to build we were about to find remains of a far more remote past, ruins that would explain why the fortress of Salapunco was placed to defend Vilcabamba against the south, and not the south against Vilcabamba and the savages of the Amazon jungles.

Passing Salapunco, we skirted the precipices and entered a most interesting region, where we were continually charmed by the extent of the ancient terraces, the length of the great *andenes*, the grandeur of the snow-clad mountains, and the beauty of the deep, narrow valleys.

The next day we continued down the valley for another twenty miles. And such a valley! While neither so grand as the Apurimac, near Choqquequirau, nor so exquisite as the more highly cultivated valleys of the Alps, the grand canon, of the Urubamba from Torontoy to Collpani, a distance of about thirty miles, has few equals

2.3 Ollantaytambo. Panoramic view showing the ancient fortress and terraces.

in the world. It lacks the rugged, massive severity of the Canadian Rockies and the romantic associations of the Rhine, but I know of no place that can compare with it in the variety and extent of its charm. Not only has it snow-capped peaks, gigantic precipices of solid granite rising abruptly thousands of feet from its roaring stream, and the usual great beauty of a deep canon winding through mountains of almost incredible height, but there is added to this the mystery of the dense tropical jungle and the romance of the ever-present remains of a bygone race.

It would make a dull story, full of repetition and superlatives, were I to try to describe the countless terraces, the towering cliffs, the constantly changing panorama, with the jungle in the foreground and glaciers in the lofty background. Even the so-called road got

2.4 Plants growing on the side of a cliff at San Miguel.

a bit monotonous, although it ran recklessly up and down rock stairways, sometimes cut out of the side of the precipice, at others running on frail bridges propped on brackets against the granite cliffs overhanging the swirling rapids (Figure 2.4). We made slow progress, but we lived in wonderland.

With what exquisite pains did the Incas, or their predecessors, rescue narrow strips of arable land from the river! Here the prehistoric people built a retaining wall of great stones along the very edge of the rapids. There they piled terrace on *andene* until stopped by a solid wall of rock. On this sightly bend in the river, where there is a particularly fine view up and down the valley, they placed a temple flanked by a great stone stairway. On that apparently insurmountable cliff they built unscalable walls, so that it should be actually, as well as seemingly, impregnable. They planted the lower levels with bananas and coca, and also yucca, that strange little tree whose roots make such a succulent vegetable. On the more lofty terraces they grew maize and potatoes.

In the afternoon we passed a hut called La Maquina, where travelers frequently stop for the night (Figure 2.5). There is some fodder here, but the density of the tropical forest, the steepness of the mountains, and the scarcity of anything like level land make living very precarious. We arrived at Mandor Pampa, another grass-thatched hut, about five o'clock. The scenery and the road were more interesting than anything we had seen so far, or were likely to see again. Our camp was pitched in a secluded spot on the edge of the river (Figure 2.6). Carrasco, the sergeant sent with me from Cuzco, talked with a muleteer who lives near by, a fellow named Melchor Arteaga, who leases the land where we were camping. He said there were ruins in the vicinity, and some excellent ones at a place called Machu Picchu on top of the precipice near by, and that there were also ruins at Huayna Picchu, still more inaccessible, on top of a peak not far distant from our camp.

The next day, although it was drizzling, the promise of a sol (fifty cents gold) to be paid to him on our return from the ruins, encouraged Arteaga to guide me up to Machu Picchu. I left camp at about ten o'clock, and went from his house some distance up-stream. The valley is very narrow, with almost sheer precipices of solid

2.5 Indians of the Chamana River.

granite on each side. On the road we passed a snake that had recently been killed. Arteaga was unable to give any other name for it than "*vivora*," which means venomous, in distinction from "*culebra*," or harmless snake.

Our naturalist spent the day in the bottom of the valley, collecting insects; the surgeon busied himself in and about camp and I was accompanied on this excursion only by Carrasco and the guide, Arteaga. At ten forty-five, after having left the road and plunged down through the jungle to the river-bank, we came to a primitive bridge, made of four logs bound together with vines, and stretching across the stream a few inches above the roaring rapids (Figure 2.7). On the other side we had a fearfully hard climb for an hour and twenty minutes. A good part of the distance I went on all-fours. The path was in many places a primitive stairway, or

2.6 Camp at Mandor Pampa.

2.7 Our guide Arteaga crossing the bridge over the Urubamba River.

crude stepladder, at first through a jungle, and later up a very steep, grass-covered slope. The heat was excessive, but the view was magnificent after we got above the jungle. Shortly after noon we reached a hut where several good-natured Indians welcomed us and gave us gourds full of cool, delicious water, and a few cooked sweet-potatoes. All that we could see was a couple of small grass huts and a few terraces, faced with stone walls. The pleasant Indian family had chosen this eagle's nest for a home. They told us there were better ruins a little farther along.

One can never tell, in this country, whether such a report is worthy of credence. "He may have been lying" is a good foot-note to affix to all hearsay evidence. Accordingly we were not unduly excited. Nor was I in a great hurry to move. The water was cool, the wooden bench, covered with a woolen poncho, seemed most comfortable, and the view was marvelous. On both sides tremendous precipices fell away to the white rapids of the Urubamba River below. In front was the solitary peak of Huayna Picchu, seemingly inaccessible on all sides. Behind us were rocky heights and impassable

cliffs. Down the face of one precipice the Indians had made a perilous path, which was their only means of egress in the wet season, when the bridge over which we had come would be washed away. Of the other precipice we had already had a taste. We were not surprised to hear the Indians say they only went away from home about once a month.

Leaving the huts, we climbed still farther up the ridge. Around a slight promontory the character of the faced *andenes* began to improve, and suddenly we found ourselves in the midst of a jungle-covered maze of small and large walls, the ruins of buildings made of blocks of white granite, most carefully cut and beautifully fitted together without cement. Surprise followed surprise until there came the realization that we were in the midst of as wonderful ruins as any ever found in Peru (Figure 2.8). It seemed almost incredible that this city, only five days' journey from Cuzco, should have remained so long undescribed and comparatively unknown. Yet so far as I have been able to discover, there is no reference in the Spanish chronicles to Machu Picchu. It is possible that not even the conquistadors ever

YALE PERU EXP. 1911

saw this wonderful place. From some rude scrawls on the stones of a temple we learned that it was visited in 1902 by one Lizarraga, a local muleteer. It must have been known long before that, because, as we said above, Wiener, who was in Ollantaytambo in the 70's, speaks of having heard of ruins at a place named "Matcho Picchu," which he did not find.

The Indians living here say that they have been here four years. They have planted corn and vegetables among the ruins and on some of the terraces. One or two families live in ancient buildings on which they have built roofs. There are also three huts of recent construction. The climate seems to be excellent. We noticed growing sweet and white potatoes, maize, sugar-

2.9 Window of the semicircular building.

cane, beans, peppers, tomatoes, and a kind of goose-berry.

Travelers like the great Castelnau, the flowery Wiener, and the picturesque Marcou, who have gone north from Cuzco to the Urubamba River and beyond, had to avoid this region, where they would have found most of interest. The Urubamba is not navigable, even for canoes, at this point, and is flanked by such steep walls that travel along its banks was impossible until a few years ago. Even intrepid explorers like Castelnau were obliged to make a long detour and to follow a trail that led over snowy passes into the parallel valleys of the Occobamba and the Yanatili. Thus it happened that the Urubamba Valley from Ollantaytambo to the sugar

plantation of Huadquiña offered us a virgin field, and by the same token it was in this very region that the Incas and their predecessors found it easy to live in safety. Not only did they find here every variety of climate, valleys so deep as to produce the precious coca, yucca, and plantain of the tropics, and slopes high enough to be suitable for maize and potatoes, with nights cold enough to freeze the latter in the approved aboriginal fashion, but also a practically impregnable place of refuge.

About twenty years ago the Peruvian government, recognizing the needs of the enterprising planters who were opening up the lower valley of the Urubamba, decided to construct a mule trail along the banks to the river. The road was expensive, but it has enabled the much-desired coca and *aguardiente* to be shipped far more quickly and cheaply than from the Santa Ana Valley to Cuzco, and it avoids the necessity of climbing over the dangerous snowy passes so vividly described by Marcou and others. This new road enabled us to discover that the Incas — and their predecessors — had left here, in the beautiful fastnesses of Vilcabamba, stone witnesses of their ancient civilization more interesting and extensive than any found since the days of the conquistadors. It is difficult to describe Machu Picchu. The ruins are located on a ridge which ends in a magnificent peak, on top of which are said to be the ruins of Huayna Picchu. There are precipices on both sides, and a large number of terraces, evidently intended for agricultural purposes. There are also *azequias* (stone-lined water-courses), although it is at present somewhat difficult to see whence the water was brought. There are three small springs here, but the Indians do not know of any running water. As it must have taken a considerable water supply to furnish water to the inhabitants of such a large place as Machu Picchu, it may be that an irrigating ditch was carried back into the mountains for many miles to some point from which an unfailing supply of water could be secured.

There is a very nicely made bathhouse, a fountain with some niches, and an adjoining retiring-room with a seat. The water was conducted into the bathhouse through a stone channel, over a nicely cut stone block. On top of a gigantic granite boulder near the bathhouse is a semicircular building, made of nearly rectangular

2.10 The three-sided building later called the Principal or Main Temple.

blocks, and containing nicely finished niches on the inside (Figure 2.9). Underneath the boulder is a cave lined with carefully worked stone and containing very large niches, the best and tallest that I have ever seen. There are many stairways made of blocks of granite. One stairway is divided so as to permit the insertion of a catch-basin for water. This stairway leads to a point farther up the ridge, where there is a place which I have called the Sacred Plaza.

On the south side of this plaza there are terraces lined with large blocks, after the fashion of Sacsahuaman, and also a kind of bastion, semicircular, with carefully cut, nearly rectangular stones, somewhat like those in the well-known semicircular Temple of the Sun, now the Dominican Monastery, at Cuzco. On the east side of the Sacred Plaza are the walls of a rectangular building, twenty-nine feet long by thirty-seven wide, containing niches and projecting cylinders resembling in many ways the buildings at Choqquequirau. It has two doors on the side toward the plaza but no windows.

On the west side is a remarkable structure, truly megalithic, entirely open on the side facing the Plaza, and entirely closed on the other three sides (Figure 2.10). The interior measurements of this building are 25.9 x 91 feet. As in the case of all the other buildings, its roof is missing. It is made of blocks of white granite, arranged in tiers. The stones in the lower tier are very much larger than those in any of the others. One block in the lower tier measures 9.6 feet in length; another, 10.2 feet, a third, 13.2 feet. As will be seen from the photographs they are considerably higher than a man and about 2.8 feet thick. The upper tiers are of nearly rectangular blocks, very much smaller, but cut with indescribable accuracy, and fitted together as a glass stopper is fitted to a bottle. The distinguishing characteristic of this building is that the ends of the walls are not vertical, but project in an obtuse angle. At the point of the angle the stone was cut away, apparently to admit a large wooden beam, which probably extended across in front of the structure to the point of the angle at the other end of the wall. This may have been used to support the roof, or to bring it down part way, like a mansard roof. This build-

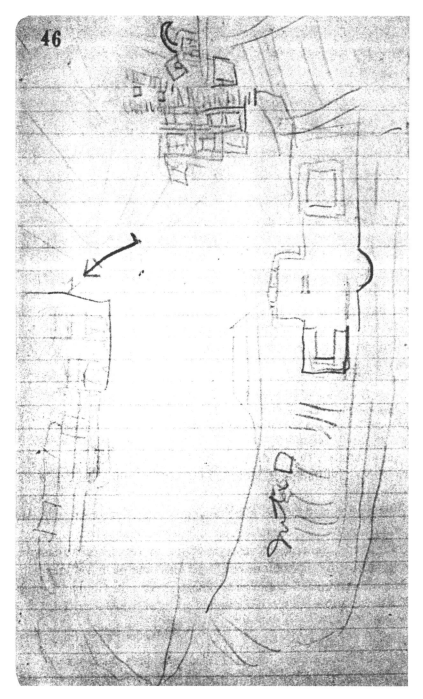

2.11 Page of Bingham's 1911 notebook with the first map made of the site.

ing is lined with small niches, high up above reach, and made with great care and precision. In the center of the back wall, and near the ground, is the largest stone of all, which measures 14.1 feet in length, and appears to have been either a high seat or an altar.

From the Sacred Plaza there is a magnificent view on both sides; to the north a tumbled mass of gigantic for-est-clad mountains, rising to snow-capped peaks, and to the South the widening Urubamba Valley, with the river winding through its bottom, protected on both sides by precipitous mountains. On the highest part of the river is a small structure, carefully built of rectangular blocks, with nicely made niches. Near it is a large boulder, carved into what is known as an intihuatana stone, sup-

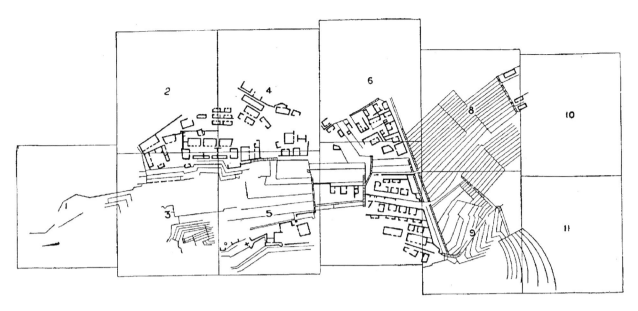

2.12 Plan of Machu Picchu (published in original 1913 *Harper's Monthly* article).

posed by some to have been a sun-dial. It has steps carved in it, and is in a fine state of preservation.

Directly below the Sacred Plaza the terraces run down to a large horseshoe-shaped plaza, evidently an ancient playground, or possibly an agricultural field. On the other side of this are a great many houses of lesser importance, although well built and huddled closely together. Many of the houses are simple in construction. Some have gabled ends. Nearly all have niches. A few are of remarkably fine workmanship, as fine as anything in Cuzco. The material used is nearly uniformly white granite. The finish is exquisite, and the blocks are fitted together with a nicety that surpasses description. The work is of the same character as that which so aroused the marvel of the Spanish conquerors. Some of the structures are nicely squared, like the palaces at Cuzco. Others have niches which resemble the best at Ollantaytambo. Cylindrical stone blocks, projecting from the wall, are common, both inside and outside the structure. In general they are larger and very much better fashioned than those at Choqquequirau. In places the ruins are almost labyrinthian. The plan gives a better idea than can be expressed in words of the extent and character of Machu Picchu (Figures 2.11 and 2.12).

On the north side of the Sacred Plaza is another structure, somewhat resembling that described as being on the west side in that the side facing the plaza is entirely open. Outside of the building are cylindrical stones projecting from the wall. Huge stones were employed in the lower tier, as in the similar building on the west side of the plaza, and their ends — that is to say, the ends of the side walls — are followed out in an obtuse angle, as in the other structure. Similarly, the point of the angle contains a hole cut into the stone, evidently intended to permit the admission of a large wooden beam. In order to support this beam, which extended across from one end of the building to the other, a single block was erected, half-way between the ends, and notched at the top, so as to permit the beam, or the ends of two beams if such were used, to rest upon it. This structure has an internal measurement of 14.9 x 33.7 feet. Its most striking feature is its row of remarkable windows (Figure 2.13). Three large windows, 3.1 feet wide and nearly 4 feet high, are let into the back wall, and look out upon a magnificent prospect over the jungle-clad mountains. Nowhere else in Peru have I seen an ancient building whose most noticeable characteristic is the presence of three large windows. Can it be that this unique feature will help us solve the riddle of this wonderful city of granite?

Sir Clements Markham, in his recent and valuable book on the Incas of Peru, devotes a chapter to a myth

2.13 Niches in one of the larger buildings.

which was told to all the Spanish chroniclers by their native informants, which he believes is the fabulous version of a distant historical event. The end of the early megalithic civilization is stated to have been caused by a great invasion from the south, possibly by barbarians from the Argentine pampas. The whole country broke up into anarchy, and savagery returned, ushering in a period of medieval barbarism. A remnant of the highly civilized folk took refuge in a district called Tamputocco, where some remnants of the old civilization were protected from the invaders by the inaccessible character of the country. Here the fugitives multiplied. Their descendants were more civilized and more powerful than their neighbors, and in time became crowded, and started out to acquire a better and more extensive territory. The legend relates that out of a hill with three openings or windows there came three tribes. These tribes eventually settled at Cuzco and founded the Inca empire. Tampu means "tavern," and toco a "window." The Spaniards were told that Tamputocco was not far from Cuzco, at a place called Paccaritampu, but the exact locality of Tamputocco is uncertain. So far no place

answering to its description has been located. It seems to me that there is a possibility the refuge of this pre-Inca fugitive tribe was here in the Vilcabamba mountains, and that Machu Picchu is the original Tamputocco, although this is contrary to the accepted location.

Certainly this region was well fitted by nature to be such a refuge; unquestionably here we have evidences of megalithic occupation; and here at Machu Picchu is a "tavern" with three windows. A view taken of this Temple of the Three Windows from below makes it easy to suggest that this was the hill with the three openings or windows referred to in the myth of the origin of the Inca empire. I may be wholly mistaken in this, and I shall await with interest the discovery of any other place that fits so well the description of Tamputocco, whence came the Incas.

In the meantime it seems probable that Machu Picchu, discovered while on a search for the last Inca capital, was the first, the capital from which the Incas started on that glorious career of empire that eventually embraced a large part of South America.

3.1 Machu Picchu among the peaks of the Andes, 1989. Photo by Marilyn Bridges.

III Machu Picchu Mysterious Royal Estate in the Cloud Forest

Lucy C. Salazar

Machu Picchu is probably the best known archaeological site in the western hemisphere, visited annually by hundreds of thousands of visitors, many of whom have traveled to Peru from Asia, Europe, and North America in order to see this magnificent Inca site buried deep in the cloud forest of the eastern Andean slopes. Machu Picchu has been described as one of the most mysterious places on earth, not only because of the otherworldly atmosphere of its white granite ruins, precipitous slopes, tangled forest, and dense mists, but also because of the many questions we have about it (Figure 3.1).

Why was it built on what seems to be an inconceivable location, a narrow ridge high above the heavily forested slopes of the Urubamba River? What led the Incas to invest large amounts of labor to build one of the most beautiful settlements known anywhere in the world in such a gorgeous landscape? Why was its spectacular mountaintop site unknown to the Spanish conquerors of the Incas? Who were its builders? What role did Machu Picchu play in Inca society (Figure 3.2)?

Since its rediscovery by Hiram Bingham on a cold morning of July 24, 1911 — its existence before this had been largely unknown to the world beyond local inhabitants — and despite the fact that thousands of visitors have journeyed to Machu Picchu, these mysteries remain unresolved. Travelers, Peruvian and foreign, continue to receive implausible and misleading information and perpetuate it. Bingham himself held and advanced many of these still current misconceptions, which, despite the evidence, have persisted for close to a century.

The ruins of Machu Picchu have inspired many myths, some of which are outgrowths of the limitations of Hiram Bingham's training and early-twentieth-century scholarship. The redoubtable leader of the Yale Peruvian Expedition was a professor of Latin American History at Yale, a geographer, explorer, and mountaineer, but he was not an archaeologist. His first journey to South America was across Venezuela and Colombia following the route of Simon Bolívar, the great South American emancipator (Bingham 1909). Bingham later began lecturing in South American history at Yale, his alma mater. Although he was highly intuitive, he was dependent on confusing and often inconsistent Spanish colonial narratives. He used these materials to draw a number of conclusions that archaeological research and other kinds of investigation contradict. His reliance on this one type of evidence and his lack of

3.2 Machu Picchu during the clearing of the forest, September 18, 1911. Photo by H. L. Tucker.

training in the other led Bingham to convince himself that what he had found was indeed what he had been seeking, the legendary Old Vilcabamba, or "Vilcabamba la Vieja," the citadel where Manco Inca, the last Inca king, rallied the resistance to the Spanish Conquest. But to this confirmation Bingham added a potentially incompatible interpretation: "Until further light can be traced on this fascinating problem it seems reasonable to conclude that at Machu Picchu we have the ruins of Tampu-tocco, the birthplace of the first Inca King, Manco Capac, and also the ruins of a sacred city, of the last Incas" (Bingham 1922: 339).

Because of the vagaries of history, Machu Picchu, whatever it may have been, remained in a near pristine state between its abandonment in the sixteenth century and its recovery in the early twentieth. Consequently the site offers the most complete example of classic Inca architecture and planning known to date. As a result of Bingham's three expeditions (the expeditions of 1912 and 1914–1915 were co-sponsored by Yale and the National Geographic Society), the Machu Picchu materials have offered opportunities for new studies, which in many cases have refuted Bingham's theories. Current studies of these materials continue to shed light on the settlement and administration of the Inca empire, the life of its elite and its retainers, and the nature of Inca society and culture.

More than ninety years after Bingham's first expedition, the mist is at last rising from Machu Picchu. While from the perspective of archaeological research this process is just beginning, the insights it has produced have already transformed our understanding of the site and the empire of which it was a part.

The Expedition

Hiram Bingham III was born in 1875 in Honolulu to a family of missionaries. He graduated from Yale in 1898 and returned to Hawai'i to serve as a pastor at the Palama Chapel. After marrying an heiress to the Tiffany fortune, Alfreda Mitchell, he traveled to Peru in 1909 and visited the great Inca ruins of Choqquequirau in the Apurimac Valley. Back in New Haven, in a letter to the editor of the *Yale Alumni Weekly* on March 10, 1911, Bingham suggested the possibility of developing fieldwork and exploration in the Andean region to improve the quality of teaching and instruction in Latin American history (Figure 3.3).

In 1911, with support primarily from Yale University and Yale alumni funds, Hiram Bingham organized an expedition with members from different academic backgrounds: Isaiah Bowman, assistant professor of geography at Yale; Dr. William Gage Erving, a physician specializing in orthopedic surgery; Harry Ward Foote, assistant professor of chemistry at Yale and an avocational naturalist; Kai Hendriksen, Danish topographer; Herman Tucker, mountain climber and assistant to Hendriksen; Paul Baxter Lanius, Yale undergraduate in the Sheffield Scientific School; Casimir Watkins, British naturalist; and Frank Hinkley, a Yale undergraduate assistant who was forced to leave the expedition only a few days into it after having an accident. Hiram Bingham personally selected the members and led the expedition to the Cuzco region in southern Peru, the capital of Tahuantinsuyu, as the great Inca Empire was called. He was looking for Vilcabamba, the neo-Inca capital on the forested eastern slopes of the Andes; from this city, descendants of the Inca emperors had opposed the Spanish conquerors for forty years. The Spaniards ultimately subdued the resistance and sacked Vilcabamba in 1572, and the area around it became depopulated. In fact, the city's location had remained lost to scholars. Bingham hoped to find old Vilcabamba by using sixteenth-century Spanish historical narratives (Bingham 1912, 1916b). Aided by a new road built in 1890 to facilitate the coca leaf and alcohol trade from

3.3 Hiram Bingham at the main camp, September 1912. Photo by Ellwood C. Erdis.

the *haciendas* (large landed estates) Huadquiña, Maranura, and Santa Ana, Bingham followed the Urubamba River into an area particularly favored by the Inca royal family, and previously inaccessible to exploration.

On July 23, 1911, Melchor Arteaga, a local farmer at Mandor Pampa, told Bingham of Inca ruins high on a ridge over the river, hidden by secondary growth, and he wrote in his journal the names Maccu Picchu/Huayna Picchu (Figure 3.4). On the next day, Bingham, accompanied by Arteaga and the military escort assigned him by the Peruvian government, Sargent Carrasco, climbed 2,000 feet above the river. Exhausted, they arrived at the site and were welcomed by a group of residents who offered them sweet potatoes, called *cumara*, and gourds filled with cold water. Bingham described his discovery as:

Two pleasant Indian farmers, Richarte and Alvarez, had chosen this Eagle's nest for their home. . . . The Indians said there were two paths to the outside world. Of one we already had the taste; the other, they said, was more difficult — a perilous path down the face of a rocky precipice on the other side of the ridge. . . . Without the slightest expectation of finding anything more interesting than the stone face terraces. . . . I entered the untouched forest beyond, and suddenly found myself in a maze of beautiful granite houses! . . . Under a carved rock the little boy showed me a cave beautifully lined with the finest cut stone. . . . To my astonishment I saw that this wall and its adjoining semicircular temple over the cave were as the finest stone work in the far-famed Temple of the Sun in Cuzco. (Bingham 1922: 317–321)

Bingham returned the following year to clear and excavate the site.

Although the name Machu Picchu did not appear in any of the Spanish historical narratives with which Bingham was familiar, he nevertheless connected the site to the places described in them. He proposed — incorrectly, as it turns out — that Machu Picchu was the birthplace of the Incas, based on the link he perceived between an unusual three-windowed building at the site and the myth that the ancestors — the four Ayar brothers and their sisters — had emerged from three windows or caves in a mountain called Tampu Toco located in Pacaritambo, south of Cuzco (Bauer 1991; Bingham 1912: 326–331; Sarmiento 1944; Urton 1990). Eventually, Bingham also interpreted Machu Picchu as "Vilcabamba La Vieja" (Vilcabamba the Old), where according to Augustinian priest Father Antonio de la Calancha, a University of Idolatries was occupied mainly by cloistered women (*acllas*) devoted to the Inca religious cult of the sun (Bingham 1912: 334–338). Bingham's gifts as a popularizer of his own work had the unfortunate effect of establishing his errors as facts in the public consciousness. It was he who described Machu Picchu as a lost city, although, in fact, it was not a city — its population had been 750 at most — and it was not "lost" in any meaningful sense. Although Bingham's theories were often flawed, he was an exceptionally dedicated, intrepid, and, some might say, lucky explorer. In addition to the discovery of Machu Picchu, the same expedition of 1911 discovered the important archaeological sites of Vitcos and Espiritu Pampa (Bingham 1912).

Rediscovering Machu Picchu

Contrary to Bingham's speculations, Machu Picchu's origins appear to have been quite recent, perhaps some time in the 1450s or 1460s, preceding by less than a century Pizarro's conquest of the Incas' vast Andean Empire. The site's origins also appear to have been less spectacular than Bingham's grandiose theories would have it. In 1982, Richard Burger and I concluded on the

3.4 Machu Picchu, with the Cerro Putucusi in the background. Photo by H. L. Tucker.

July 30, 1912. 11:30.

3.5 Panoramic view from the top of Mt. Machu Picchu showing the ruins on the ridge, and the Huayna Picchu hilltop in the center with the Urubamba River. Photo by Hiram Bingham, 1912.

basis of the archaeological evidence that Machu Picchu, far from being the Inca birthplace, was merely one of a number of personal royal estates built by an Inca king in the remote countryside from the imperial capital, Cuzco.

In fact, ninety years of scholarship have radically transformed our understanding of the Inca Empire and of Machu Picchu's position in it. These studies have confirmed some of Bingham's intuitions and substantially refuted others. Machu Picchu can only be properly understood in the larger context of the Inca social, economic, and political structure (Figure 3.5).

Machu Picchu does not resemble any of the five types of settlement that account for 99 percent of the sites within Tahuantinsuyu, the empire between 1450 and 1532 AD, when the Incas held sway:

- It was only a tiny fraction of the size of Cuzco, the Inca capital, and lacked Cuzco's large temples and fortresses.
- Its form and size were not comparable to such Inca provincial administrative capitals as Huanuco Pampa, Hatun Xauxa, and Pumpu.
- Its location and strongly religious character — given the quality of stonework, the high-altitude setting, and the numerous shrines — set it apart from places like the administrative wayside stations, called *tambos*, the Incas had placed along their more than 30,000-mile road network.
- It was far too elaborate to have been either a rural village or one of the planned state agricultural sites on which the Incas forcibly settled alien ethnic communities as a development strategy.

- Its classic Inca architecture and the artifacts recovered from it show that Machu Picchu could not have been one of the non-Inca villages that paid tribute to the empire through their labor on public works, state lands, mines, and other projects.

Machu Picchu, however, does have features consistent with one special type of Inca settlement: the royal estate. These estates — there was a group of them in the empire — were defined as being outside the state administrative system and its support area, belonging instead to a specific Inca ruler and his descent group segment (see Chapter 4). These kin groups, called *panacas* (royal corporations or royal lineages), were each headed by an Inca king and supported in luxury by the lands and retainers acquired through conquest during that king's reign. This adulation continued after the king's death, because in his role as an ancestor he was part of court politics.

These royal retreats were associated with lands farmed for the panaca, the produce of which supported the centers and their visitors. There seem to have been many of these settlements in a number of areas, but the Urubamba Valley, to the north of Cuzco, was favored, perhaps because of its proximity to the capital and its warmer climate. Descriptions of the estate of the eleventh Inca ruler Huayna Capac, located in Yucay, upstream from Machu Picchu, tell of forests where exotic lowland plants and animals — such as deer, fish, chili peppers, coca, and peanuts — were kept for the emperor's pleasure (Farrington 1995; Niles 1988, 1999; Rowe 1987). According to the Spanish chroniclers, these centers were used as country estates for relaxation when the Inca ruler or his descendants traveled out of Cuzco. Hunting, entertaining other Inca nobles and foreign dignitaries, and other activities are mentioned.

The fine Inca masonry, small size of the settlement, absence of features tied to the economic infrastructure, and other elements lead us to conclude, solely on the basis of archaeological evidence, that Machu Picchu was probably such a royal estate. This working hypothesis was confirmed by John Rowe's study of a 1568 document, written only thirty-six years after Pizarro's arrival, that mentions a site "Picchu," approximately where Machu Picchu is located today. The term *Machu*, that

3.6 **The ninth Inca ruler, Pachacuti Inca Yupanqui, creator of Machu Picchu, as drawn by the native writer Felipe Guaman Poma.**

precedes *Picchu* means "old" and was used by locals to differentiate it from the hill at its northern extreme, called Huayna Picchu, which means "young." The entire area in which the site is located, according to Rowe, was apparently collectively called Picchu, or Pijchu (Rowe 1987: 14). These documents say that the lands in the bottom of the valley belonged to Inca Yupanqui (also known as Pachacuti Inca Yupanqui, the ninth ruler) and his panaca — Inaca Panaca Ayllo (Sarmiento de Gamboa 1944: 14). Although Machu Picchu is not mentioned per se, the documents imply that it would have fallen within Pachacuti's estate. Pachacuti Inca Yupanqui conquered this region in the course of his military campaign into the areas of Vitcos and Vilcabamba (Cobo 1979: 135–137). Under Pachacuti's leadership the Inca armies subjugated the Urubamba drainage in an effort to protect the Cuzco basin from a sneak attack by their principal adversaries, the Chancas. It is generally believed that Pachacuti conquered only the middle and lower Urubamba after his conquest of the Chancas, probably sometime in the 1450s. As a result of his military conquests he took the land along the river and built a series of royal estates (Figure 3.6).

Machu Picchu was the most spectacular commemoration of Pachacuti's war conquests. It had strategic importance for the neighboring highland groups. His other royal estates, Pisac and Ollantaytambo, were also constructed to glorify his military campaigns, but Machu Picchu was the symbol of his divine power, legitimacy, and authority. Rowe's hypothesis that Machu Picchu was founded by Pachacuti is consistent with our preliminary ceramic analysis, indicating the absence of Kilke, Lucre, and the other ceramic pottery styles immediately antecedent to the imperial Cuzco style of Inca pottery (Bauer 1999). The area had been only lightly settled before the Inca conquest, and it seems reasonable to suggest that Machu Picchu, built sometime between 1450 and 1470, had been in use for only some eighty years when Tahuantinsuyu crumbled and the site was abandoned.

The Royal Haven

A royal palace is a formal architectural symbol of the power of the ruler and his elite. It is also an example of a formal architecture created and maintained by the ruler. Studies of the structure and the functioning of the Machu Picchu household indicate that members of the Inca royalty and their retainers engaged in celebrations, diplomatic feasting, religious ceremonies and rituals, astronomical observations, and administrative affairs of the empire in Machu Picchu's warmer and more pleasant climate. The land around the retreat at Machu Picchu was terraced and farmed and otherwise made delightful to the rulers, their families, and visiting Inca nobility. In modern American terms Machu Picchu, as well as the other royal estates, served as a kind of Inca "Camp David," except that the estates did not pass to the king's successor upon his death.

The Inca ruler traveled through the empire with his court and his courtiers, which consisted of hundreds of retainers and advisors and thousands of troops. After the

Inca's death, he was regarded as a living ancestor, and his body was embalmed and his mummy was cared for by hundreds of attendants. As during his lifetime, he was dressed in *cumpi* (fine textiles) — made of camelid fiber, gold, and feathers — and was carefully tended, fed, and given a daily change of clothing. Pachacuti, who established the restricted use of the vicuña wool for himself and his panaca (Garcilaso de la Vega 1958: 407), presumably wore garments woven of this remarkably fine fiber (Rowe 1977; Rowe and Rowe 1996; Salazar and Rousakis 2000). In the same spirit, Pachacuti may have been responsible for the creation of a symbolic system of geometric designs, called *tocapos*, depicted on the royal textiles. This distinctively imperial clothing illustrates how garments could communicate rapid and effective social information without the use of language. The most complex tocapos were used exclusively by the royal elite, and probably made by them, because of their secret symbols and meanings. These textiles embodied the power and authority of the Inca Empire. They were given by the Inca himself as the most valuable gifts, to the loyal members of Tahuantinsuyu.

What implications does the identification of Machu Picchu as a royal estate have for the interpretation of its archaeological remains? First, the general layout becomes comprehensible from a functional perspective. It would be expected that the site would have been used for part of each year, perhaps during May to September, when nightly frosts are common in Cuzco. During this period, the royal court and courtiers would have resided at the site along with a much larger number of retainers (*yanaconas*) to serve them. In addition to a permanent population of caretakers and servants who likely lived at the site throughout the year, specialized workers (*camayocs*) were brought by the Incas for their skilled craftsmanship. Some, from Peru's north coast, home of the Chimu, lived in the southwest section of the palace complex, near where the schist stone ritual paraphernalia was produced (Zapata 1983: 53–57).

Indeed, when we look at the layout of Machu Picchu, we can immediately identify a sector of high-status households in the northeast sector of the site. The residences utilized the classic architectural form, which the Incas referred to as *kancha*. These were composed of rectangular units arranged within a walled compound

3.7 Ingenuity Group. House 494, interior, from the southeast corner showing stone mortars cut into the boulders in the floor. Photo by Hiram Bingham, 1912.

just as each family differed in size, history, and status. Many of the kanchas of the Upper sector housed the elite, a message conveyed by the use of double-jamb entryways and walls of finely cut and polished stone. Many also incorporated household shrines. The masonry in these domestic constructions and other exquisite buildings used the locally available granite, but it is possible that stonework specialists (*pirca camayocs*) from the *altiplano* of Lake Titicaca may have participated in their construction. This possibility is consistent with the *altiplano* presence in Machu Picchu's burials (Salazar 1997a).

At Machu Picchu, three elite compounds on terraces to the east of the central plaza probably housed members of the Inca elite. Bingham labeled these compounds the Clan Groups, and he assigned names to them based on their distinctive characteristics, such as the Ingenuity Group and the Three-Doors Group (Figure 3.7). The three residential compounds are located adjacent to one another in the northeast sector of the site. Each is unique, and none conform to a simple kancha pattern such as that known from the elite housing at Ollantaytambo.

The three elite residential compounds are located on terraces overlooking Machu Picchu's central plaza. The largest and most southern of them, the Ingenuity Group and Private Garden Group, can be divided into four sections (Figure 3.8). The compound is surrounded by a perimetric wall, however, with only a single entrance on its southern wall. The imposing entry by way of a double-jambed doorway topped by a massive lintel immediately distinguishes this as a high-status compound. The back wall of a *huairona* (a three-sided room) has been placed to obstruct vision of the compound from the entrance, thereby enhancing privacy. Both the houses and the *huaironas* have numerous interior trapezoidal wall niches, up to eighteen in some of the larger buildings, alternating with cylindrical stone tenons. The sections of this compound are connected by narrow stone staircases, one of which is carved from a single block of bedrock. One notable feature of this large compound is the presence of two shrines focused on natural stone outcrops; another is the two unique circular mortars carved into the bedrock. Six windows in the western wall of the compound provide a view of the Temple of

around a central open-air patio, and various roofed buildings were used for sleeping, cooking, and household storage. Each kancha group typically had a single main entrance and would have been used by a single family group. Bingham identified fourteen groups of kanchas divided into two sectors: Upper (Hanan) and Lower (Hurin). Aware of this Inca custom, he referred to these groups as *ayllus* (kin groups).

As one might expect, each house group was unique in its room arrangement, decorations, and other features,

3.8 Ingenuity Group. General view, showing a high-gabled double house. Photo by Hiram Bingham, 1912.

the Sun (the Torreón) and the Temple of the Three Windows.

The adjacent compound, the Three-Door Group, covers an area of 111 by 170 feet. The entrance consists of three massive stone doorways, each of which has a double jamb with carved sockets with stone bar-holds. Its layout is basically three adjacent and interconnecting kanchas in which houses and huaironas surround a central patio on four sides. The few buildings with windows offer a view towards the eastern terraces and mountain landscape. The third and final elite compound at Machu Picchu, not named by Bingham but referred to as the Upper Group or *Conjunto Superior* (Buse 1978), has two sections. It has a single entry, which, like the others features the distinctive double jamb and carved stone bar-holds. The main entrance leads into a blind corridor, ensuring maximum privacy, while a secondary entrance provides access to the lower level of the compound. The most important section of this compound is a central patio flanked by huaironas and a roofed dwelling. The main dwelling measures 42 by 26 feet and has twenty large vertical niches (*hornacinas*).

The largest of the compounds, the Ingenuity Group, has eleven buildings that could have housed fifty or sixty elite residents. In contrast, the upper group probably held fewer than twenty people. It is unlikely that the three elite compounds held more than one hundred twenty members of the Inca nobility. The houses in these elite compounds average between 344 and 904 square feet, more than twice the size of the rustic dwellings outside the compounds that were occupied by the retainers. Many of the elite houses have finely fitted cut and polished stonework.

An unusual feature of these elite households is the bar-sockets that were carved in the entryway to each compound (Figure 3.9). These are believed to have been used to block entry to the compound, either symbolically by holding a cord or wood bar, or, literally, by supporting a massive wooden gate across the space (Bingham 1930: 76–79). Also, it is significant that behind each of these elite household compounds, outside the compound walls, there are rows of buildings lacking patio areas or any kancha-like arrangement. Such buildings at other Inca sites have been identified as resi-

3.9 Gateway, interior, showing two bar sockets. Photo by Hiram Bingham, 1912.

dences of the yanaconas and camayocs (Niles 1987; Rowe 1982; Villanueva 1970: 139). The ethnohistoric evidence available indicates that one prerogative of an Inca panaca responsible for the conquest of new zones and populations was to have a number of individuals of the conquered group for its own service or to give these people to other panacas as a symbol of their newly acquired power. The rustic terrace buildings were probably occupied by these workers, associated with the adjacent households.

At most, 150 possible domestic dwellings have been identified within the site. Even if they were all residential in function and all were occupied, it is difficult to argue for a maximum population at any time in excess of 750 people within the "palace walls," and it is likely that the actual number was closer to 500 people, most of whom were yanaconas and camayocs. This number, of course, does not include the inhabitants of the land surrounding Machu Picchu whose agricultural fields probably provided much of the necessary food for the people living there. The terraces at Machu Picchu, which con-

stituted only about 12 acres of agricultural land, could not provide a sufficient amount of food for the estimated population (Wright et al. 1997c: 47). Also, there is no evidence within the palace walls of houses for the farmers who tilled the terraces of Machu Picchu, nor did Bingham's excavations recover the diverse types of stone and metal tools used by this agricultural labor force.

Unlike the elite compounds, the residence of the emperor Sapa Inca (Unique Inca) is set apart physically in the southwest sector from all other domestic architecture. Above the complex to the west are broad terraces, and below it to the east is a small walled garden. Running along the north and south of the complex are deeply inset staircases leading to the plaza below. Thus, there was no housing adjacent to or even near the royal compound. This spatial isolation would have given the sovereign a degree of privacy absent from the elite compounds, perhaps a feature necessary to maintain the myth of divine kingship. Bingham appears to have been correct when he labeled it the King's Group (Figure 3.10).

3.10 King's Group. General view from the northwest. Photo by Hiram Bingham.

Significantly, this royal residential complex is adjacent to the Torreón. The dwelling of the sovereign is no larger than that of his elite relatives; in fact, the building in which he probably slept measures only 75 by 52 feet and the interior patio covers only 300 square feet (Figure 3.11). Entrance into the Inca ruler's complex. however, is more difficult than into the elite compounds. A large gateway is found in the compound's entryway, and another gateway limits access into the sector of the site in which the compound is located. The buildings in this royal complex also are set apart from the others by the care with which the white granite was selected for the walls, the superior quality of their fitted stonework, and the massive size of the stone lintels. Its lintels are twice the size of those used in the other residential compounds, and Bingham estimated their weight at three tons (Bingham 1930: 96).

Machu Picchu was supplied with fresh springwater brought from a perennial spring on the north slope of the Machu Picchu mountain and a series of smaller springs along the way, and channeled to a stone-lined gravity canal from its source 2,456 feet to the south (Wright et al. 1997a: 838). Reaching the royal estate, it was channeled into a descending series of sixteen ritual fountains, the first of which is adjacent to the doorway of the royal compound. Thus, the water reached the Sapa Inca from the spring in its pure state, uncontaminated by prior usage (Figure 3.12). The highly elaborate fountain is unique at Machu Picchu in its unusual cut stone walls forming an enclosure that might have been used as a ceremonial bath. Like the other fountains at Machu Picchu, a cut stone channel delivers the springwater at the top of the fountain and a sharp-lipped rectangular fountain spout creates a falling jet of water into a small cut stone basin at the bottom of the enclosure (Wright et al. 1997a: 842). Rising 5 feet high, the walls of the fountain would have allowed the Inca ruler to take a ceremonial purification bath in absolute privacy, a concern referred to explicitly in the early chronicle of Pedro Pizarro (1978: 32).

While the Inca's quarters do not bespeak of a fondness for luxury, the exclusive garden and adjacent bath,

3.11 King's Group. House interior and entrance to toilet area. Photo by Hiram Bingham.

3.12 Fountains and Torreón before clearing. Photo by Hiram Bingham.

as well as the more private setting and the site's private toilet arrangement, attest to the special comforts provided for the Inca ruler and roughly match the descriptions of royal dwellings in the Spanish chronicles. Pollen analysis of the soil of the Inca private garden and adjacent terraces has revealed that beans, corn, and potatoes were grown, perhaps along with some of the ninety species of orchids, found in the Machu Picchu Historic Reserve (Alfredo Valencia, personal communication). In designing the garden, the Incas may have been taken in consideration the gurgle of the running water of the fountains nearby for the relaxation of Inca Pachacuti, whose fondness for flowers has been

recorded in the *cantares* or *haravec*, songs dedicated to the memory of the events of his life, and sung especially at the time of his death. Pedro Sarmiento de Gamboa (1944: 140) notes that at the time of his death, Pachacuti began to sing a cantar: "I was born as a lily in the garden, and like the lily I grew, as my age advanced / I became old and had to die, and so I withered and died." (*Nací como lirio en el jardín, y ansí fuí criado, y como vino mi edad, envejecí, / y como había de morir, así me sequé y morí.*).

Another distinctive architectural feature of the king's compound is a deep incised line grooved in the large lintel of the entrance (Figure 3.13); this kind of line appears also in the entrance of the main building of the Ingenuity Group, and this sort of visual signal has also been noted in one of the rooms of the Coricancha of Cuzco (Valencia and Gibaja 1992: 67). In 1980 a cave underneath the lintel was uncovered containing the remains of a woman (Valencia, personal communication). Other architectural details like friezes or wall murals and furnishings made of perishable materials have not survived. However, Bingham found remains of red paint on the stucco plastered walls of a house in the Ingenuity Group (Figure 3.14), and red bitumen-like paint were observed by the Spanish conquerors in the Inca residence at Cajamarca (Xérez 1968: 233).

During the process of restoration in the King's Group, in the core of a wall, an offering of a guinea pig (*cuy*) was found pierced through by two shawl pins (*tupus*), one of gold and one of silver (Eusebio Mendoza, personal communication). This ritual offering is analogous to the offering made to commemorate the ritual burial of a wall that served as the foundation of a late terrace, where one such offering, a laminated gold bracelet, was found in pristine condition in the rubble of chipped stones (Elba Torres, personal communication).

Judging from the architectural evidence, besides the domestic architecture used by the elite and their retainers, the most common structures at Machu Picchu are those involved in the various religious rituals central to the royal court. The Incas, like most conquerors, claimed that their deities — the Sun and the Moon, among others — had instructed them to go forth and subdue all the nations to their north, south, east, and west. Their claim to legitimacy was closely tied to their ideology of being descended from the Sun and having special links to the cosmos and its manipulation. Inca rituals required a core of specialists and involved complex astronomical observations and carefully specified sequences of prayers and sacrifices. Pachacuti himself participated in the design and building of a new house for the worship of the Sun. After his visit to the shrine of Susurpuquiu, a natural spring (*pacarina*), a deity in the form of a man dressed in puma skins, serpents, ear spools, and a headdress in the form of the sun's rays, appeared through a crystal tablet or mirror and called him by his name saying he was his father, the Sun, and

3.13 Doorway with monolithic lintel in the King's Group. Also shown is Melquiades Richarte, the child who guided Bingham through the site. Photo by Hiram Bingham, 1911.

granted him the power and legitimacy of his divine kingship (Molina 1916; Sarmiento 1944; Betanzos 1987). In memory and celebration of this oracular event, which predicted his victory over the Chancas and his future conquests, Pachacuti rebuilt the Temple of the Sun in Cuzco, called the Coricancha. In this temple, a figure the size of a year-old child was made of solid gold during a month of fasting, sacrifices, and ceremonies. These rituals were carried out by the Inca ruler, himself a priest of the newly founded religion (Betanzos 1987). Some years later after the Chancas War, Pachacuti initiated new religious reforms as a way of organizing the dif-

3.14 House in the Ingenuity Group, with red stucco showing in the windows on the left. Photo by Hiram Bingham.

3.15 Interior wall of the Main Temple. The stone block near Sergeant Carrasco is 10.2 feet wide, 8.0 feet high, and 2.8 feet thick. Photo by Hiram Bingham.

3.16 Intihuatana stone, from the southwest. Photo by Hiram Bingham.

3.17 View of the side of the Torreón after Bingham cleared it of vegetation. Photo by Hiram Bingham.

3.18 The Torreón with terraces and expedition tent in the background. Photo by Hiram Bingham.

to events of an astronomical nature such as the solstices or zenith passages dates, as well as events that involved celestial observations to determine crucial times, such as when to plant or to carry out sacrifices.

The Temple of the Sun, or the Torreón, as Bingham called this unique building, is a curved structure of carefully fitted masonry that encloses a carved rock outcrop in a form that resembles a feline, probably a puma. Pachacuti himself dressed for the wars with a puma skin over his head to show his ownership of this totemic ancestor. This mythical affinity reflects Pachacuti's superior spiritual status as a cultural hero (Helms 1998).

The Torreón has a clear view to the east (Figure 3.17). The two windows in this wall have symmetrical stone pegs projecting very close from the four corners. The Torreón's northeastern window is aligned to a declination of +21.6 degrees, providing an interesting similarity to the Coricancha (Dearborn and White 1982, 1983). Another special feature is the straight edge cut in the bedrock platform that points through the center of the window. Its orientation is precisely to the rising point of the sun on the June solstice. The solstitial alignment of the central stone is accurate to approximately 2 arc minutes, the best precision possible using the naked eye (Dearborn, Schreiber, and White 1987). But, to cast a shadow through the window and onto the stone for observations of the setting stone, they probably used a plumb bob that hung from a stick supported by the stone pegs; this or any other vertical object acted as a hand on a clock until the day of the solstice when the shadow could become parallel with the edge of the bedrock (Figure 3.18). Bingham found silver and bronze plumb bobs at the site (Bingham 1930: 184). Another instrument that could be used for casting a shadow is the plated bronze "mirror" (Bingham 1930: 182; Salazar 2001a). In addition, another window in the Torreón was used for the observation of the first morning rise of the constellation Pleiades (Dearborn and Schreiber 1986; Reinhard 1991; Urton 1982). It has been suggested that a similar astronomical observation was made at Pisac, also a royal estate of Pachacuti. A structure called Intimachay, located on the eastern side of Machu Picchu, or the Hurin, seems to have been created to monitor the sunrise on and around the December solstice (Dearborn, Schreiber, and White 1987). Also, the second win-

ferent ethnic groups he was integrating under his imperial rule.

As Bingham (1930: 56–66) and others have observed, the entire upper section of Machu Picchu to the west of the main plaza is dedicated to an impressive set of structures or special features designed for ceremonial activities (Figure 3.15). These include the Main Temple, with its massive granite altar, and the Intihuatana, an elegant carved stone with a tall vertical shaft, that may have served to follow the movements of the Sun (Figure 3.16). Such early chroniclers as Cristóbal de Molina (1916), Juan de Betanzos (1987), and Polo de Ondegardo (1916) describe the Inca religious celebrations and refer

3.19 Rainbows are common over Machu Picchu. Photo by Sir Charles Chadwyck-Healey.

dow of the curved wall allowed visitors to view several constellations, such as the tail of Scorpio, called *Collca*, or Store House.

The Torreón and its associated features were a symbol of the Inca cosmological order as conceived by Pachacuti. I would like to argue that the form of the Torreón as seen from above corresponds to the Rainbow (*Kuychi*, "el arco del cielo"), one of the main deities of the Inca religion. It is relevant that the Coricancha in Cuzco housed a special shrine for the worship of the Rainbow. The Incas believed the rainbow originated from the Sun, and they displayed it as an emblem on their shields

and coat of arms, a reference to the myth that they were descendants of the Sun. The rainbow was a celestial phenomenon that, like lightning, united the three spheres of the cosmos: the sky, the earth, and the underworld (Figure 3.19). Many investigators have assumed that the Torreón's curved wall symbolized the circular shape of the sun, but the form of the building is distinctively hemispherical, despite the ability of the Inca masons to create circular structures, such as the site of Ingapirca in Ecuador. On the colonial Inca ritual wooden vessels called *qeros*, the Sapa Inca is often shown beneath a rainbow — sometimes imagined as a two-headed

3.20 Cave with fine niches beneath the Torreón. Photo by Hiram Bingham.

3.21 Rock carved as a stairway beneath the Torreón. Photo by Hiram Bingham.

3.22 The emperor and queen worshipping such ancestral places as Tampu Toco. Drawing by Guaman Poma.

3.23 Shrine inside the Ingenuity Group. Photo by Hiram Bingham.

3.24 Ellwood C. Erdis in the rock outcrop shrine that resembles Mount Yanantin in the background. Photo by Hiram Bingham.

serpent (*amaru*) — because the rainbow was said to be the Inca's means of communicating with the Sun (Isbell 1978). The cave beneath the Torreón (Figure 3.20) conceptually corresponds to the underworld from which rivers and ancestors like the mythical Inca Manco Capac emerged from in Inca mythology (Figure 3.22). The carved stair in this chamber could have served as a small platform to support portable sacred images (Figure 3.21).

All these unusual architectural features at Machu Picchu, including the sixteen cut stone fountains, suggest the centrality of worship to the activities at Pachacuti's country palace. Similar features are well known from sites in Cuzco, where they were interpreted as reified elements from myth or history. Spanish chronicler

Bernabé Cobo lists 328 shrines (*huacas*) in Cuzco's landscape, about 30 percent of which corresponded to natural stone formations (Cobo 1964). Significantly, the boulders and the rock outcrops all over Machu Picchu informed the planning of the buildings by the Inca architects and stonemasons. In a physical sense, they were probably a stabilizing feature, but at the same time these boulders were crucial elements in the animistic Inca religious philosophy (MacLean 1986: 72). The fine masonry platforms surrounding analogous features at Machu Picchu dispel any doubts that might exist concerning their ceremonial function (Figure 3.23). Moreover, religious features are not limited to the ceremonial sector. Natural stone outcrops that served as the focus of shrines occur on the eastern side of the site both within and adjacent to the principal areas of elite residence (Figure 3.24). But why should religious activity be so crucial to a country palace where hunting and other nonurban pleasures might be expected?

It is very significant that a large number of architectural structures, around thirty, were used for religious activities. This total is very high when compared to the remains of other royal estates, such as Chinchero, Huamanmarca, Pisac, and Callachaca (see Chapter 4). Pachacuti dedicated substantial amounts of skilled labor and prime real estate to these religious elements within the palace complex at Machu Picchu. It suggests that from the outset Pachacuti and his panaca may have played an exceptionally important role in the ceremonial life of the Cuzco elite. The claim by Inca Pachacuti and later rulers that a special relationship existed between the Inca royal lineages and the supernatural forces immanent in the landscape and the celestial sphere was so important that it had to be actively reaffirmed through daily ritual. It may be significant that one of Pachacuti's sons, Yamque Yupanqui Topa, was said to have devoted his life to Inca religious activities

rather than political rulership. If a special link existed between Pachacuti's panaca and the Inca religious cult, it might help explain the presence of unusual ritual constructions like the Temple of Three Windows, whose architectural metaphorical reference to the Inca mythical origins is unparalleled at other royal estates (Figure 3.25). Encoded within Machu Picchu's architecture lies the structure of the Inca ideology upon which Pachacuti's legitimacy rested.

Inca sites were carefully located and landscaped into alignment with mountain peaks and constellations. From the summit of the Huayna Picchu, the magnificent peak of Salcantay is visible. It is the most prestigious snowcapped mountain in the Andes and regarded today, with its brother the Mount Asungate (20,905 feet above sea level), as the ancestors of all mountains and as deities to the people of Cuzco and Apurimac. Today Salcantay is considered a male deity invoked by male healers in rituals to cure illnesses, increase crop yields, and ensure livestock fertility (Reinhard 1991). Another snowcapped peak to the east of Machu Picchu visible from the Intihuatana is Mount Veronica (18,865 feet

3.25 Temple of Three Windows. Photo by Hiram Bingham.

3.26 Mount Salcantay and Mount Veronica. Photo by Hiram Bingham.

above sea level) to the east of Machu Picchu, which to-day is considered a female deity (*apu*) (Figure 3.26).

It is not surprising, then, that a royal estate such as Machu Picchu would feature numerous places for ob-serving solar, lunar, and stellar activity (the windows of the Torreón), for making ritual offerings (the Principal Temple) (Figure 3.27), or for the temporary placement, worship, and sacrifices to their deities and ancestors (the cave beneath the Torreón). It is interesting, however,

that in addition to such public areas of worship and cer-emony on the upper northwest sector of the site, there are small shrines within each of the elite compounds, where more intimate family rituals could be carried out.

Demystifying Machu Picchu
Investigations of recent years have convincingly dis-proved Bingham's dual identifications of Machu Picchu as either the last Inca capital (i.e., Vilcabamba) or the

mythic Inca birthplace (i.e., Tampu Toco). But what about Bingham's rather passionate claim that the so-called Virgins of the Sun occupied Machu Picchu? This theory, not particularly consistent with his other two theories, derived primarily from George Eaton's conclusion that the skeletons recovered from the Machu Picchu burials in 1912 had almost all been women, with a few "effeminate men" (Eaton 1916).

These burials were discovered mainly in walled-up crevices beneath or adjacent to the large boulders strewn along the edges of the site. Bingham was familiar with the Inca custom of selecting young girls at the age of seven or so, and assigning them to a state-run female institution or *acllahuasi* (house of the chosen women) created by Pachacuti, where they were trained and educated to become priestesses, were sacrificial victims, or, in most cases, were kept as secondary wives of Inca emperors or to be distributed as a sign of favor to successful

3.27 Excavations at the Main Temple in 1912. Photo by Hiram Bingham.

generals, administrators, or allies. These houses, which the Spaniards compared to nunneries, were the focus of many Spanish accounts.

Understandably, Eaton's findings brought this group to Bingham's mind. At the site of Huanuco Pampa, Craig Morris found a distinctive structure of barrack-like form. It is a large compound with a single entrance that encloses a densely packed set of rooms. The excavation yielded high numbers of spindle whorls and shawl pins, artifacts associated primarily with the female sex (Morris and Thompson 1985). But no such architectural arrangement exists at Machu Picchu, nor did Bingham encounter large numbers of weaving implements or other artifacts related to females in any particular sector. How then can we explain Eaton's findings? Reanalysis

of the skeletal materials has documented the presence of 174 individuals; the ratio of men to women was 1:1.5, rather than the asymmetric 1:4 Eaton calculated. The skeletal evidence also indicates that many of the adult women recovered had given birth, and there are skeletons of fetuses, infants, and young children (Verano 2003) (see Chapter 6). Bingham's theory of the Virgins of the Sun was an attempt to explain a nonexistent anomaly in the evidence.

Although the burials of men and women do shed light on life in Machu Picchu, royal estates were not the preferred burial grounds of the Inca elite. Inca royalty who died suddenly while visiting Machu Picchu would have been borne back on litters (as they had been brought there) for mummification and burial in Cuzco, the imperial capital. One would expect only retainers to be interred at a place like Machu Picchu, and this expectation accords well with the archaeological evidence. First, little energy was expended in preparation of the burial chambers, which, in most cases, was simply an unmodified natural space with a few rocks piled around the body to keep wild animals out. Second, most of the goods left with those found buried at Machu Picchu were modest at best. Because the dead were believed to use the items interred with them in their journey to the next world, even low-ranking officials—burials of the lowest Incan bureaucrats (*curaca pachaca*), who had charge of 100 taxpayers—were interred in the Ica Valley with precious metal cups, more than a dozen pieces of pottery, and other offerings (Menzel 1977: 97). In contrast, only a few modest offerings accompanied the bodies buried at Machu Picchu—rarely more than four to six pots, and even these typically were vessels that had been repaired during the life of the deceased. On burial goods alone we can infer that the majority of those buried at Machu Picchu were people of relatively low status.

Also, some of these skeletons bear the traces of broken bones and bad backs, which mark common laborers, such as retainers. The retainers—*yanaconas, mitimaes*, and *camayocs*—of the Inca elite are known to have been drawn from throughout the provinces. For example, the royal estate upstream from Machu Picchu at Yucay was said to have had retainers brought from Quito, Ecuador. The nonlocal origin and heterogeneity of the retainer population also fits well with the Machu Picchu burial sample. For example, several types of cranial deformation are represented, including types not typical of the Cuzco region. By far the most common ethnic groups represented in the Machu Picchu cemeteries are from the area surrounding Lake Titicaca (Collas, Lupaqas, Pacajes). There also significant numbers of Chimu from the north coast, Cañaris and Chachas from the northeastern mountains, and groups from the central coast. The number of burials of people from Cuzco appears to be small (Salazar 2001b).

Although the role of retainer was not prestigious within the vertical hierarchy of Inca society, documents from the sixteenth century mention that the Cañaris and Chachas were exempt from tribute and labor tax

(*mita*) (Espinoza Soriano 1978; Villanueva 1971). At Machu Picchu, the mortuary treatment of the retainers suggests the multiple levels of individual identity and their real implications for daily life in a way not possible even through a close reading of Spanish historical narratives. At Machu Picchu some retainers were buried with pottery bearing the emblems of the Inca state: silver shawl pins, tweezers, and plated bronze mirrors (Salazar 2001). At the same time, these individuals retained their original ethnic identity, symbolized by the presence of pottery and other personal items made in the style of their homeland; the use of these ceramics was a public expression of their identity. Significantly, the burials of the retainers followed the Cuzco style of entombment rather than that of their homelands. This conformity suggests the degree of dominance of a retainer's native culture in the asymmetric world in which these people lived and died. Also, there is evidence that many of the Machu Picchu dead were regularly worshipped in their capacity as ancestors, and that the burial caves were the focus of post-inhumation visits. As expected, evidence also shows that ritual feasting involving food and drink was carried out around the entrance and periphery of the burial caves. The remains recovered there consisted mainly of animal bones, drinking vessels, and serving dishes (Figure 3.28). In Andean ideology, the mummified remains of ancestral dead (*mallquis*) were the object of great veneration because they provided for the continuation of life for their communities (Salomon 1996). The mallquis were considered the ultimate source of food, water, and agricultural land, and their burial places were located in natural or modified caves (*machays*). This belief system survived the Spanish Conquest. Mary Doyle, in her analysis of seventeenth- and eighteenth-century documents, encountered numerous descriptions of the performance of ceremonies at the entrances of machays honoring the dead with corn beer (*chicha*), llama blood, and guinea pigs (Doyle 1988).

Archaeological artifacts recovered from the graves and refuse argue against workers' involvement in agriculture, but the studies by Gordon and Rutledge (1987) indicate the production of tin bronze alloys at the site. Metalworking by-products, raw materials, and tools for creating metal artifacts provide strong evidence of an

3.28 Burial named the Gran Salon. Photo by Hiram Bingham.

unexpected component of daily life at Machu Picchu. Spanish chroniclers identified the ethnic groups in the tombs as having special metallurgical skills; many of them were brought to the royal estate because of this technical knowledge (Salazar 1997b). The identification of the Machu Picchu burials as basically belonging to specialized retainers helps to explain why Bingham failed to encounter large quantities of precious metal objects, because their inclusion would have been restricted largely to the elite.

The creation of highly valued craft items may have been part of an intentional strategy by Pachacuti's panaca to use these wealth objects in establishing or reinforcing alliances with other groups. The link between metallurgy and magical transformation has been observed cross-culturally and, in the Andes, the use of metals to represent supernatural forces is a feature not only of the Incas, but of many of their predecessors for over two millennia. And, in addition to this ideological dimension, metallurgy played a special role in the political economy of the Inca court.

Why Machu Picchu Was Perceived as "Lost"

Machu Picchu's location is indeed spectacular, and it was probably for this reason that it was selected for settlement. Whether or not it was couched in sacred geography or cosmological determinism, the Incas appreciated the aesthetic qualities of highland landscapes as much as or more than do modern-day archaeologists and travelers; their fascination with the site's location may have been based on the same features we find fascinating today.

Yet the choice of this spot had disadvantages as well as advantages. For example, it was located 60 miles from Cuzco in a lightly settled region; as such, it was particularly vulnerable to surprise attack from either rebellious highland groups like the Chancas or unconquered jungle groups downstream. With few prospects for reinforcements in the immediate area, the elite staying at Machu Picchu would have had to be concerned about security even during a short sojourn at the site.

This concern is reflected in Machu Picchu's architecture. The building atop Huayna Picchu was positioned to enable detection of approaching armies far in advance of their arrival. The major road leading to Machu Picchu features a drawbridge spanning a chasm from which attendants could remove the requisite logs in case of a threat. The site itself is inaccessible from three sides because of the steep slopes; the fourth side is protected by a deep, dry moat, which has since been largely filled in by eroding soil. Beyond the stone-lined trench are two high stone walls. The single entrance into the inner city could have been lashed and defended even if the moat and the first wall were breached. As other scholars have noted, while Machu Picchu is not laid out as a military installation, it is undeniable that, in contrast to many Inca sites, special design features made the site defensible in case of attack.

As this discussion suggests, the relationship between the elite and the surrounding rural population may have been perceived as sensitive, a tension reflected in the way hospitality was provided to these groups. Inca rule was premised on the myth of royal generosity. Inca bureaucrats spent much of their time feasting the taxpayers at state centers, providing them with corn beer, coca leaves, alpaca meat, and music. Studies at Huanuco Pampa and other Inca administrative centers have demonstrated that the structures most commonly found around the main open plaza areas are long hallways (sometimes called *kallankas* by archaeologists) used for this ritual feasting. What distinguishes these as kallankas are their many doorways and the large numbers of broken serving vessels found surrounding them.

In Machu Picchu, such kallankas are not found in the plaza area. Instead, smaller versions of the kallankas are associated with each of the elite compounds, as if the royal families created facilities only to entertain one another, excluding the larger agricultural population that likely inhabited the countryside. There is, however, one large kallanka in the Machu Picchu complex, located outside of the city walls about 400 feet to the south above the agricultural terraces. Although small by Inca standards, this ten-door kallanka is twice the size of any inside the city; it would have been perfect for entertaining a large group of farmers without allowing them inside the town walls. In front of the kallanka is an open plaza space with a carved stone, probably used for religious rituals on these occasions.

The reason for Machu Picchu's abandonment, so mysterious to many visitors, is easy to understand. The site was never a self-sufficient center with an economic base. Its very existence was a luxury made possible by the surplus labor and goods at the disposal of the Inca elite. When Tahuantinsuyu was conquered, the socioeconomic system underlying it collapsed, and royal estates like Machu Picchu lost both its reason and the resources to continue to function. Some royal estates closer to Cuzco such as Ollantaytambo were transformed into simple rural villages and continued to survive into the seventeenth century as part of the emerging colonial economy. Others, like Machu Picchu, were too far from the main road system and urban markets to make continued utilization feasible; by the time the farmers finally abandoned the area, the Inca elite and their retainers had long since fled, taking with them whatever portable objects were of value.

The reason Machu Picchu is not mentioned in any of the early Spanish historical narratives of the conquerors is not particularly mysterious either. Historical records of that time were the work of Spanish writers who wrote mainly of those settlements perceived as being of special economic or military importance. Royal estates, of which Machu Picchu was but one of many, had little reason to attract their attention, particularly if it had been abandoned before large numbers of Spaniards had entered the region. Other impressive royal estates, such as Pisac, are similarly ignored by these chronicles, even though they were nearer to Cuzco and continued to be used in colonial times.

Detail from Figure 4.15. The entrance gate to Machu Picchu.

IV The Nature of Inca Royal Estates

Susan A. Niles

Many of the archaeological sites visited by Hiram Bingham III and best known to modern travelers were the Inca royal estates. These complexes, built by an individual Inca ruler and used by him and his family, had significant economic and social functions in addition to their importance as pleasant places where the king and his courtiers could rest and enjoy themselves. Machu Picchu was one such estate, built by the king Pachacuti. This chapter explores the nature of Inca royal estates so that Machu Picchu can be understood in its historical and social context.

What Are Royal Estates?

Although they encompassed only a small portion of the territory that fell within the Inca Empire, royal estates were especially significant kinds of properties. They embed important notions of caste, privilege, and religion, and — better than any other kind of Inca construction — display the engineering prowess of their builders.

During the reign of the Incas, relatively little land was owned by individuals, and in this regard, royal estates operated differently from most holdings. There are particular reasons why estates were unusual, and why this pattern of ownership and design made sense. In order to understand Inca royal estates, we have to look at how Inca royal families were organized, and explore some of the activities that members of these families enjoyed.

Although nominally owned by an Inca king, royal estates were managed by and for the benefit of his family. The families acted much like a corporation, working to conserve their resources and their reputation and assigning management functions to various members. The head of the family and owner of its property was its founder, the Inca king, whether he was alive or dead. The corporations reflected the structure of Inca royal families. As was the case for their contemporaries in the royal houses of Europe, Inca descent was theoretically patrilineal. That is, a child inherited his or her most significant family identity from the father. This royal lineage was known as the *panaca*. In order to preserve the purity of the royal families, the late Inca kings (after the mid-fifteenth century) were expected to take their principal wife from among their full sisters. The marriage to the sister-wife was theoretically designed to produce a pure and unambiguous heir, but in practice, only one Inca king (Huayna Capac) was the product of such a union.

One of the most important rules of Inca royal descent

stated that each ruler must establish his own panaca. As soon as a son succeeded his father in office, he left the panaca of the father and became head of his own. The position was marked symbolically by his official marriage to his sister, which took place at the same time he succeeded to office. From this point on, he was the founder of a panaca, a potential ancestor. The sons who did not succeed their father in almost all cases remained as part of the father's descent group. The job of running the estate included managing the real property, plus managing the reputation of the dead owner, as the well-being of the living members of the descent group was directly related to the prestige accorded the dead ancestor. Posthumous grants to dead kings were made in cases where his reputation advanced — very likely owing to the strategic management of both the reputation and political alliances by important living members of the family. The produce of the land on royal estates sustained the living members of the descent group and, most important, maintained the cult of the dead lineage ancestor. He remained on his property, moving from palace to palace on his various estates, enjoying the food, beer, and other goods produced on its lands. The land belonging to dead kings remained their property. In fact, their holdings were so vast that the later rulers complained that the best property belonged to the dead, and there was little left to sustain the living kings. Huascar, the last king of Cuzco, scandalized the royal families by taking some of the estates that had belonged to the dead and using them for his own purposes.

The son who succeeded his father in office started out with power, but without wealth. One of his first acts was, of necessity, to find property that could be developed to support his family and his court. In short, he had to found a royal estate. The estate each king developed was designed to suit his own taste and his own social, economic, and political needs. Because the estates around Cuzco were developed sequentially, they are of particular interest to archaeologists who hope to examine differences that might be attributed to particular reigns.

How Were Estates Acquired?

The Incas loved to tell stories about their leaders' accomplishments, including legends that account for the founding of royal estates. These stories show the variety of ways in which particular members of royal families came to own property.

The creation of estates is, in many cases, associated with Inca military triumphs. Whenever they conquered new regions, the Incas embarked on construction projects that would serve their political agenda: roads and bridges facilitated the movement of the army into the region, and of tribute goods out to the capital; administrative centers housed the government overseers and provincial workers doing temporary service to the Inca state. Such constructions were the tangible proof of Inca superiority. Built in an alien style, by conscripted labor, they were monuments to Inca control of the provinces. Although not created exclusively to further the political agenda of the state, the royal estates served an equivalent function. They were reminders to local people of the new political order. The rich agricultural developments that were part of them, as well, were models of how the Incas could improve upon local practices.

Pachacuti, who ruled from around A.D. 1438–1471, celebrated each of his early military excursions by creating an estate (Rowe 1990: 143). Early in his reign, Pachacuti set out to conquer the Urubamba Valley. Consolidating control would give him access not only to the rich agricultural lands of the valley, but also to passes that would lead to the coca lands of Antisuyu and the silver and gold mines of Vilcabamba. Defeating first a group called the Cuyos, and later, the Tambos, Pachacuti marked each of those conquests with a permanent memorial of his victory: near the Cuyos' capital he created an estate and a palace at Pisac; in the old Tambo domain, he created an estate and palace at Ollantaytambo (Rowe 1990: 141). Machu Picchu was almost surely another example of Pachacuti's policy of building a monument to commemorate his conquest of this hard-won region (Rowe 1990: 141). Like Pisac and Ollantaytambo, it was a "jewel in his crown" that stood as a permanent memorial of his victory.

In other instances, royal estates were carved out of land that was not especially useful. In such cases, we assume the Inca reclamation of the land was more a demonstration of engineering prowess than of military expertise. This was the case in an estate created by Pachacuti's grandson, Huayna Capac, on a piece of for-

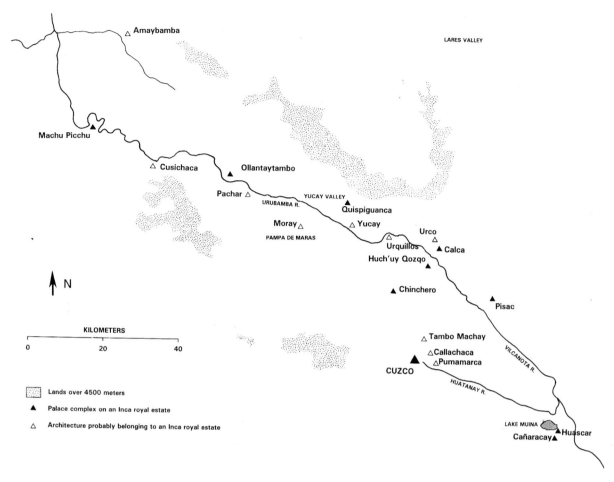

4.1 Royal estates near Cuzco.

merly worthless land in the meander plain of the Urubamba River. Although the property was in a region that had long been pacified, the land had been overlooked by his predecessors, probably as unworthy of their attention. But Huayna Capac made it productive by drafting 150,000 workers to canalize the river and to move soil onto agricultural terraces created in the formed swampland (Betanzos 1996: 170). When finished, the estate was one of the richest of the royal developments near Cuzco. Most likely, this ruler employed ambitious engineering and architectural innovations on his estate because of his interest in demonstrating his ability to control resources and improve upon the technological inventions of his ancestors (Niles 1999: 293–297).

Some royal land was acquired in the form of grants. When estates were created, the ruler sometimes left

pieces of the land to be used for the benefit of others. For example, the estate of Huayna Capac's father, Topa Inca, included grants to his principal wife, to other royal men, and to the Incas' chief divinity, the Sun (Niles 1999: 149–150; Villanueva Urteaga 1971). Huayna Capac was especially lavish with his grants. His estate near Urubamba included grants to his sister-wife, his dead mother, a favored secondary wife, and various unnamed lords and ladies (Niles 1999: 150–151). Many of the grants were probably made to reward the loyalty of the owners or their descent group in the wake of the various coup attempts that plagued Huayna Capac's early reign.

Estates were theoretically inalienable; that is, ownership was private and could not be transferred. However, grants could be expanded by later rulers who wished to honor an illustrious ancestor, and could be removed by

51

Table 4.1 Inca Holdings in Regions Surrounding Cuzco

Ruler	Reign	Estates
Manco Capac	Mythical	
Sinchi Roca	Unknown	
Lloque Yupanqui	Unknown	
Mayta Capac	Unknown	
Capac Yupanqui	Unknown	
Inca Roca	Unknown	Larapa
Yahuar Huacac	Unknown	
Viracocha Inca	Pre-1438	Huch'uy Qozqo
Pachacuti Inca Yapanqui	1438–1471	Pisac
		Pachar
		Picchu
		Tambo Machay
Topa Inca	1471–1495	Chinchero
Huayna Capac	1498–1527/8	Yucay/Urubamba
Huascar	1527/8–1532	Calca
		Muina
Atahualpa	1532–1533	None near Cuzco

Source: Information is based on a variety of sources. For full references see Niles (1999: 3, 76–77, 120).

a ruler when a dead owner fell from favor. For this reason, managing the reputation of the ancestor was an important part of the work of his descendants.

Where Were Estates Built?

The physical location of Inca royal estates mirrors the expansion of the empire carved out by these brave warriors. Historical documents — supplemented by archaeological surveys — verify the location of estates in most of the region surrounding the Inca capital, Cuzco (Figure 4.1). Located at the head of the Huatanay Valley, the capital was ringed by property that belonged to the Inca kings and nobles. Tracts were owned by the earliest known Incas, those who ruled prior to the mid-fifteenth century, when, under the leader Pachacuti, the Incas began to systematically expand their domain; the region continued to be developed for the latest Inca kings

(Table 4.1). Terraced fields and isolated architectural compounds surrounding the capital very likely belonged to these individuals. By perhaps the 1430s, the Incas were making conquests in the nearby, and considerably more lush and fertile, Vilcanota-Urubamba Valley. Rulers from that point onward added extensive developments from that region to their holdings closer to the capital. By the middle of Pachacuti's reign, lands in the forested regions north and east of Cuzco were also incorporated in the empire, and coca-growing estates were later established in the Amaybamba, Tono, and Qosñipata valleys. There may well have been royal estates in some provinces much farther from the capital, built as the empire expanded, but to date, no work has been done to identify any such holdings, if they existed.

Although we often think of the modern limits of archaeological sites as coterminous with ancient bound-

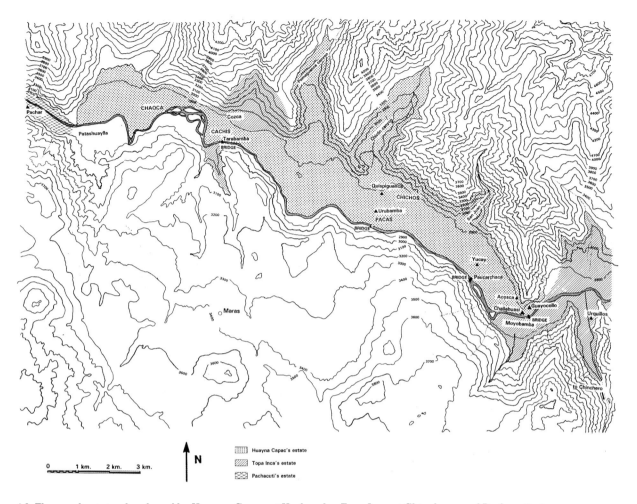

4.2 The royal estates developed by Huayna Capac at Urubamba, Topa Inca at Chinchero, and Pachacuti at Ollantaytambo.

aries, this is not the right way to view them. Rather, ancient palaces, such as those at Pisac, Chinchero, or Machu Picchu, were simply parts of a whole system of properties developed and owned by an Inca king as part of an estate.

Archaeological surveys, coupled with legal documents, suggest that the Incas conceived of estates as strings of fields located in arable spots along a valley floor, owned by an individual who had a palace nearby, and sustained by farmers in support communities built within the estate's boundaries. A single estate could consist of dozens of named plots of land, along with the infrastructure — roads, bridges, terraces, towns — needed

to make it profitable. The documentary evidence for estates — especially those from Urubamba and Chinchero (Villanueva Urteaga 1971) — shows that the Incas conceived of them as a string of named places organized in a logical way as an individual's properties. Estates were not the only kinds of properties conceived of as individual named places related in a logical way. The shrine system of the Inca capital that formed the focus of royal devotion was organized this way, as well. There, over three-hundred-fifty named shrines (*huacas*) were believed to be arrayed on forty-one lines (*ceques*) that were thought to emanate from the capital. In both cases, the records of properties (whether royal or sacred) could be

4.3 Terraces near the palace on Topa Inca's estate at Chinchero. Photo by Susan Niles.

easily recorded on *quipus*, the knotted string cords the Incas used to keep records. Some of these places included architecture, others included fields. On large estates, productivity figures and censuses were kept. The parts of the estate were related by access — whether by roads or rivers. Ownership was scrupulously recorded — whether the ruler, his associates, his children, or a deity was the nominal owner of the property. The quality of the land was noted, as well, with observations on whether it was good land or bad, used for maize or for collecting firewood, or to grow coca or hot peppers.

Because of the documentary evidence of the structure of these properties, it is possible to map the boundaries of estates. Estates were developed following major topographic features (Figure 4.2). Topa Inca's estate at Chinchero, for example, included the edge of a high plain, and continued down an adjacent canyon and to the fields immediately across the river from the canyon's mouth. Huayna Capac's estate at Urubamba began at

one constriction in the river valley, and ended more than nine miles down valley at the next significant constriction. Pachacuti's developments at Ollantaytambo began on the far side of the constriction where Huayna Capac's ended (at Pachar), and continued as far as the narrowing of the Urubamba canyon just beyond Ollantaytambo. Today, all these boundaries coincide with flow patterns of irrigation sources and with administrative boundaries; such features may have been relevant, as well, in antiquity.

Estates included fields as well as other kinds of developments. For example, at Ollantaytambo, palaces for the nobles, lodgings for the king, and shrines — the part of the site best known to visitors today — were but part of the estate: it included over nine miles of river-bottom land from Pachar to just below Ollantaytambo, reclaimed by canalizing the river and terracing the fields. It also included roads and bridges to provide access to them, and storehouses for the produce. (See Protzen

4.4 Overview of the terraces at Yucay that were part of Huayna Capac's estate. Photo by Susan Niles.

1993 for a discussion of Ollantaytambo.) Developments in the adjacent Patacancha Valley probably also relate to this estate.

How Were Estates Used?

Because the main purpose of the estates was to provide physical support for the ruling Inca and his descent group, they generally included substantial developments devoted to production of crops. Estates also included pastures, forests, and mines that were privately owned by a ruler (Rostworowski 1970: 253). Archaeologically it is easiest to identify many of the agricultural fields associated with estates. Some fields remained unterraced, but most estates included vast tracts of agricultural land, some of which was terraced to increase its productivity (Figures 4.3 and 4.4). On Huayna Capac's estate, for example, one terraced field measured over one-quarter mile in length by nearly one-tenth of a mile in width, and there were dozens of such fields. Terraces

provided level land in the mountainous region. They also helped to facilitate the movement of water across fields. In the highest regions, fields were devoted to potatoes; the bulk of the land in the Urubamba-Vilcanota Valley was devoted to maize, a staple valued in its own right, and also used to make the beer that was an important part of Inca ritual and entertaining (Figure 4.5).

In at least one case, we have evidence of salt production areas on an estate: Topa Inca owned land near Maras, at a town called Cache (which means "salt"), and some residents of the town were royal salt makers (Levillier 1940: 108). The extant system of terraces on which salt is produced by evaporating water from salty springs in the area probably makes use of the old royal Inca saltworks (Figure 4.6).

The efficiency of the state-level economy the Incas imposed on the captured provinces impressed their Spanish conquerors. Goods collected in tribute were

4.5 Maize grown on the terraces that were part of Topa Inca's estate in the valley below Chinchero. Photo by Susan Niles.

gathered in administrative centers, where they could be redirected to support such state endeavors as outfitting the army or provisioning the conscripts who were building Inca roads and bridges. The administrative efficiency of the Incas is seen in the compounds of storehouses that surround provincial administrative centers, such as Huanuco Pampa and other sites in the central highlands (D'Altroy 1992; LeVine 1992; Morris and Thompson 1985).

Just as goods from the state economy were stored in large complexes of carefully guarded storehouses, the produce of the royal economy was similarly warehoused. Recent work has identified a number of massive complexes of storage facilities adjacent to royal estate lands belonging to Pachacuti (Protzen 1993: 111–135), Topa Inca (Niles 2001; Niles and Batson 1999), and

Huayna Capac (Niles 2001; Niles and Batson 1999). Both the sheer size of the buildings as well as the capacity of the complexes attest to the quantity of goods produced on estates. In fact, the storage capacity of some royal storage compounds dwarfs the capacity of even the large administrative center. The scale of the storage facilities near royal estates suggests that, in the heartland of the empire, the royal economy far outpaced the state economy.

Several styles of storehouses are associated with royal sites. One compound noted by Bingham's contemporary at the site called Peñas, or Piñasniyoq, includes a group of fifty-one contiguous square chambers (Cook 1918: 108; and see Huaycochea Núñez de la Torre 1994: 130–172). This style might have been used to store tubers, such as potatoes (Protzen 1993: 119–121). The location of the site adjacent to the Inca road from Ollantay-tambo (Pachacuti's estate in the Urubamba Valley) and lands in Quillabamba and Amaybamba, where there were royal coca fields, suggests at least the possibility that it could have been used to warehouse this ritually important commodity, although the route may also have been used to transfer goods from the silver and gold mines of Vilcabamba to the Inca capital. Other groups of large, rectangular storehouses are related to the estates of Topa Inca and Huayna Capac, where maize was a major product, though, like the storehouses of Peñas, they could also have been used to warehouse goods needed to sustain workers or residents on the estates or to store goods in transit from other royal lands and the capital (Figure 4.7).

The presence of storehouses adjacent to royal estates, as well as the size of the structures and magnitude of the sites, reminds us that the royal economy was a very significant influence, and that estates had an important role in sustaining the elite families of Cuzco.

Estates as Social Cosmos

Estates, created as private patrimony for members of royal families, confirmed the belief of the Incas that they were special, their gods' chosen ones. Their special place relative to people of other ethnic groups was further affirmed by the social working of the estates.

Estates were created by conscripted labor and staffed by retainers who served the owner in perpetuity. These retainers (known as *yanacona*) farmed the land, maintained buildings, carried produce to storage, and served in the palace when the king and his courtiers were in residence. The support population mirrored the structure of the expanding Inca Empire.

As the Incas conquered new provinces, portions of the existing population were granted the status of *mitima*, or colonist. Colonists were removed from their natal villages and moved to communities to serve the Inca cause elsewhere. Some of the mitima settlers became retainers on Inca royal estates. For example, two thousand households of colonists of various ethnic

4.6 Terraces at Maras used for the production of salt by evaporation. They were probably originally part of Topa Inca's royal estate.

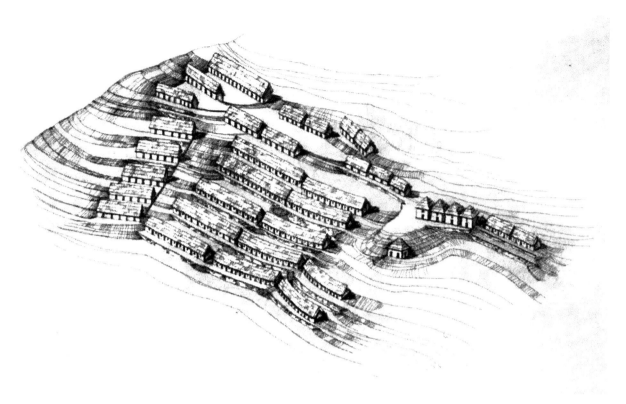

4.7 Reconstruction drawing of Mama Collca, a massive complex of storehouses associated with Topa Inca's royal estate near Chinchero. Drawing by Robert N. Batson.

groups were settled on Huayna Capac's estate; these settlers came from provinces in which he had active military campaigns (Collasuyu and Chinchaysuyu). An additional fifty households of colonists were brought from Ecuador—where Huayna Capac was consolidating conquests at the time of his death—to serve his mummy as retainers (Niles 1999: 131–133). While we do not always know the ethnic identity of the yanacona on estates, it is likely that some of the retainers on Pachacuti's estates were Soras, Lucanas, and Chancas. These were regions in which he had made early conquests, and from which additional servants were granted by his grandson to attend to the needs of his mummy (Betanzos 1996: 167). In addition to colonists from conquered provinces, estates had resident populations of ethnic Incas, brought to oversee projects on the estates.

The policy of moving people from the provinces to the estates meant that their population was made up of workers from varied ethnic backgrounds. Although we believe that workers were moved into settlements built for them by estate owners, we might expect that some of the patterns of their use of this space would show the inhabitants' status as foreigners. We might also expect that some heirloom objects might have been brought from their native land to leave a physical trace in the material record of the settlers' life. We have documentary evidence for the massive relocations of these retainers, yet relatively little archaeology has been done to identify the ethnicity of the support populations on estates. We can, however, suggest that the estates were maps of the Inca social cosmos.

Estates as Pleasant Places

While the importance of estates to the royal economy has dominated the discussion thus far, it is important to note that a major function of royal estates had to do with creating a place where the Inca ruler and his associates could relax between military ventures and indulge in activities they found pleasurable. Estates had palaces, parks, lakes, gardens, and dovecotes. Inca rulers are described as receiving and entertaining ambassadors at their country palaces, and Topa Inca spent most of his later years — after consolidating his conquests in the north — at his estate in Chinchero, gambling and dallying with a favored concubine. Spanish chroniclers noted the pleasurable function of estates, comparing them to Aranjuez, the summer palace of the Spanish court. We might make analogies to Camp David, where American leaders retreat to get away from the press of official business, as well as to entertain visiting dignitaries.

The activities in which the Inca indulged were varied: Topa Inca and Huayna Capac played gambling games on their estates. Rahua Ocllo, Huayna Capac's consort, raised doves and gardened on his estate. Both Huayna Capac and Pachacuti had hunting lodges on their holdings, as well, so they could indulge in that royal privilege. From sixteenth-century descriptions of Huayna Capac's palace, we know it was surrounded by lakes and parklands, and fountains and carefully tended gardens were also part of the landscape (Niles 1999; Villanueva Urteaga 1971). Gardens had flowers, trees, and exotic crops as well as crops of ritual importance like the hot peppers used in mourning ceremonies and the reeds used to ritually pierce the ears of young noblemen.

The heart of the estates was a palace, which we can often identify archaeologically and which is also mentioned in historical sources. It is somewhat frustrating that even when we can identify estates and associate them with rulers, it is often difficult to identify which particular complex within them would have been the palace structure. At best, we can use documentary evidence to locate the building, identifying features more commonly found in prestigious architecture to guess at which buildings may have served the ruler. In contrast to the palaces of their European contemporaries, in which a single structure had multiple rooms that served different functions, Inca rulers tended to build compounds in which discrete buildings served varied functions. For example, Hatun Cancha, in Cuzco, was said to have hundreds of component buildings within it, and Huayna Capac's town palace was large enough to include an artificial pond. But within these compounds, the specific quarters of the king cannot be identified with any certainty.

At Ollantaytambo, for example, the nine extant

4.8 At Ollantaytambo, stone-paved streets are shaded by the austere surrounding walls of palace compounds, probably built by Pachacuti for his nobles. Photo by Susan Niles.

groups of courtyard houses are described in historical sources as the palaces of nobles (Figure 4.8). Which — if any — actually belonged to the builder, Pachacuti, is unknown (Protzen 1993: 64). At Calca, the formally planned town had perhaps as many as twenty-three walled blocks of houses (Niles 1989). Two compounds have the double-jambed entrances and better-fitted masonry that make them more likely candidates for palaces of the site's builder, Huascar, but, again, the specific palace in which he may have spent time is not known. Even in the case of Huayna Capac, where documents make it clear exactly where the principal palace would have been, we have only surrounding walls and a few remnants of the component buildings by which to identify the compound (Niles 1999). And at that site, the palace in which the mummy of the dead owner was housed—which is, again, very specifically located in historical documents—cannot be identified at all.

If the imposing remains of palaces provide indefinite answers to archaeologists, we are even less secure in identifying the houses of the legions of retainers who served the estates. For example, the retainers who served Huayna Capac were settled in nine such towns, whose locations can be approximated; still, there is no physical trace of the residences where the support population lived.

Estates also had facilities for ritual, which was an important part of a ruler's duties and an even more important part of the duty of the custodians of his mummy. Huayna Capac, for example, had a water garden on his estate where he grew a particular kind of reed used to pierce the ears of young boys in the rite of passage that marked the move to manhood for noblemen. Some of the fields on his estate were almost certainly used to support the mummies of his dead mother and principal wife. Other fields were dedicated to the Sun, to produce the goods required for his worship.

Inca kings were divine, and demonstrations of piety—to both human and divine ancestors—were important. It is likely that much of the produce from their estates went to sustain their ritual obligations. It is also likely that any devotions that were required by circumstance (such as petitions to a deity or commemorations of a death) or by calendar (regularly occurring celebrations) would have been performed at estates if the ruler was in residence. Thus, in addition to the inherent sacredness of a particular location on an estate, estates likely had provisions for royal worship. There were also provisions for the devotions attendant upon the custodians of the royal mummy, when it was in residence on the estate.

Architecture on Royal Estates
Each ruler who developed an estate put his mark on it by creating structures that matched his vision of himself in the world. It is illustrative to compare the palaces of two Inca rulers whose handiwork is relatively well known. In the architecture built by Pachacuti and by his grandson, Huayna Capac, we see reflections of their differing concerns.

The first king to rule an empire, Pachacuti came to power by repelling an invasion of the Inca capital, displacing his father, and quashing at attempted usurpation of the position by his brother. More than any of the other Inca rulers, Pachacuti chose to present himself as a creator, with the formalized histories that retold his life focusing on his invention of laws, his creation of rituals (especially the funeral ritual), and his work as a builder. Pachacuti also embarked upon projects to physically reshape the world. He redesigned the Huatanay Valley, providing it with irrigation canals and terraces so that it could be more productively farmed. He rebuilt the Inca capital of Cuzco so that it would suit its new position as seat of an empire. In doing this, he devised a new architectural style, one which, according to some chroniclers, may have been based upon his impression of the smoothly fitted stonework of Tiahuanaco, an ancient site near Lake Titicaca with which the Incas had mythical ties (see, e.g., Cobo 1979: 141). Pachacuti's style was used in his redesign of some of the principal buildings of the capital, including its most sacred place of worship, the Temple of the Sun (Figure 4.9). In the stories that tell of his work as a builder, Pachacuti is described as laying out the plan of the city in clay models, joining his closest associates in taking up cords to measure out the building foundations personally (see especially Betanzos 1996: 44–45, 69–71). Whether or not the stories are true, they show that Pachacuti liked to portray himself as intimately involved in physically reshaping his world.

Many of the design features evident in Cuzco's style are seen in Pachacuti's royal estates. For example, the style of fitting blocks in perfect courses is seen in some of the buildings at the Inti Huatana sector of Pisac (Figure 4.10) and perfected at the "Semicircular Temple," or "Torreón," at Machu Picchu (Figure 4.11).

More than any other Inca builder, Pachacuti incorporated natural outcrops of bedrock into beautifully fitted walls at his country palaces. In some cases, for example, the cave that forms the "Royal Mausoleum" at Machu Picchu, masonry was fitted into the interstices of a natural cave or crevice (Figure 4.12). Other buildings seem

4.9 One of the structures in the Temple of the Sun in Cuzco, designed by Pachacuti. Photo by Susan Niles.

4.10 Inti Huatana sector of Pisac, one of Pachacuti's royal estates, showing the coursed, fitted masonry style he developed for important buildings. Photo by Susan Niles.

4.11 The exterior wall of the "Semicircular Temple" at Machu Picchu is another example of the coursed, fitted masonry Pachacuti favored. Photo by Susan Niles.

4.12 "Royal Mausoleum" at Machu Picchu shows a natural rock crevice completed by fitted masonry. Photo by Susan Niles.

to grow organically out of the bedrock (Figure 4.13). In such spaces, the architecture seems to complete a work left unfinished in nature: the boundary between the work of architect and Creator is blurred.

In this approach to design, Pachacuti is probably revealing something of his image of himself in relation to the spiritual forces that shaped his world. Bernabé Cobo tells a story about Pachacuti: on the eve of battle he had a vision of the Sun god in which it was revealed that he was that deity's chosen son. Later he devoted himself to the superior power of Pachayachachic, the Creator, to whom he dedicated temples and handiworks (Cobo 1979: 134–135). It does not seem too far a stretch to suggest that Pachacuti was emulating the Creator god in his

handiworks. Much as he took credit for establishing the social and religious order of the Incas, he also developed an architectural style that improves upon the handiwork of Creator. What the deity had left unfinished, Pachacuti completed. What the deity made good, Pachacuti made better, by framing a good view and making it perfect.

Pachacuti's work as a social reformer is suggested in the design of his palaces. He claimed to have invented Inca notions of caste, establishing the purity of the rulers by enforced brother-sister marriage, defining the Incas as a chosen people, elevating important allies to nobles of a lower rank (Incas-by-privilege), and imposing marriage and sumptuary laws to maintain and reaffirm these ranks. His architectural expression of this be-

4.13 Detail, Inti Huatana sector of Pisac, showing the incorporation of bedrock into the architectural structure, a design feature Pachacuti favored. Photo by Susan Niles.

4.14 Gateway through the wall that encloses portions of Pisac. Photo by Susan Niles.

lief system is seen in the pervasive use of walls and doorways in the structures he built. Walls and gateways are a prominent feature at such sites as Puca Pucara, his hunting lodge, which is ringed by a wall pierced by a single entrance. The ceremonial Pisac, built on a narrow ridge of land, is approached through a series of gateways that flank the formal pathway along the promontory (Figure 4.14). And anyone who has entered Machu Picchu on the "Inca Trail" has first encountered it through a splendid view framed by a formal gateway that shapes the visitor's first experience of the site (Figure 4.15). More symbolic definitions of the sites than effective fortification walls, such gateways and adjacent bits of wall do serve to define the royal precinct of Pacha-

cuti's estates, and at least symbolically control access to these sites.

Further, discrete compounds at sites devised by Pachacuti show arrangements of buildings that vary with respect to their size, building materials, and complexity of arrangement. For example, at Machu Picchu, some groups are composed of single structures arrayed along a terrace, while other parts of the site include buildings disposed around a courtyard (see Bingham's plan shown in Chapter 2, Figure 2.12). I have argued elsewhere that such variations in building size and arrangement most likely reflect differences in prestige among the residents of buildings or among the activities that took place within them (Niles 1987: 40–58).

4.15 The entrance gate to Machu Picchu framing a view of Huayna Picchu. Photo by Richard Burger.

Drawing on the principles of design devised by his grandfather, Huayna Capac developed an estate quite different in character (Niles 1999). Huayna Capac, who came to power around sixty years after Pachacuti began to build his empire, could benefit from a long-established tradition of architecture to design his palaces and could make use of time-tested principles of engineering to create the physical infrastructure of his estate. Still, having taken the helm of an empire that had virtually climaxed during his father's reign, Huayna Capac faced many problems. Within the first several years of his father's death, Huayna Capac had to quash two coup attempts spearheaded by highly placed members of Cuzco's nobility. His rule was so tenuous in some provinces that, according to one chronicler, he maintained control through the power and charisma of the Inca governors who had been placed there. In the early

years of his rule, Huayna Capac devoted his efforts to establishing his authority and reconfiguring the relations among the panacas of Cuzco. Later, he followed the tradition of leading the army to war, first consolidating control of rebellious provinces, and later pushing the empire's border farther north.

The estate Huayna Capac commissioned reflects the concerns that dominated his life. In particular, it provided the wherewithal for the especially lavish ritual and entertaining obligations of a late-Inca king, and it included architecture designed to inspire second thoughts in any fractious noble who might have questioned Huayna Capac's right to rule. His estate, centered at Yucay, covered nearly ten miles of the Urubamba River (see Figure 4.2). Although the region had been conquered by his grandfather (it is located between Pisac and Ollantaytambo in the same river valley), the Incas had not done much to reclaim the meander plain in this part of the valley. Huayna Capac saw the possibility of rehabilitating this seemingly worthless swampland, for to do so would be an unambiguous statement of his position: his land was fitted in to abut estates created by his father (on the eastern boundary) and his grandfather (on the western edge), just as he was fitted into the dynasty of Inca kings. Further, the task of making the land useful was a job worthy of his most ambitious ancestors. Basing his mid-sixteenth-century account on native descriptions, Juan de Betanzos writes: "He had the river moved along the side [of the valley] facing Cuzco making it stronger and making a bed where it went. Along the path of the river the Inca had hills leveled. Thus he made the valley flat so that it could be planted and harvested. There he had houses built and lodging where he could go to enjoy himself" (1996: 170).

The fields that were so prepared were worked by two thousand households of retainers settled permanently in towns built for them. The impressive agricultural works at the site (see Figure 4.4) would have amply supported the king's entertainment obligations while at the same time serving as a visible monument to his ability to command the labor of the farmers who worked on the terraces, and the builders who created them.

The lodgings to which Betanzos refers were similarly built to impress. Though no longer as well preserved as the palaces Pachacuti built, portions of the compound

4.16 Artist's reconstruction of the exterior of Huayna Capac's palace at Urubamba. Drawing by Robert N. Batson.

4.17 Artist's reconstruction of the triple-jambed portal into Huayna Capac's palace at Urubamba. Drawing by Robert N. Batson.

where Huayna Capac and his closest associates spent time can still be seen. The compound is built on a huge terrace, its rectangular area delineated on three sides by a tall wall (Figure 4.16). The palace was built within the walled area. In contrast to the architecture of Pachacuti, in which cut and fitted stone was commonly used in the most important buildings, here the major structures are composed of sun-dried adobe brick built on stone foundations. Walls were mud-plastered, and traces of bright red pigment in protected corners attest that the entire compound would have been painted. The most interesting feature at the site today is the gateway that provided access into the palace compound. The road that approached the palace was ramped so that visitors would pass through it at terrace-level (Figure 4.17). From the outside, the surrounding wall would have provided a forbidding façade. Its central feature, the massive triple-jambed portal, was formed by two-story towers (Figure 4.18). The only other openings in the surrounding walls would have been in the oversize windows high in these towers, and in the decorative doorways of the paired gatehouses that flanked it.

Within the compound's perimeter wall, the buildings of the palace compound were similarly built to impress. The north side of the plaza was dominated by a pair of halls, each built with a single wide opening in the wall overlooking the plaza (Figure 4.19). Measuring nearly 144 feet long and 45 feet wide, each structure would have had a gabled roof with a peak that towered over the plaza. This kind of building — and especially, its wide end-wall opening — was a triumph of Inca engineering principles. Its architect devised technical solutions to make such large buildings stand up; he also used visual tricks to make them seem even larger, by placing them next to smaller buildings and more intimate terraced spaces.

4.18 Remains of the adobe towers that form the triple-jambed portal at Urubamba. Photo by Susan Niles.

4.19 Artist's reconstruction of the great halls of the northern side of Huayna Capac's palace compound. Drawing by Robert N. Batson.

There were other buildings in the palace compound — at least one walled courtyard group, and a small pair of structures built between the great halls — but they are not as well preserved. Still, what can be observed reinforces the impression left by the better-preserved gateway and great halls: the buildings on Huayna Capac's estate were large and arrayed to focus inward, toward plazas and other constructed spaces; they were brightly painted; and they were built solidly, using right angles, on artificially created terraces. The structures were large and colorful, and oriented toward the central plaza, in the case of the great halls and the buildings along the surrounding wall, or toward a smaller plaza, in the courtyard group.

Although they are clearly related to the canons of prestigious Inca architecture, Huayna Capac's "lodgings" are quite different from the palaces designed by his ancestors. It is instructive to compare his creations to the palaces built by his grandfather, Pachacuti. Where Pachacuti chose to build on ridge tops and enhance views of impressive peaks by framing them, Huayna Capac's palace literally turns its back on the tallest snow peaks; the impressive views framed by its buildings were not of mountains and rocks, but of human-built spaces.

Where Pachacuti reveres nature by bending terraces, building groups, and even individual structures to conform to the existing terrain (Figure 4.20), Huayna Capac carves a new topography, moving rivers and building platforms to accommodate huge structures. While we do not know how Pachacuti might have modified the surfaces of his palaces, today their fitted stone walls grow in a seemingly organic way from the bedrock, echoing the form of nature. By contrast, Huayna Capac's adobe palaces boldly trumpeted their character, their broad walls brightly painted in colors that contrasted with the hues of the landscape around them. Huayna Capac's architecture uses scale, as well, to assert the triumph of the built form. Any pedestrian entering the portal would have felt dwarfed by the architecture. By contrast, a visitor to one of Pachacuti's palaces, though surely awed by the mastery of materials in the buildings, would have felt dwarfed by the mountains that were visible from nearly any point in the compound. Significantly, the most enduring impression Huayna Capac's palace evokes is of the triumph of culture over nature, while Pachacuti's works seem to continue the act of creating the landscape itself.

The palaces on Inca royal estates exemplify perhaps

4.20 Detail of a building group from Pisac, showing Pachacuti's propensity to conform building groups to the terrain. Photo by Susan Niles.

the most important function of such properties: they were places for the ruler to relax and enjoy himself and to rest in the company of his courtiers. It should be no surprise that the design of these most personal of creations would reflect the place of the royal owner. It is in such spaces that we come closest to seeing the builder's self-image, and where we can approach an understanding of the historical and social challenges that shaped him — and, by extension, the structures he created.

Inca royal estates served varied functions. They were part of the infrastructure of empire, serving to sustain the military agenda of the ruler and figuring in the political position of the Incas relative to other groups. Estates were also central to the domestic politics of the royal families of Cuzco, providing the setting for entertainment and the wherewithal for a ruler to support his descendants and to honor his ancestors. For archaeologists, they provide a rich source of information — both architectural and documentary — that permit us to better understand the workings of an ancient American empire.

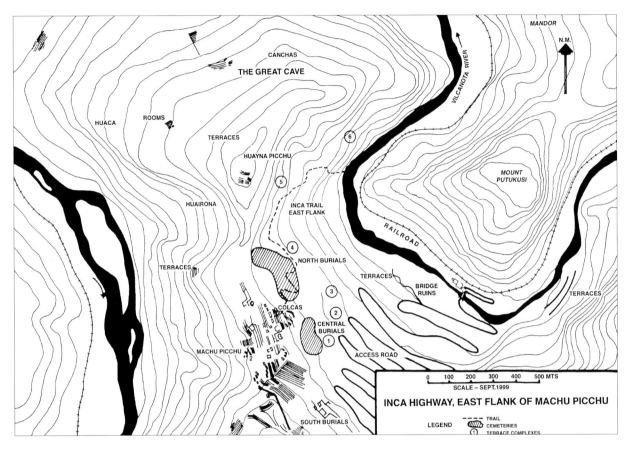

5.1 Plan of the Inca road, East Flank of Machu Picchu.

V Recent Archaeological Investigations at Machu Picchu

Alfredo Valencia Zegarra

Translated by Richard L. Burger

Considerable archaeological research has been carried out at Machu Picchu since the 1912 Yale Peruvian Expedition, often in conjunction with efforts to adequately conserve and develop the site for visitors. I have been fortunate to be involved in many of these investigations (Valencia and Gibaja 1992). In this chapter, I offer a brief overview of the recent archaeological explorations of Machu Picchu's Lower East Flank agricultural terraces and walls, the site's caves, the field surveying and mapping of the extension of the Inca Road beyond Machu Picchu, and other new archaeological evidence found on the eastern flank of Machu Picchu that included hydraulic and hydrologic analyses of its aquifers, pollen, and construction (Figure 5.1). Civil engineer Kenneth R. Wright of Wright Water Engineers, Inc. (WWE), and I, jointly carried out these investigations between 1995 and 1999.

The East Flank of Machu Picchu represents an area rich in new archaeological finds, a botanical and wildlife treasure and a civil engineering masterpiece, all occurring in conjunction with an Inca road of remarkable design and construction (Wright and Valencia Zegarra 2000). The East Flank's lush forest habitat supports much flora and fauna, including the rare and endangered spectacled bear (*Tremarctos ornatus*), within several hundred feet of one of South America's most visited archaeological sites. In 2001, one of these rare bears wandered into the main Machu Picchu site before returning to the forest via the Inca Road's long granite staircase, described below (Figure 5.2).

The numerous terraces and walls on the East Flank, over a vertical distance of 1,723 feet, are associated with the Inca Road, just over a mile long, which traverses the forest from top to bottom. The terraces and walls provide great stability on the steep landslide-prone slopes as well as pleasant visual impacts associated with creating permanency and control of the mountainside. Fountains, way stations, drains, and agricultural-worker buildings provide impressive additional infrastructure for the road.

Agricultural Zone on the Eastern Slopes

Along the eastern slopes of Machu Picchu six large *conjuntos* of Inca agricultural terraces can be found united by a major Inca Road (Hatun Ñan). I use the term *conjunto* to represent a group or a whole — a complex. This road links the center of Machu Picchu with the six agricultural terrace complexes, which we numbered 1

5.2 **Sighting of the rare spectacled bear in the Machu Picchu Historical Sanctuary. Photo by Ken Wright.**

through 6. These included the two distinct lower groups of terraces 5 and 6 reaching all the way down to the left bank of the Urubamba River. These terrace complexes were never explored by Bingham and the Yale Peruvian Expeditions and had been overlooked by previous investigators, likely because of the steep slope and thick forest. Nevertheless, as a student in 1969, I was able to roughly map them after a forest fire had denuded the area. The maps, unfortunately, were somehow lost.

Complex 1 is found downhill of the lowest of the six barracks and storehouses of the agricultural center of Machu Picchu, and adjacent to the northeast wall. This *conjunto* has a triangular form and consists of nineteen terraces in its central part and other terraces in the lower and upper parts. A road and doorway through the wall provide access to a secondary road to the Urubamba River. The WWE excavations carried out in September

of 1998 resulted in the discovery of a fountain with a rectangular layout (Figure 5.3). It is located at the base of a terrace wall with a channel that, when cleaned, allowed the discharge of underground waters. This excavation also permitted us to learn of the existence of three stratigraphic layers within the fountains: a superficial humus layer with fallen stones from the partially destroyed upper part of the fountain, a second layer of brown soil with fragments of monochrome Inca ceramics, and the third stratum of soil deposited at the bottom of the fountain.

The duct for draining the water is small and has a trapezoidal form with a width of 14 inches and a height of 20 inches. The water flowed at a rate of up to 2.64 gallons per minute, and its analysis indicated that it had a pH of 7.0 and an alkalinity of 9. According to Wright, the analysis indicates that this water was of high quality

5.3 Fountain 1, collecting samples of water. Photo by Alfredo Valencia Zegarra.

with a low content of dissolved solids (Wright, Valencia Zegarra, and Crowley 2000: 9).

On the upper surface of some of the terraces we observed the untouched foundations of several small buildings that were likely the modest dwellings of the farmers. Archaeological excavation of these enclosures could provide important information concerning their contents and may also provide evidence about the daily lives of the farmers at Machu Picchu.

Dr. Linda Scott Cummings of the Paleo Research Institute in Golden, Colorado, analyzed the samples of pollen the WWE recovered from different terraces at Machu Picchu during the 1998 and 1999 field seasons. A sample taken on the eastern slopes on a terrace in complex 1 above the fountain yielded evidence of the cultivation of maize (corn), potatoes, and a type of legume (Wright, Valencia Zegarra, and Crowley 2000: 15).

In terrace complex 2, to the north of complex 1, we found a zone of terraces smaller than all the others, with semi-curved terraces that conformed well to the topography. Terrace access is by means of stairs made of large, flat stones set into the retaining walls of the terraces. We call these "flying stairs." One of the terraces has a kind of niche, owing to the accommodation of the wall construction on top of a large stone. On one terrace we uncovered a large semi-circular building that measures 115 feet in length and 16 feet in width and whose entryway is on the north. This enclosure likely served as a living area for farmers. No evidence of water supply was found in this complex, although fountain 1 was nearby.

Complex 3, located north of complex 2, has a general pentagonal form and is made up of various narrow terraces that are internally connected by way of flying stairs (Figure 5.4). In its middle section is a fountain without a reliable water source, but it has a receptacle at its base

5.4 Alfredo Valencia Zegarra standing in front of terrace complex 3. Photo courtesy of Alfredo Valencia Zegarra.

that channels its waters to the next terrace by way of a narrow duct. The waters of the channel were caught at the foot of the terrace and then carried to the lower part of the complex. Its flow was irregular, and in the southern hemisphere's winter months (May, June, and July), its waters diminished but then increased notably in the summer season.

Complex 4, the next complex to the north, is the most impressive and beautiful, and one of the most extensive along Machu Picchu's eastern slopes (Figure 5.5). It is some 820 feet long by 328 feet wide. Two narrow staircases permit one to go down each of the lower terraces, which extend to the edge of a vertical granite precipice. The southern section of this complex is composed of large terraces, but the northern is more important because here we found two fountains of excellent stonework (fountains 3 and 4) and a viewing platform

terrace with a perennial water source (Figure 5.6). At the interface with terrace complex 5 is a water tunnel that furnished water to fountain 5. An excellent portion of the Inca Road passes through complex 4 longitudinally. It is 6.5 feet wide, and along its length it contains stairs and a ramp of fine construction that range up to almost 10 feet wide.

The laboratory analysis of the water from the two interconnected fountains in complex 4 produced the following results: a pH of 7.0, a water flow of 1.8 gallons per minute, 56 parts per million (ppm) of dissolved solids, 16.2 ppm alkalinity, 0.41 ppm chlorides, and 0.49 ppm sulfates. The dissolved metals consist of 3.1 ppm sodium, 0.98 ppm potassium, 3.0 ppm calcium, and 1.3 ppm magnesium. The water is judged to be of high quality (Wright, Valencia Zegarra, and Crowley 2000: 9).

The excavations of these fountains allowed us to de-

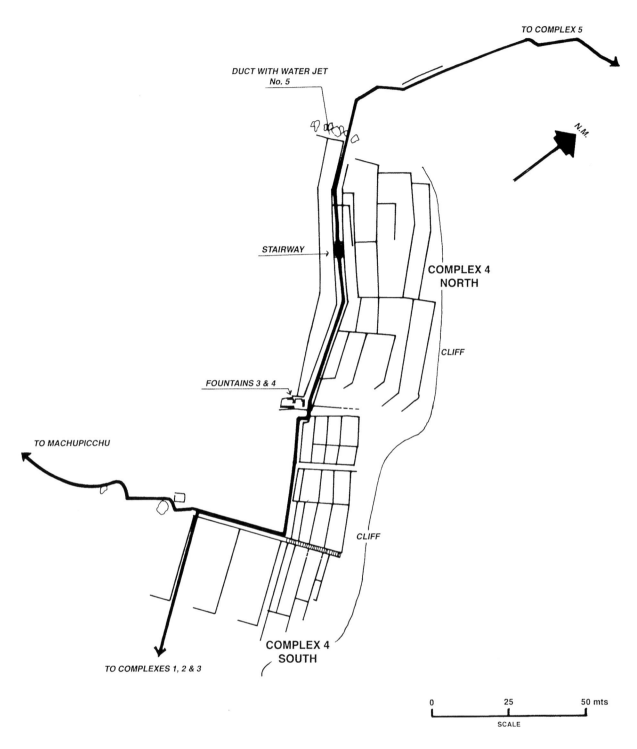

TO COMPLEX 5

DUCT WITH WATER JET
No. 5

N.M.

STAIRWAY

COMPLEX 4
NORTH

CLIFF

FOUNTAINS 3 & 4

TO MACHUPICCHU

CLIFF

COMPLEX 4
SOUTH

TO COMPLEXES 1, 2 & 3

0   25   50 mts

SCALE

EAST FLANK OF MACHU PICCHU

COMPLEX 4 – WRIGHT, CROWLEY & MARSHALL
DATE 1999

5.5 Plan of complex 4, East Flank of Machu Picchu.

5.6 Fountain 3 after excavation. Photo by Alfredo Valencia Zegarra.

lineate their forms and become familiar with their stratigraphy. The surface layer was made up of soil humus and stones fallen from adjacent walls. The second layer consisted of finer and very moist brown soil and a fine gravel, mainly at the base of the fountains and in the small canals. Three lithic artifacts were recovered; a pestle of a mortar, an ovoid mortar, and a polished granite slab fragment. There were also fragments of Inca ceramics in clear association with the archaeological features.

Fountains 3 and 4 were square with four small walls that defined them above a quadrangular base and a well-polished stone spout (Figure 5.7). In their interior walls were small niches. The water, after it was carried from its source via a channel, was used in the first fountain, then spilled to the adjacent lower one and finally over a high stone wall onto the lower-lying terrace. At the base

of the wall were numerous pieces of broken pottery. These two fountains were very similar to those in the center of Machu Picchu as well as those at other sites such as Choquesuyuy, Chachabamba, Wiñay Wayna, Sayacmarca, and Phuyupatamarca — all of which indicate common design standards. As dramatic proof of the quality of the Inca hydraulic design, after we had excavated the fountains and cleaned out the earth-filled stone channel, the two fountains burst into operation after being buried for some 450 years. The spouts of both fountains were designed with a narrowing of the channel width to create a water jet. We used this water for our much needed daily water supply.

Excavations have also been carried out in the extreme northern section of complex 4 in the area of the water tunnel where the spring and a small channel were completely covered by earth and debris and the relatively re-

5.7 Fountain 4 shortly after excavation. Photo by Alfredo Valencia Zegarra.

cent collapse of large rocks falling from far above, from around the fissure near the beginning of the Inca Road up to Huayna Picchu. A stone-lined conduit had been constructed beneath the terrace until it reached the base of a large rock where the flow from the spring can be noted. The conduit is 8 feet long and 3 feet wide, and is quadrangular in cross section.

Above the duct is a small cave blocked off with an Inca wall and completely filled in with a type of gravel that seems related to it. In this cave was a small amount of Inca pottery and the skull of an agouti, a kind of rodent also found at Machu Picchu by George Eaton in 1912 (1916). Eaton indicates that during his excavations in the burial caves and refuse deposits at Machu Picchu, he found the bones of at least eight rodents. He highlights the discovery of a skull of the genus *Agouti* in a small garbage deposit at the eastern limit of the urban

center of Machu Picchu, which is to say in the upper part of the terraces of the eastern slopes. Eaton writes of this skull, "It is different from all of the species known up to now described under the genus *Agouti*. For that reason, I have selected this cranium (C.O. 3227) as the type specimen of a new species that I have the honor to name Agouti Thomasi [sic] in honor of Mr. Oldfield Thomas of the British Museum (of Natural History)" (Eaton 1916: 62). The skull of the agouti we recovered was found in good condition, although we did not encounter the lower mandible; it belongs to an adult animal with heavy tooth wear. Excavation at the water duct was terminated prematurely when we came across venomous snakes.

Complex 5 was located at the foot of Huayna Picchu Mountain at an altitude of 6,890 feet above sea level (Figure 5.8). Covering an area of 59,255 square feet, it

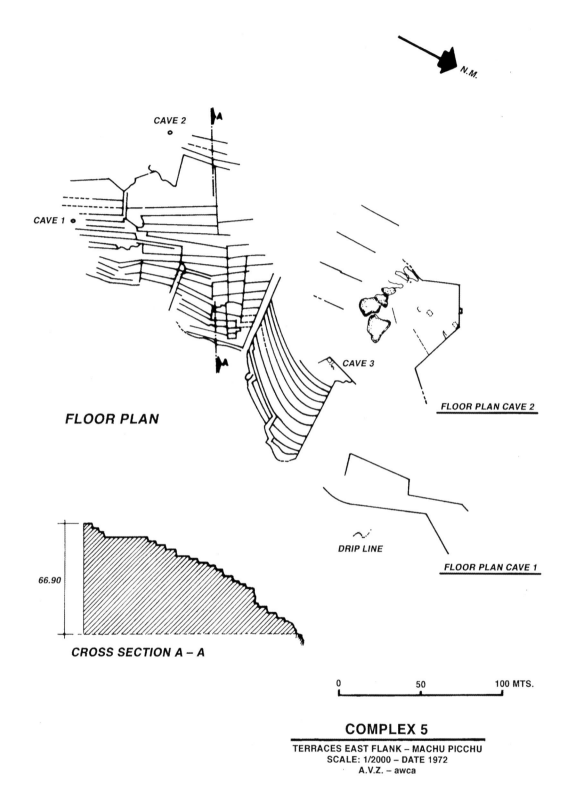

N.M.

CAVE 2

CAVE 1

CAVE 3

FLOOR PLAN

FLOOR PLAN CAVE 2

DRIP LINE

FLOOR PLAN CAVE 1

66.90

CROSS SECTION A – A

0   50   100 MTS.

COMPLEX 5

TERRACES EAST FLANK – MACHU PICCHU
SCALE: 1/2000 – DATE 1972
A.V.Z. – awca

5.8 Plan of complex 5, East Flank of Machu Picchu.

consists of two large sectors of handsome terraces divided by a large, well-built staircase that crosses through the terraces from east to west. Nearby is a large cave and two rock shelters, one in the extreme southeast and the other in the extreme north. The terraces have a rectangular layout and are connected to one another by an impressive case of inset stairs. These stairs provide access to the Inca Road, which leads to complex 6.

Complex 6 is one of the largest and most complicated sectors of terraces (along with complex 4) on the eastern slope of Machu Picchu. It consists of a series of terraces that have long been hidden by dense forest. Extending from cave 3 in complex 5 down to the left bank of the Vilcanota River, it includes both wide and narrow terraces accessible by the main road and also by flying stairs and ramps. It is likely that in the road's lower section it would have been possible to cross the river by way of an Inca bridge in order to join the known Inca Road at the bottom of the valley. In the lower part of complex 6 and next to the road, which in this section is carved into an outcrop of granite, is a spring. The water of this aquifer was analyzed and yielded the following results: a flow of 2.6 gallons per minute and a dissolved solids analyzed at 24 parts per million. Near the spring is a well-designed staircase carved into the granite bedrock.

The calculation of the agricultural production of maize on the recently investigated terraces of the eastern slopes of Machu Picchu is only approximate because we do not have detailed topographic maps of all the terrace complexes. Nonetheless, based on the sketch maps completed thus far, we have established that terrace complexes 1, 2, and 3 cover an area of 32,280 square feet; complex 4, 64,560 square feet; complex 5, 36,200 square feet; and complex 6, 32,280 square feet. Totaling 3.7 acres, these six terrace conjuntos could have yielded an annual harvest of approximately 5,280 pounds of shelled maize along with other minor crops that would have complemented this highly valued crop. The maize harvested was likely brought to the center of Machu Picchu and stored at the six large two-story storehouses found at the very beginning of the main road, for later distribution and consumption.

The complexes present traces of rustic buildings constructed on some of the terraces, which were probably used to provide housing for the farmers of these terrace systems. This fact is important inasmuch as it offers us the opportunity to study that part of the population of Machu Picchu that lived in the vicinity of the agricultural terracing. These buildings, although few, could also have been used for temporary storage of agricultural products before they were transferred to the center of Machu Picchu.

The Inca Road

The newly discovered Inca Road extends from the staircase of the storehouse complex down to the edge of the Vilcanota River at the foot of Huayna Picchu Mountain. The road along the sloped terrain is a little over a mile long, although when seen in a horizontal plan, it appears to be just under a mile long. Over this stretch of road, the elevation drops 1,723 feet. The slope of the road is surprisingly uniform if we consider the rugged topography of the mountainous environment (Wright, Crowley, and Marshall 1999). The construction of the road was a remarkable work of engineering. It was paved with stone slabs and includes sections with finely finished staircases and paved ramps. At certain intervals along the road are platforms, apparently created to serve as rest stops, as well as caves and buildings. In several of the terrace complexes, the road passes by springs and fountains providing fresh water to travelers.

From its origin in the upper main Machu Picchu site, the Inca road descends by way of a steep, narrow granite staircase until it reaches a small Inca building that we judged to be a control station. This structure was studied in 1997. Following this, a stairway leads in a zigzag to a ramp supported by a retaining wall 82 feet long and completely paved with stone slabs. After a descent by extensive straight and curved stairways and ramps that have been well constructed with blocks of stones united by clay mortar, one arrives at complex 4 (Figures 5.9 and 5.10). At this point, the main road branches into two sections. The primary road descends and leads northeast toward complexes 4, 5, and 6. The minor branch of the road has only a slight slope and continues on to complexes 1, 2, and 3, thereby interconnecting the southeast side of Machu Picchu Mountain.

After passing complex 4, one arrives at the middle section of complex 5, and then on its extreme south the road passes below cave 1. This cave is 16 feet long and 10

5.9 Staircase of the main road in sector 4. Photo by Alfredo Valencia Zegarra.

feet wide. Cave 2, located in the upper central part of this complex, is pentagonal and delimited by two walls of fine granite masonry. On the surface, it is possible to observe various finely worked stones from destroyed masonry, perhaps disturbed during the Bingham explorations. Cave 3, a cathedral-like formation of vertical granite slabs, is found in the extreme north at the edge of complex 5. It consists of a large space that covers 270 square feet. At the bottom of this space, at ground level, are two large, flat stones worked into the form of seats. Nearby is a long, perfectly formed curved wall. From there, the road continues on to complex 6. This last section of the road merits additional exploration because it is covered with heavy vegetation and we were not able to fully explore it. The road in the lower part runs along the frontal face of the Huayna Picchu geological fault, passing by a section of polished, natural stone where one observes various depressions or cavities upon which rest the stones of the staircase where the road continues.

Nearby is fountain 6, which is completely destroyed, and only the water flow is observable.

The road ends at the bank of the Urubamba River where Inca walls still exist. It permitted connection to the main river route road at Machu Picchu that ran along the right bank of the river until Ollantaytambo, passing by various intermediate sites. Along this route, after passing the control site of Piscacucho, it is possible to observe the cave painting near Luqmachayoq and the buildings of Canabamba. Downstream, along the Urubamba River, the road continues to Antisuyo, which connects with the capital of Tahuantinsuyo and permitted communication with the historic territory of Vilcabamba, the bastion of the last Inca rulers. This road permitted the penetration of the extensive but little explored valleys of the tropical forest in the province of La Convención. The tropical and semitropical plants, the great variety of fruit trees, and the sacred leaf of the coca, used for ritual activities, were also important to

5.10 Steep staircase, part of the Inca road leading down to the Urubamba River. Photo by Kenneth R. Wright.

the inhabitants of Machu Picchu. The camelids from the high grasslands (*puna*) were important for their diet, as was meat from the wild animals of the cloud forest (*ceja de selva*). Copper and tin, as well as gold and silver, were utilized in their metallurgy.

To the economic function of the Inca road, we can add a military and strategic function, considering that in the vicinity of Machu Picchu these roads are protected by a large wall that runs along the eastern slopes. The road is also protected naturally by dangerous precipices. Strict control of human movement was also maintained by the existence of only one entryway to complex 1 and by the bridge, which must have been well guarded. The East Flank Inca road of Machu Picchu could be observed by strategically placed lookout stations.

Ceremonial Function of the Road

This Inca Road permitted easy access between the Machu Picchu center and the extensive cemeteries ex-

plored by Eaton (1916) and Bingham (1930). The map of the geography where Machu Picchu was found, made by Hiram Bingham during the 1912 Yale Peruvian Expedition, allows us to appreciate three large complexes of tombs along the eastern slopes: one to the north, another at the center, and a third to the south. The first two of these, located just below the archaeological monument of Machu Picchu along its eastern slopes, are accessible by way of the Inca Road, whose path was first mapped by the WWE in 1999. The northern conjunto of Inca tombs contained those Eaton numbered in the following manner: 1–8, 12–17, 45, 47, and 48. In the central group, tombs 28–40 were found, and in the south caves, tombs 9, 11, 18–22, 26, 49, and 52 were found. The burial structures varied in form from simple or individual tombs to composite structures for two individual subterranean burials resembling a kind of gallery covered by stones. Cave 79 contained a type of ceramic urn.

The majority of buried individuals have been found on the eastern slopes of Machu Picchu, in a flexed, seated position without a defined orientation. These sites revealed a high percentage of ceramic objects (56 percent of the offerings) such as cooking pots, serving plates with two handles, small plates, plates with bird's head handles, plates with a ring base, small bowls, jars, and so forth. The next most common burial objects were metal artifacts (20 percent) such as bronze pins, silver pins, knives, tweezers, broaches, mirrors, and bronze crowbars. Some artifacts were related to textile production (8 percent) such as bronze bone awls, cactus spine needles, vegetable fibers, textiles of camelid wool, and fine textiles. Lithic artifacts (2 percent) such as hammerstones, mortars, and pestles were also recovered. The remains of animals (11 percent) such as llamas, deer, dogs, and edible land snails were noteworthy, as was carbon and other plant materials (3 percent) (Valencia and Gibaja 1992: 257). The function of these objects was related to death and was required as part of the rites and social activities defined within the ceremonial calendar.

Evaluation of the many terraces, fountains, and other structures on the East Flank of Machu Picchu demonstrates that the Inca road, found here, is the most important of the numerous roads leading out of Machu Picchu. It is also evident that the Inca builders were good civil engineers. The excavations and archaeological exploration described here have allowed us to affirm with confidence that, from the spatial perspective, there existed a well-defined relationship between the six fountains, six terrace groups, and way stations. From the point of view of relative chronology based on the study of architecture, cultural materials such as pottery, lithic artifacts, and stratigraphic contexts by means of archaeological excavation, we are able to validate the affiliation of this area to the Inca culture, which corresponds to the Late Horizon.

At this point, it is worth emphasizing John Rowe's publication of a sixteenth-century document in the historic archive of Cuzco, where it is indicated that the cultivated lands at the bottom of the narrow valley from Torontoy downstream were the property of Pachacuti. According to Rowe, "If the lands from the bottom of the canyon belonged to Inca Yupanqui, it is probable that the neighboring lands at higher elevations but not far from the river such as Machu Picchu would have also formed part of the royal estate of the Inca Yupanqui" (1987a: 16). As our recent research has shown, this royal property also included the six complexes of agricultural terraces, described here for the first time, as well as the administrative, political, and religious center of Machu Picchu, documented by Hiram Bingham and the 1912 Yale Peruvian Expedition.

Additional archaeological research potential on the East Flank of Machu Picchu is significant, the 1995–1999 archaeological exploration being limited primarily to the route of the main Inca road and a few of its branches. However, any additional access and research in this area must be balanced against possible adverse effects on the forest habitat there with particular attention to protection of the home of the spectacled bear, a treasure of the Machu Picchu archaeological site.

6.1 Naturalist and chemist Harry Foote, in search of insects. Photo by Hiram Bingham.

VI Scientific Insights into Daily Life at Machu Picchu

Richard L. Burger

For most of the twentieth century, our understanding of Machu Picchu was shaped by the ideas of Hiram Bingham III and the results of the expeditions he led. Bingham considered himself an explorer first and a historian second. He never had pretensions to being a scientist (A. Bingham 1989). Most early-twentieth-century archaeology had a strongly humanistic orientation, and Bingham's work was far from being exceptional in this regard. In thinking about the Incas, Bingham had a natural inclination to comb historical narratives for clues and, perhaps, draw upon his ethnographic observations among the Quechua-speaking farmers of the Urubamba drainage.

Almost a century has passed since Bingham's discoveries. In the United States, archaeological study of the Incas has become the domain of scholars trained in anthropology. As a consequence, the questions formulated and the techniques used to answer them have become strongly influenced by currents in the social and physical sciences. Over the past two decades, much progress has been made in archaeological analysis and it is now possible to ask and answer questions about Machu Picchu that would have seemed inconceivable to Bingham and his colleagues.

Beginning in 1983, the Yale Peabody Museum facilitated a series of new technical analyses by a variety of specialists in order to explore the scientific potential of the Bingham materials; other scientific studies were initiated independently at Machu Picchu itself. Questions focusing on diet, technology, and patterns of interaction have now been explored based on laboratory studies of the Machu Picchu collections recovered in 1912 and in the more recent field investigations. The findings of these studies give a much fuller and more accurate idea of the life of the people who lived at Machu Picchu. The purpose of this chapter is to provide a summary of these technical analyses and consider how they modify our understanding of daily life at the Inca royal estate at Machu Picchu.

Antecedents from the Yale Peruvian Expeditions

While not a scientist, or even an archaeologist, Hiram Bingham III was not a stranger to the idea of utilizing state-of-the-art scientific knowledge in order to shed light on Machu Picchu. As a historian focusing on modern Latin American development, Bingham had a detailed knowledge of the economic geography of South America. He had great respect for the technical knowledge necessary to evaluate and develop the natural resources in this continent and, in 1908, he was chosen as the youngest member of the United States delegation to the Pan-American Scientific Congress in Santiago, Chile. In organizing the Yale Peruvian Expeditions of 1911, 1912, and 1914–1915, Bingham put together teams of specialists from a wide range of fields. For example, the expedition of 1911, which resulted in the "scientific discovery" of Machu Picchu, included geographer Isaiah Bowman, chemist Harry Foote, and naturalist Casimir Watkins (Figure 6.1). The expedition of 1912, which focused on the excavation of Machu Picchu, included George Eaton, curator of osteology at the Yale Peabody Museum, and Herbert Gregory, a professor of geology at Yale. It would not be an exaggeration to characterize Bingham's archaeological projects as interdisciplinary investigations, and, in some respects, Bingham's historic expeditions foreshadowed an interdisciplinary archaeological approach that did not become popular in Peru until the 1970s, with projects such as Richard MacNeish's Ayacucho-Huanta Archaeological-Botanical Project.

The three Yale Peruvian Expeditions were interdisciplinary not only in staff composition but also in the discoveries they produced. Thus, the publications stemming from the expeditions included studies of the natural history of reptiles, amphibians, insects, mammals, land snails, and cacti, as well as the geography and geology of Cuzco, Andean terracing, and the physical anthropology of contemporary highland and lowland indigenous peoples (Bingham 1922). The biological investigators encountered numerous species never before documented. Most important from the perspective of this chapter, the specialists Bingham engaged used their expertise to analyze the archaeological materials from Machu Picchu with techniques that were sophisticated by the standards of their time. George Eaton (1916) produced an influential volume on the human skeletal material recovered in the Inca tombs at Machu Picchu, and Foote and Buell (1912) and Mathewson (1915) carried out chemical studies of the metal artifacts. These pioneering scientific analyses had a powerful impact on Bingham's interpretations, and they provide the antecedents for the research discussed here. Although these early analyses have now been partially superseded,

when used critically they continue to provide insights and information of lasting value.

Curiously, the interdisciplinary character of the Yale Peruvian Expeditions has received little attention in studies of the history of archaeology. Most scholars have dwelled on the technical limitations of Bingham's archaeological training and practice. Bingham's conscious decision not to include professional archaeological personnel on the staff of the expeditions undermined his efforts and was responsible for some of the flawed interpretations that resulted. Nevertheless, the broad focus of Bingham's three expeditions is noteworthy, reflecting his distinctive vision of archaeology as part of a larger geographic endeavor. His involvement of first-class technicians was consistent with his pride in the technological prowess of the United States. The team that made up the 1912 Yale Peruvian Expedition stands in sharp contrast to that of other archaeological projects carried out in Peru in the early twentieth century by such investigators as Max Uhle, Julio C. Tello, Alfred Kroeber, and Luis Valcarcel. For these scholars, archaeological field research was a largely self-sufficient enterprise that might involve complementary historical research but did not require specialists from more scientific disciplines. The publications stemming from their research were limited to descriptions of excavations and artifacts, rarely involving technical studies of any kind. Thus, the scientific work described in the following sections can be seen as following the trail blazed by Bingham and the Yale Peruvian Expeditions.

Health and Diet at Machu Picchu

The archaeological site of Machu Picchu corresponds to a royal estate built by the emperor Pachacuti and controlled by his descendants (or *panaca*) roughly until the Spanish Conquest (Burger and Salazar-Burger 1993; Rowe 1990). The best-known portion of that estate is a finely constructed architectural complex that was created on the ridge crest between Machu Picchu Mountain and Huayna Picchu Mountain to serve as a country palace for the royal family, their guests, and their retainers. Although Bingham referred to it as a "lost city," probably no more than 750 people lived there at any given time. During the rainy season (November–April), the population probably dropped to only a few hundred people, most of whom were religious specialists and members of the support staff.

During the Yale Peruvian Expedition of 1912, over a hundred tombs were encountered, most of them hidden by the dense cloud forests of the site's eastern slopes. Concentrated in three clusters, these interments were usually placed within crevices beneath large granite boulders. In many cases, coarse walls were added to seal these simple tombs and protect them from animals and other intruders. The small number of grave goods, the modest quality and nature of these objects, and the variability of the skeletal materials indicate that these are the graves of Machu Picchu's retainers rather than interments of the members of the royal family or their guests (Burger and Salazar-Burger 1993; Salazar and Burger 2003; see also Chapter 3). Subsequent archaeological work at Machu Picchu has failed to uncover tombs that are significantly more elaborate than those found in 1912 (Valencia and Gibaja 1992). This mortuary pattern is not surprising, for if members of the Inca elite had died while residing at the country palace, they would have been transported to their principal residence in Cuzco rather than buried at Machu Picchu. Because the elite were transported on litters and because the journey to the capital took only three days, this option would not have presented serious obstacles.

This background information is necessary to understand the significance and limitations of the recent analysis of the human skeletal materials recovered by the Yale Peruvian Expedition. This osteological analysis can illuminate many aspects of the lives (and deaths) of Machu Picchu's retainers, but it does not cast an equivalent light on the elite residents for whom the site was built. Because the Spanish chronicles devoted slight attention to the Incas' retainers and other staff, however, the information the osteological analyses provide is particularly welcome. It should be emphasized that the group of people buried at Machu Picchu was not homogeneous in status or ethnicity, as evidenced from the burials themselves. Despite this variability, however, it is first useful to consider the burial results as a group in order to obtain a general picture of what this population was like.

George Eaton, one of Bingham's colleagues at Yale, was the project osteologist on the 1912 expedition, and in

1916 he published a detailed study of the human remains that were recovered. Unfortunately, Eaton had not worked previously with skeletal materials from the Andes, and he was hampered by the lack of a large comparative sample of Peruvian skeletal remains that could be used as a baseline for his study. Bingham (1948) seized upon Eaton's main conclusion that the vast majority of the skeletons were female to support the hypothesis that Machu Picchu was occupied by the *aclla*, a group of cloistered women sometimes referred to as "Virgins of the Sun" or "Chosen Women." Because of Eaton's lack of experience and the limitations of the techniques he utilized as well as the incompatibility of a community of aclla with other aspects of the archaeological record, we were convinced that Eaton's sexing of the skeletons required reconsideration, as did his controversial claim that some of the individuals showed evidence of syphilis.

A definitive resolution of these and other issues was provided by a reanalysis of the entire osteological collection by John Verano, a physical anthropologist on the faculty of Tulane University. Verano has had more extensive experience working with osteological collections from archaeological sites in Peru than any other U.S. scholar in the field. He was enthusiastic about reexamining the Machu Picchu collection, one of the oldest and most complete osteological repositories of an Inca population, and was able to complete his initial observations while a visiting professor at Yale in the spring of 2000. In the detailed presentation of his findings, Verano (2003) concluded that a minimum of 174 individuals were represented in the Machu Picchu osteological sample. Contrary to Eaton's findings, a significant proportion of these individuals were males. In the new analysis, the ratio of females to males proves to be 1.46:1 rather than the 4:1 ratio cited in Eaton's work. The sex ratio documented by Verano is relatively balanced and does not suggest the need to posit the presence of a community of "Chosen Women" to explain it. The presence of children in the Machu Picchu sample, including newborns, and the osteological evidence that some of the women had given birth further undermines Bingham's "Virgins of the Sun" hypothesis.

In determining the ages of the Machu Picchu dead, Verano encountered a diverse population of infants,

Table 6.1 Machu Picchu Age Distribution

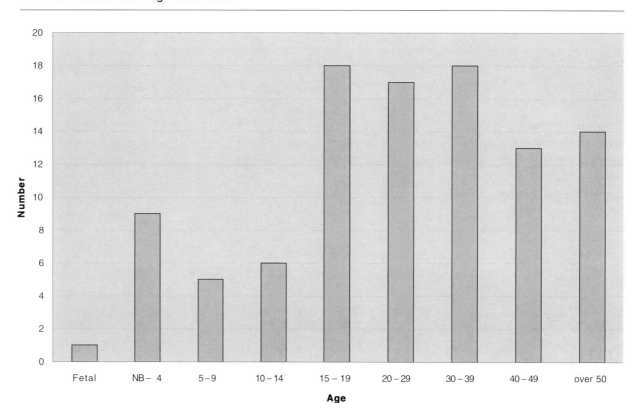

children, young adults, and elderly (Table 6.1). The burial population was dominated by adults (78 percent of the skeletons), with at least fourteen individuals who were over fifty years of age. The latter were old by the standards of the prehispanic world. Significantly, twenty individuals were under the age of fifteen, and one of the twenty was apparently a fetus. Given the underrepresentation of children's burials common in archaeological samples, the population of Machu Picchu appears to be a fairly normal one. Contrary to its traditional image, it in fact had its share of children playing at least along the margins of the settlement.

The stature of Machu Picchu's retainers was small by United States standards: men were an average of 5 feet 2 inches tall, and women averaged 4 feet 11 inches. None of the skeletons studied by Verano were over 5 feet 6 inches. It should be kept in mind, however, that studies of modern Quechua-speaking peoples in the Department of Cuzco found that the average height of an adult male was 5 feet 2.5 inches and an average female was 4

feet 9 inches tall (Stinson 1990, cited in Verano 2003). These contemporary highland farmers are remarkably close in height to those from Machu Picchu some five hundred years ago.

Judging from Verano's findings, the population at Machu Picchu was a fairly healthy one. Dental caries, however, were a common problem, which suggests the consumption of sticky, high-carbohydrate foods such as maize (corn). More severe pathologies, such as skull fractures of the kind produced by armed combat, are completely lacking at Machu Picchu (Verano 2003). This absence contrasts sharply to the findings at other late prehispanic sites in Cuzco. Similarly, osteological evidence of advanced arthritis and other markers of occupational stress was surprisingly limited. This suggests that the work load for retainers at Machu Picchu was reasonable, and somewhat less than the physical demands at other kinds of Inca sites. Although Verano failed to confirm Eaton's claims for syphilis, he did find evidence of tuberculosis and possible parasitic infections such as tapeworm. Nonetheless, the retainers appear to have enjoyed generally good health. This conclusion received independent support from the low frequency of growth disruptions in the formation of tooth enamel. The scarcity of hypoplasias similarly suggests that the retainers experienced few severe illnesses during their childhood.

It is reasonable to assume that the good health of the Machu Picchu retainers was based upon an adequate diet. Because little organic material has survived the heavy rains and temperature fluctuations at Machu Picchu, our understanding of their diet remains limited. Nevertheless, recent breakthroughs in the study of bone chemistry have provided some insights into what they were eating. The chemistry of human bone collagen reflects the foods consumed during an individual's lifetime, but it is often difficult to interpret these data because of similar results produced by different foods. In the Andes, however, maize is the only major food plant characterized by C4 photosynthesis. All the other dietary plants in prehispanic Peru utilized a C3 photosynthetic pathway (DeNiro and Hastorf 1985). C3 plants make 3-carbon molecules from atmospheric carbon dioxide, while C4 plants make 4-carbon in the first photosynthetic step. C3 plants discriminate against ^{13}C, the heavy carbon stable isotope, so that their delta ^{13}C (δ^{13}C) values are lower (more negative) than those of C4 plants. The differences in the C3 and C4 pathways are mirrored in the contrasting carbon isotope ratios of these plants, which, in turn, shape the carbon isotope ratios of the bone collagen of animals that consume these plants as food. The ratio between the stable carbon isotopes (^{12}C and ^{13}C) is measured relative to a marine carbonate standard known as PDB, and the result is reported as a delta 13 value in parts per thousand (per mil). The carbonate standard has a high ^{13}C content, so the measurement of most living or formerly living things consequently yields negative numbers. The collagen of C3 plant eaters has δ^{13}C values of approximately −21.5 parts per thousand, or per mil, while animals that eat only C4 grasses have δ^{13}C collagen values of around −6.5 per mil. Some complicating factors existed such as contamination from the soil and confusion resulting from the chemical signature of marine foods, but it is possible to control for these variables. Thus, at least high

in the Central Andes, it is feasible to use stable carbon isotope values of human bone to calculate the relative importance of maize in the diet. An earlier bone chemistry study of early pre-Inca cultures in the Peruvian highlands (2000–200 BC), for example, encountered δ^{13}C values of −18.7 per mil −19.0 per mil. Based on these figures, we have concluded that although corn was consumed, it was not a major staple crop, probably constituting less than 25 percent of the diet (Burger and Van der Merwe 1990).

The results of the Machu Picchu bone chemistry analyses provide a fascinating contrast to this earlier study. Bone samples from fifty-nine individuals of both sexes and different ages and cranial forms were analyzed in collaboration with Julia Lee-Thorp and Nikolaas van der Merwe at the Archaeometry Laboratory at the University of Cape Town. The carbon isotope figures ranged from −9.61 to −18.8 per mil, averaging −11.9 per mil (Burger, Lee-Thorp, and Van der Merwe 2003). The results indicate that most of the carbon in the bone collagen was derived from consuming C4 plants. Apparently, maize constituted the staple food for the retainers at Machu Picchu and, for most individuals, maize constituted 60 to 70 percent of the diet used to produce bone collagen. Although remarkably high, this figure probably underestimates the importance of maize in the total diet.

Although the importance of consuming corn beer (*chicha*) in Inca rituals has long been appreciated, the relative importance of maize in the diet has been the subject of debate. Potatoes and other high-altitude crops native to the Andes are better adapted to the mountain environments of Cuzco than maize, whose origin appears to have been in the lower and more tropical environments of Mexico (Pearsall 1994). In contemporary highland Peru, maize is viewed as a luxury to be consumed on holidays to break up the tedium of a diet dominated by tubers. Among the Inca, the elite associations of maize raised the possibility that even if it was the staple among the upper class, corn might be less important for the retainers serving the royal family and their guests than high-altitude foods such as potatoes, quinoa, and *chocho* (a lupine). One well-known Inca specialist, John Murra (1960), suggested that the prominent role of maize in Inca rituals reflected its special symbolic im-

6.2 Inca terraces at Machu Picchu where maize was grown along with other crops. Photo by Richard L. Burger.

portance and its association with the state, rather than its importance in the daily diet. While Murra's argument is plausible, the large sample and the consistent results of the stable isotope analysis of human bone leaves little doubt not only that the servants and other staff at Machu Picchu had access to maize, but that it constituted the core of their daily diet.

When combined with beans, lupines, and other crops, maize is an extremely rich source of protein and other nutrients. The good health of Machu Picchu's retainers, both men and women, was to some degree the result of this imperial diet. Much to our surprise, in contrast to an earlier study of provincial Inca populations in the central highlands (Hastorf 1990; Hastorf and Johannessen 1993), there was no significant difference in maize consumption between Machu Picchu's male and female retainers. The equivalence of C4 foods in their diet suggests that male and female retainers drank

chicha and were involved in the activities associated with its consumption. The overall role of maize as the staple of Machu Picchu's population is consistent with Verano's (2003) documentation of numerous dental caries, which were probably the by-product of this maize-rich diet.

Judging from the carbon isotope study, plant foods other than maize constituted a small but significant proportion of the diet. Unfortunately, stable carbon isotope analysis does not shed light on their identity. One alternative source of relevant evidence comes from microscopic pollen that has been preserved since Inca times in the terraced fields on the eastern slopes of Machu Picchu. Pollen analysis is still rare in Central Andean archaeology, but it has become more common over the past two decades. Because the structure of pollen is largely inorganic, pollen does not decay the way most food remains do and, depending on the composition of the earth, it can remain intact, mixed with the soil for millennia despite heavy precipitation. During a study of the agricultural terracing on the slopes of Machu Picchu by Peruvian archaeologist Alfredo Valencia Zegarra and American hydrologist Ken Wright, soil samples were taken and pollen was successfully extracted (Figure 6.2). When these samples were analyzed, the results indicated that the crops planted there included potatoes and an unidentified legume as well as maize (see Chapter 5).

At Machu Picchu, meat would have been another source of protein and nutrients for the Inca elite and their staff, although early Spanish historical accounts indicate that meat was not the focus of Inca cuisine. According to the Spanish chroniclers, drinking, rather than eating, was the central feature of Inca foodways (Coe 1994). Nevertheless, the Incas did eat meat, and the abundant residue of animal bone at Inca and pre-Inca sites dispels any doubt about its presence in the diet. What animals were being eaten at Machu Picchu, given its unusual location in the cloud forest environment of the eastern Andean slopes? Bingham had little interest in this question, and his speculation on this subject was based on a small number of bones and local observations while at the site.

In contrast to the archaeology of Bingham's time, the analysis of faunal remains has become an important part of contemporary archaeology and analysis of animal bone has become an effective tool for studying diet and other cultural patterns. Bone is more resistant to the elements than plant material, but the animal bones encountered in the center of Machu Picchu were not kept by the 1912 Yale Peruvian Expedition. Fortunately, the animal bones that were recovered in or around the cave burials were carefully catalogued and preserved at the Peabody Museum of Natural History in New Haven. A few of these, like the rare remains of a paca (*Agouti thomasi*), were studied by Eaton (1916: 87–89) and others, and used to identify several previously unknown taxa and species native to the cloud forests around Machu Picchu. The Yale Peruvian Expedition paid much less attention to the more common animal remains that reflect the dietary habits of the residents of Machu Picchu.

Beginning in 1994, zooarchaeologist George R.

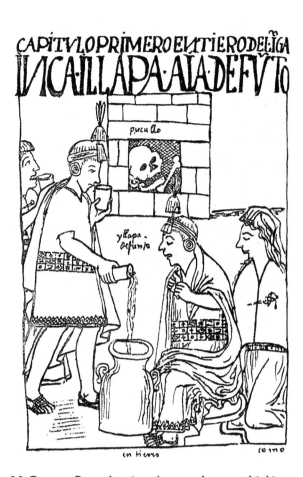

6.3 Guaman Poma drawing of men and women drinking corn beer (*chicha*) at a funeral.

Miller initiated the first systematic analysis of the faunal remains from Machu Picchu. The sample consisted of 2,169 bone fragments, over a thousand of which could be identified at the family level or better. Because most of these came from the burial caves, Miller assumed they were the remains of food presented to the dead ancestors or consumed during graveside rituals. Such banquets for and with the dead were described by the Spanish chroniclers, and they continue to be a feature of traditional Andean ceremonial life (Figure 6.3). Although these faunal remains from the burial caves probably do not constitute an exact reflection of daily diet, they do suggest the range of animals that were eaten and their relative importance as food. According to Miller's analysis, by far the most abundant animal remains from the Machu Picchu burial caves were those of the do-

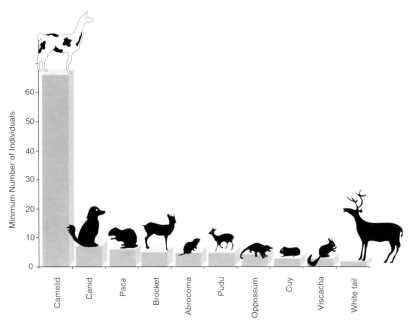

6.4 Relative abundance of animals recovered from the Machu Picchu burial caves. Courtesy of George Miller.

mesticated camelids (llama and alpaca). In terms of the total number of bones, they account for 88 percent of the remains. When these numbers are converted into the amount of meat they represent, camelids constituted over 90 percent of the remains. Miller (2003) believes that over 95 percent of the meat consumed at Machu Picchu came from alpaca or llama herds, or both (Figure 6.4).

The natural habitat of both the llama and the alpaca is the high, open pastureland above 12,500 feet (3,800 meters) above sea level, known as *puna*, rather than the densely forested slopes below Machu Picchu between 6,600 and 8,000 feet (2,000 and 2,400 meters) above sea level. Some patches of high grassland are within a day's walk of Machu Picchu, and it is likely that llamas and alpacas would have been herded in these and more distant puna areas. Domesticated camelids were essential for transport and for wool production throughout the Inca Empire; one of the species, or both, would likely have been a common sight near Machu Picchu. Both llamas and alpacas were eaten in Inca times, although their role as a food source is traditionally thought to be secondary to their other economic functions.

At some point in the distant past, the llama and alpaca had a common wild ancestor. In fact, they can still interbreed and produce fertile offspring, although under normal circumstances such crossings are uncommon and avoided by both the herders and the animals themselves. From the perspective of archaeologists, an unfortunate result of this similarity is that it is extremely difficult to distinguish between the remains of llamas and alpacas on purely morphological grounds, particularly using archaeological samples. There is, however, a size differential between them; using biometrics, it is possible to determine with a fair degree of accuracy the kind or kinds of camelid represented.

In the case of the Machu Picchu sample, the camelids appear to have been mainly alpacas. Today, the alpaca is valued for its fine wool, as well as being prized as food. Alpacas are usually herded in the pasturelands above 14,000 feet above sea level so, at Machu Picchu, whose elevation is only 8,000 feet above sea level, alpacas are an exotic species brought from another, much higher ecozone. Some camelid remains are between modern alpacas and llamas in size. Miller believes these were a special variety of llama that may have been raised in Inca times and no longer exists in Peru. Based on his study of the skeletal elements represented in the Yale Peabody Collection, Miller concluded that the alpaca and llama remains represented were whole animals. Apparently, alpacas and small llamas were brought to Machu Picchu on the hoof to be slaughtered there and then prepared for funerary ceremonies. The sixty-six camelids identified among the Machu Picchu remains represent at least five tons of meat prepared during the funerary rituals of Machu Picchu's retainers.

Using the same skeletal remains, Miller was able to determine the age of the alpacas and llamas when they were slaughtered. This is of interest because young animals are more tender and less gamey than older animals, particularly when the latter have been herded year after year over vast distances. Of course, by slaughtering young animals, the Incas would lose the most productive years of wool production. This trade-off was appreciated early in Peruvian prehistory. In the Janabarriu Phase (400–200 BC) at Chavín de Huantar, for example, the elite consumed young camelids, while the less prosperous feasted on the tougher, older animals that were no longer suitable for other purposes (Miller and Burger 1995). At Machu Picchu, over a millennium later, none of the camelids recovered were under two years old, and 83 percent of them were over age three (Miller 2002). Thus, old alpacas and llamas appear to have been the meat offered as a final meal to dead retainers and their mourners at Machu Picchu. Perhaps these animals were herded for their wool and made available for slaughter and distribution to retainers only when their value as fiber producers had diminished. Alternatively, Miller suggests, a symbolic rationale could underlie the selection of older animals for sacrifice (a possibility discussed later in this chapter). It would be fascinating to analyze a sample of camelid bone from the daily refuse from the households or banqueting areas at Machu Picchu to see whether younger and more tender animals were being served. Such a study, unfortunately, must be left for the future.

The sixteenth-century Spanish accounts leave no doubt that hunting was one of the main activities the Inca royalty enjoyed while staying at their country palaces. The forested mountain slopes surrounding Machu Picchu would have provided an excellent setting for such activities, which has been confirmed by faunal analysis. Also, judging from the faunal remains, the royal retainers buried at Machu Picchu were al-

lowed to consume some of the wild game that was bagged within the dense vegetation of the cloud forest (*ceja de selva*) below the royal palace. Among the bones Bingham's crew recovered is evidence of two types of deer (*Mazana americana* and *Pudu mephistopheles*). Both these species of deer are native to the cloud forest. It is significant that there is only an antler fragment of the white-tailed deer (*Odocoileus virginianus*) that are usually found at archaeological sites on the coast and highlands of Peru, and no examples of the *taruka* (*Hippocamelus antisensis*) that populate the high grasslands. Among the Machu Picchu remains are examples of the subtropical paca, or agouti (*Agouti paca*), which is a culinary delicacy of modern topical forest groups. In addition, the Inca retainers sometimes were able to capture the tasty rabbit-like viscachas (*Ligidium peruanum*), animals that still inhabit the rocky prominences surrounding the Machu Picchu ruins (Figure 6.5).

6.5 Viscacha at Machu Picchu, in 2001. Photo by George Miller.

These wild animals were complemented by the occasional opossum (*Didelphis albiventris*) and subtropical selva rodents, such as the *Abrocoma oblativa*, a distant relative of the chinchilla rat (Miller 2003). This evidence suggests a pattern of hunting in the lands immediately surrounding the royal palace.

The domesticated guinea pig (*Cavia porcellus*), or *cuy*, was valued as a delicacy by the Incas and their ancestors, probably because its meat and delicate taste offered a welcome break from the low-fat, high-carbohydrate diet that constituted the daily fare in the Andes. It is for this reason that the *cuy* remains a popular party food in the Peruvian highlands. At Machu Picchu, guinea pig teeth were found in two cave environments, thus confirming that its meat was consumed as part of funerary rituals. Given the small size of guinea pig bones, their vulnerability to the natural elements, and the absence of screening during the 1912 excavations, it is likely that cuyes, like viscachas, were underrepresented in the faunal sample recovered by the Yale Peruvian Expedition.

Some animals were probably kept at Machu Picchu as pets rather than as sources of food. The Spanish chroniclers indicate that tropical forest birds and monkeys were favorites of the Inca court. Although the archaeological evidence from Machu Picchu is silent on this, it offers an eloquent testament to the special relationship between the burial population at the site and their dogs. Six dogs were recovered from Machu Picchu's burials, and it is evident that these creatures served as companions to the dead, not as meals for the departed and their mourners. Miller (2003) reviewed the contexts in which dog remains were found; in all those instances where it is possible to determine the sex of the deceased, the tomb was always that of an older woman (Salazar 2001a). This conclusion, which draws upon excavation results, faunal analysis, and human osteology, illustrates the degree to which our understanding of Machu Picchu can be enriched by archaeology and laboratory analysis.

The Multi-Ethnic Character of Machu Picchu

Traditional characterizations of Machu Picchu have tended to focus on the Inca elite for whom the site was built and maintained. It is clear from the Spanish chronicles and the archaeological evidence that the Inca rulers drew upon their small ethnic group for imperial leadership. Consonant with this, the distinctive architecture of Machu Picchu embodies the cultural and social values of the ruling Inca ethnic group from the Cuzco Valley. Nevertheless, historic documents make it equally clear that retainers (*yanacona*) belonging to royal panacas were drawn from a wide range of ethnic groups that had been incorporated into Tahuantinsuyu by conquest or peaceful means. Because the great majority of the occupants of Pachacuti's royal estate at Machu Picchu were probably yanacona serving as support staff and craft specialists, it would be expected that the site population would have been a multi-ethnic mix reflecting the complex makeup of the empire, particularly those parts of it acquired by the military and political activities of Pachacuti (Chapter 3). On the basis of her analysis of grave goods, Lucy Salazar (1997a, 1997b) has argued that most of the individuals buried at the site came from areas outside of Cuzco. This conclusion, derived from a stylistic analysis of the ceramics that accompanied the dead, has received independent support from morphological and chemical research on the human osteological collections.

One of the most common ways of expressing ethnic identity in the prehispanic Andes was through cranial deformation. This was achieved through the binding of infants in cradle boards or with other devices while the skull was still relatively flexible. The result would have been visually conspicuous but would not have had an impact on the mental capacity of the individual. Such practices have a long history in the Andes and go back at least three millennia before the Inca (Burger 1992). Because cranial deformation was a function of culturally determined child-rearing practices, it is not surprising that specific kinds of cranial deformation were more common in some regions than others, and that a homogeneous population tended to favor a single kind of skull modification. In his 1916 monograph, Eaton identified the presence of different forms of cranial modification at Machu Picchu and plausibly attributed this to the mixed ethnic population in the burials.

John Verano (2003) reexamined the presence of multiple types of cranial deformation at Machu Picchu by using more scientific procedures. He concluded that al-

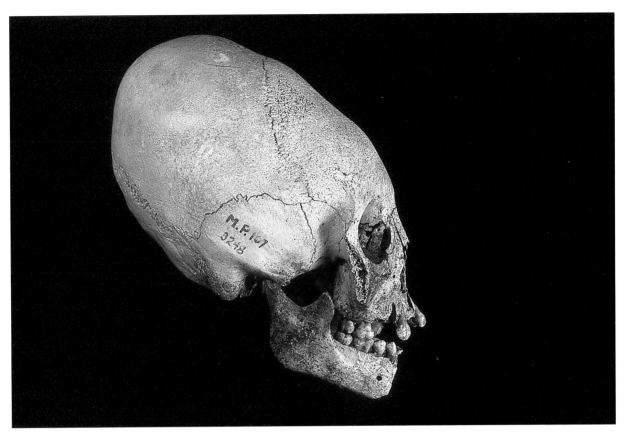

6.6 Cranium from Machu Picchu illustrating annular deformation, which is associated with the highlands, especially the altiplano. Photo by John Verano.

though most skulls sufficiently intact for analysis were not deformed (55 percent), several types of cranial deformation were found (Figure 6.6). The most common type of deformation (23 percent) was annular or circumferential, a type of skull shaping linked to the wrapping of the head with cloth bands during infancy. This kind of deformation was imposed more commonly in the highlands than the coast, and it was particularly popular in the altiplano area of Lake Titicaca. The second kind of deformation, known as occipital flattening, occurs in some 22 percent of the samples. It is linked to the use of cradle boards and was associated with the ethnic groups from the central and north coast of Peru. Another analysis by Verano focusing on a statistical analysis of the facial portions of crania reveals that roughly half the Machu Picchu skulls can be classified as coastal. Many of these are similar to samples from the Jequetepeque

Valley on Peru's northern coast, but others more closely resemble samples from Peru's central coast. Based on these two independent lines of evidence, Verano concluded that the burial population at Machu Picchu was ethnically heterogeneous.

A third line of evidence on population diversity is provided by an analysis of the bone chemistry of the Machu Picchu burials (Burger, Lee-Thorp, and Van der Merwe 2003). As already noted, the isotopic composition of collagen in human bones directly reflects diet, and archaeological studies have demonstrated that small villages show little variability in their bone chemistry, owing to their shared foodways. Because the isotopic composition of bones reflects the average diet of individuals over many years, it follows that if the individuals buried at Machu Picchu had been drawn from different ecological habitats, geographic regions, and cultural traditions

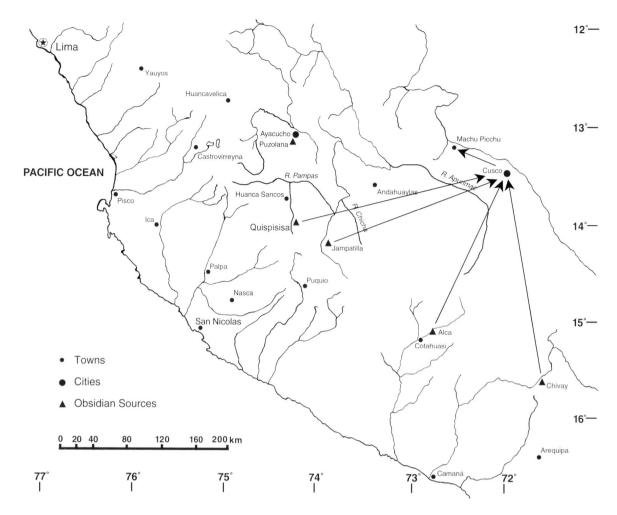

6.7 Location of sources of obsidian used at Machu Picchu. Drawing by Rosemary Volpe and Kim Zolvik.

there would be a significant degree of isotopic variability, and if it had been drawn from a single background (e.g., Incas from Cuzco), there would be relatively little variability. Two isotopes (C^{13} and N^{15}) analyzed for fifty-nine individuals suggest a highly diverse population. The $\delta^{13}C$ results range from -18.8 to -9.61 per mil, while the $\delta^{15}N$ results range from 6.05 to 12.79 per mil. When the $\delta^{13}C$ is plotted against $\delta^{15}N$, the values are not tightly clustered as one would expect for a homogeneous cultural group, which suggests dietary heterogeneity. This variability probably reflects differences in the dependence on maize as a staple and in the consumption of marine foods by those individuals coming from the coast.

In summary, judging from new osteological and chemical analyses, the population at Machu Picchu was a diverse one. At least in this respect, Machu Picchu had more in common with heterogeneous urban centers than with the small homogeneous villages of the Peruvian highlands chronicled by anthropologists. This conclusion reinforces the importance of considering Machu Picchu within the larger context of Tahuantinsuyu. Although some features of Machu Picchu can be understood in terms of local ecology and the mineral and other resources that attracted the Incas to the lower Urubamba, most features of the site relate to a much larger frame of reference.

Just as servants, metalworkers, masons, and other retainers were brought from the length and breadth of Tahuantinsuyu, so too were items utilized there. As discussed in the following section, sheets of pure tin were imported from the southern highlands of Bolivia to Machu Picchu for the creation of tin bronze objects. Likewise, a significant portion of the pottery, particularly that recovered in the tombs, also seems to have come from distant provinces (Salazar 2001b). In the latter case, a preliminary study using instrumental neutron activation has been carried out at the University of Missouri Research Reactor to determine the difference between locally produced and exotic ceramics based on the chemistry of their clay minerals. This study, while suggestive, has not yet yielded conclusive results because of the chemical variability of clays and the numerous clay deposits that were exploited in prehispanic times.

Success has been achieved, however, in a study of the obsidian artifacts that Bingham recovered in the center of Machu Picchu. Altogether, seven cutting tools made of obsidian glass were encountered by the 1912 expedition, but the lack of recent volcanic deposits around Machu Picchu left the origin of the raw material for these tools a mystery. Fortunately, obsidian deposits are extremely rare in the Central Andes, and recent laboratory research suggests that fewer than ten of them were intensively exploited in prehispanic times (Burger and Asaro 1979; Burger, Chavez, and Chavez 2000). Fieldworkers have successfully located most of these, and the sources of the three most important quarry areas have been documented (Figure 6.7).

In 2002, all seven obsidian tools from Machu Picchu were analyzed at the University of Missouri Research Reactor in collaboration with Mike Glascock, a specialist in the application of geochemistry to archaeology. A nondestructive x-ray fluorescence technique was utilized to study the trace element composition of the artifacts, all of which were visually similar. As expected, the majority of these (71 percent) proved to be made of obsidian from the Alca source located in the Cotahuasi Valley of central Arequipa. This massive deposit, which covers over 19 square miles, is found in the deepest canyon in the world at roughly 2 miles above sea level (Burger et al. 1998a, Justin Jennings, personal communication, 2002). It is located 140 miles southwest of Cuzco

and, if procurement was direct, it would have taken about two weeks for it to have been transported over rugged terrain from the geological source to Machu Picchu. It is more likely that the obsidian tools were simply brought to the royal palace by the residents and visitors as part of their personal effects. Significantly, most people living in the Cuzco Valley depended on obsidian from the Alca source.

Much to our surprise, two of the tools did not come from the Alca source: one appears to come from the Quispisisa source and the other came from the Jampatilla source. Both these sources are located over 155 miles to the west of Machu Picchu in an area that now falls within the Department of Ayacucho. Throughout most of prehistory, the obsidian from these sources was not utilized by the residents of the Cuzco region. The Quispisisa source was the most important source for those living in what is now central and northern Peru (Burger and Glascock 2000), while the Jampatilla source was primarily of local importance for what is now southern Ayacucho and Apurimac (Burger et al. 1998c). In a comprehensive synthesis of obsidian procurement in Cuzco, the anomalous presence of Quispisisa obsidian and the single previously documented example of Jampatilla obsidian were shown to be correlated with the expansion of the Huari empire (Burger, Chavez, and Chavez 2000: 324–343). This probably resulted from the increased movement of individuals from more western areas into Cuzco for reasons of imperial administration and economy. A similar explanation can be offered to explain the presence of Quispisisa and Jampatilla obsidian at Machu Picchu, although, in this case, it would apply to the Inca rather than the Huari imperial expansion seven centuries earlier. The obsidian sourcing results suggest that visitors from other parts of the empire, particularly the central highlands of Peru, were present at Machu Picchu. An alternative hypothesis — that obsidian was being pooled through imperial taxation with the resulting admixture being redistributed to properties of the Inca state or its leaders — seems less likely, given the absence of clear documentary or archaeological evidence that the Inca state was intimately involved in the production or distribution of volcanic glass.

Craft Activity and Technological Innovation at Machu Picchu

During the dry season, daily life at Machu Picchu probably focused on the royal family and their needs. The public architecture that dominates the archaeological site continues to provide evidence of the public and private aspects of the activities required to maintain and entertain these individuals (see Chapter 3). While the nonelite residents of Machu Picchu who made up the majority of the site's occupants were primarily a support population for the elite, they also engaged in other productive activities. These mundane tasks were reflected in the artifacts recovered at Machu Picchu, and they received relatively little attention from Bingham. One can speculate that such activities may have increased in intensity during those months when the country palace was not being visited by the royal family. Among these secondary activities were textile production, as attested to by the presence of spindle whorls for spinning and bone tools for weaving (known as *wichuñas* in Quechua), and the production of stone objects, as documented by unfinished small stone carvings of locally available schist.

Metallurgy appears to have been especially important at Machu Picchu. The site is well situated for this activity because abundant fuel would have been available and its exposed setting would have favored the utilization of draft furnaces and other techniques harnessing natural wind. Some of the best evidence for the presence of metalworking at Machu Picchu comes from laboratory analyses carried out on the collections recovered by the 1912 Yale Peruvian Expedition. Of the approximately 170 metal artifacts recovered during the Machu Picchu excavations, 15 have been identified as metal stock, works in progress, and waste materials left over from metalworking. A detailed study of these pieces by Robert Gordon, a Yale professor specializing in the history of metallurgy, and his student John Rutledge has shed new light on the kinds of metalworking activities that were going on at Pachacuti's royal estate. Most were related to the creation of objects made from tin bronze, an alloy of copper linked with the Inca state.

Tin is a rare metal in the Central Andes, and its closest source is the cassiterite deposits in the northern Bolivian highlands, hundreds of miles to the south of Machu Picchu. Although tin bronze was being produced south of Lake Titicaca by the end of the Middle Horizon (approximately 900 AD), it was not until the southern expansion of the Tahuantinsuyu in the fifteenth century AD that tin became available to Peruvian metallurgists and tin bronze finally appeared in the Cuzco region (Lechtman 1997). Tin bronze was disseminated throughout the Central Andes by Inca expansion, and tin bronze replaced or complemented the arsenic bronze alloys that had been produced in earlier times. It is likely that the Inca state controlled the production of tin and, by extension, that it dominated the production of tin bronze artifacts. Thus, the tin bronze objects that were created not only represented especially hard and durable products, but also symbolized the power of the Inca rulers in their composition. This link between the tin bronze objects and the Inca state was likewise reflected in their distinctive form, which drew from a limited array of shapes found throughout much of Tahuantinsuyu (Owen 1986).

The process of tin bronze production at Machu Picchu can be partially reconstructed on the basis of the metallurgical by-products studied by Rutledge and Gordon (1987). Judging from the fragments of pure tin and nearly pure copper sheet metal, the component metals for the bronze alloy were brought to Machu Picchu in almost pure form after initial processing closer to the geological deposits. Because no finished Inca objects of pure tin are known, it is reasonable to assume that tin from the irregular sheets found at Machu Picchu was designed to be mixed with copper. A close examination of the tin sheets reveals evidence that the tin was chipped away using metal chisels. At Machu Picchu, the bronze objects have a tin content of about 6.7 percent, a mixture that rarely varies more than a few percent. Several examples of tin and tin bronze "spills" confirm the assumption that bronze was actually being cast at Machu Picchu. One piece of metal recovered at the site was the result of molten tin being poured onto straw or some other organic surface, while two other pieces were the product of a tin bronze mix being spilled or poured onto a rock surface. Perhaps these "spills" were residuals that exceeded immediate needs or the volume of the crucible being utilized.

A subsequent stage of bronze production is attested to

by fragments of work in process. Several bars of cast tin bronze have been forged by annealing and hammering but were never transformed into a finished tool or ornament. Another particularly memorable work in process is a partially completed tweezers whose blade has yet to be shaped. An analysis of its composition indicates an unusually high percentage of tin (9.7 percent), and Gordon suggests that this elevation in tin composition may have been intentional in order to ensure the hardness of the tweezer blades and the retention of spring action. In summary, there can be little doubt that tin bronze was being cast as stock and transformed into tools and decorative objects at Machu Picchu (Rutledge and Gordon 1987: 593).

Other artifacts found in 1912 at Machu Picchu indicate that artifacts of a silver copper alloy were also being produced. While these objects had a silver content of roughly only 14 percent, the surface enrichment process resulted in the even silver coloration of objects, such as the finger ring of hammered "silver" excavated at Machu Picchu. Heather Lechtman (1997) has argued that Inca metallurgy consisted basically of three components: copper, silver, and gold. As indicated by Gordon's recent studies, at least two of these were being manufactured at Machu Picchu.

Gordon's analysis of the Machu Picchu metal artifacts suggested much more than the existence of basic metalworking at the site. It provided new evidence for the innovative character of Inca metal technology, while at the same time indicating some of its limitations. The Incas, like many prehispanic cultures in the Americas, are frequently portrayed as technologically conservative. Of course, the rapid expansion of tin bronze throughout Tahuantinsuyu flies in the face of such a characterization. At Machu Picchu, a vivid example of metallurgical innovation, or, perhaps more accurately, experimentation, emerged from an analysis of a bronze ritual knife (*tumi*) with a llama head that Bingham recovered in cave burial 54 at Machu Picchu (Gordon and Rutledge 1984) (Figure 6.8). In his initial examination, Mathewson (1915) concluded that the *tumi*'s elaborate and distinctively colored handle had been cast onto the blade's stem from a high tin bronze alloy. Gordon's more recent study of the artifact showed that besides tin (9 percent), the metalworker had added an un-

6.8 Analysis of this llama-headed ritual knife (*tumi*) from Machu Picchu yielded evidence of the addition of bismuth to the tin bronze alloy of the modeled handle, perhaps as a metallurgical experiment in casting technology. Photo by Robert Gordon.

precedented quantity of bismuth (18 percent) to the mix. This is the first known use by the Incas of bismuth as an alloying element of bronze. After considering the alternatives, Gordon concluded that its inclusion was intentional. The advantages of a bismuth-rich tin bronze would have been to make a casting that adhered more effectively to the stem, and to produce a distinctively whiter color of bronze. Although this addition was a success in the case of the llama-handled *tumi*, the practice does not seem to have been extended to other objects at the site and may never have been adopted outside of Machu Picchu.

Another kind of innovation suggested by the technical studies concerns the use of metal for tools at Machu Picchu. As Lechtman (1980) has observed, metals in the Central Andes were generally employed for ideological rather than mechanical ends. Consistent with this, it is widely accepted that the considerable engineering accomplishments of Inca builders were achieved with stone tools despite their knowledge of tin bronze and arsenic bronze. This was almost certainly true at Machu Picchu judging from the abundant stone cobbles with evidence of battering found in many portions of the site (Bingham 1930). Nevertheless, the presence of large bronze crowbars suggests that these metal tools may have been displacing wooden levers in late Inca times. When Gordon (1985) examined the surface marking and microstructural damage on the bronze crowbars and other tools from Machu Picchu, he concluded that masons had used some of them in producing the site's stonework. In his opinion, the kinds of postproduction stress and damage observable in these artifacts would have resulted only from working hard materials such as stone. This finding suggests that the Incas may have been in the process of moving away from a neolithic building technology at the time of the Spanish Conquest, and that their technology was far from static.

At the same time, Gordon observed that many of the newly identified metal masonry tools showed brittle fractures and other flaws resulting from sulphide inclusions and excessive porosity. The technical limitations of these tools contrast with the remarkable sophistication that characterizes other products of Inca metallurgy. If the fabrication of metal tools for masonry and other construction activities was a late innovation, it is possible that the Inca metalworkers still lacked the experience necessary to fine-tune the earlier metallurgical techniques that were appropriate for the production of jewelry or ritual objects but were not adequate for producing tools used in heavy-duty building activities. It is likely that with time, the Incas would have modified their alloys and casting processes to produce metals that were well suited for working stone and other hard materials.

Inca Science and the Construction of Machu Picchu

The remarkable beauty of Machu Picchu and the mystery concerning the reason for its creation and abandonment have overshadowed the investigation of basic questions concerning its construction and the technological knowledge underpinning its successful comple-

tion and maintenance. Such issues were touched upon by the 1912 Yale Peruvian Expedition, but only recently have scholars in the field begun to focus on issues such as the nature of Machu Picchu's hydraulic system, the character of the terracing along Machu Picchu's slopes, and the way in which the natural terrain at Machu Picchu was modified in order to support the construction of the royal palace complex. Drawing upon contemporary knowledge of engineering, Alfredo Valencia Zegarra and Kenneth Wright have pioneered technical studies of Inca engineering at Machu Picchu (Wright and Valencia Zegarra 2000). Their findings are so intriguing that a brief review of some of their conclusions is warranted in this overview of recent scientific advances in the understanding of Machu Picchu.

The picture that emerges from a study of Machu Picchu's hydraulic system is particularly compelling. Geological studies indicate that two principal faults, known as the Machu Picchu fault and the Huayna Picchu fault, transect the site; the saddle-like piece of flat land upon which the main Inca constructions were built is actually a block or graben wedged between the faults. The faults and the associated rock fractures increase the ability of precipitation to infiltrate this landscape, and this collected water in the subsoil becomes available at a spring located on the steep north slope above Machu Picchu (Wright, Witt, and Valencia Zegarra 1997b).

In Inca times, water from this perennial spring was carried 2,457 feet to Pachacuti's royal palace complex by way of a stone-lined canal. This water is remarkably pure, and its flow varies seasonally from 6 to 33 gallons per minute. The natural spring is a mere 60 feet above the central ridge-top settlement, so the creation of a gravity canal with the appropriate gradient to carry water required considerable skill and knowledge. The route and slope of the canal had to be determined before the design of Machu Picchu itself in order to ensure the availability of water to the elite and their retainers, and to avoid conflict between the canal's path and the elaborate architecture within the complex. Along most of the route, the grade of the Inca canal varies from 2.5–4.8 percent, but on the terraces adjacent to the center it is reduced to only 1 percent. To support the stone-lined canal and to maintain the appropriate gradient, a stone terrace 6–18 feet high was built. The well-fitted stone

6.9 Main canal carrying water from the natural spring to the palace complex at Machu Picchu. Photo by Richard L. Burger.

lining of Machu Picchu's canal would have minimized seepage and reduced maintenance requirements (Figure 6.9).

Once inside the palace complex, the canal fed a series of sixteen fountains, each of which was equipped with a sharp-edged fountain spout. These cut stone spouts created a jet of water that fell into each of the carved stone basins below. Such an arrangement would have been optimal for collecting water in ceramic jars. The water carried by the Machu Picchu canal system would have been adequate to meet the basic hydraulic needs of Machu Picchu's residents even during peak season (Wright, Kelly, and Valencia Zegarra 1997a; Wright and Valencia Zegarra 2000; Wright, Witt, and

Valencia Zegarra 1997b). Nevertheless, the construction of an additional branch canal was under way at the time of the site's abandonment. Valencia Zegarra and Wright's recent research indicates that the Machu Picchu canal was built to meet the needs of the palace inhabitants and not to irrigate crops on the terraces adjacent to the site.

The terracing system at Machu Picchu, like the canal system, reflects considerable engineering know-how and was designed to support cultivation using the natural rainfall at Machu Picchu. Evidence from the Quellcaya ice cap (Thompson et al. 1986) suggests that rainfall early in the history of Machu Picchu (AD 1450–1500) may have averaged 72 inches, while during the site's later history (post-AD 1500), precipitation increased to 82 inches, which is slightly above the current level (Wright and Valencia Zegarra 2000: 50–51). Such levels of rainfall were more than sufficient to support the cultivation of maize and other crops (see Chapter 5).

Excavations of the Machu Picchu terraces show that they were carefully built with layers of different materials to ensure adequate drainage and soil fertility (Wright, Kelly, and Valencia Zegarra et al. 1997a). The constructed terraces typically began with a layer of large stones covered by a layer of medium gravel. Above this, the builders placed a layer of fine sand mixed with gravel. This was topped by a thick layer of topsoil probably brought from the valley floor and placed by hand behind the stone retaining wall on the top of the terraces. Basically, the Inca agricultural terracing system surrounding Machu Picchu constitutes a series of flat surfaces designed to create a human-made environment optimally suited to agricultural cultivation in this moist cloud forest environment. The stone retaining walls that supported the terraces commonly leaned inward by approximately 5 percent, thereby reinforcing the stability of these features. The fact that they have survived over five hundred years in this difficult terrain and climate is ample testament to the success of the engineering principles employed.

One final set of insights into the construction of Machu Picchu by Wright and Valencia Zegarra (2000: 36–46, 59–62) merits consideration. Improved geological understanding of the site indicates that the ridge-top encountered by the Inca at Machu Picchu would have

6.10 Gold bracelet, discovered at Machu Picchu in 1995 by archaeologist Elba Torres, buried deep within the construction fill of Machu Picchu's plaza. Photo by Kenneth R. Wright.

been an irregular surface, quite different from the flat, mesa-like configuration currently observed. If this were the case, much work would have been required to transform Machu Picchu into a landform that could sustain the elaborate architecture that fills the site's urban core. When excavators from the Instituto Nacional de Cultura penetrated the surface below one of Machu Picchu's plazas, they encountered a 3-foot layer of loose rock and stone chips. This unconsolidated fill was stabilized using construction walls unseen from the ground surface. In total, the excavations extended some 8 feet below the surface without reaching bedrock. This research suggests a massive investment in reshaping the site surface and providing it with drainage infrastructure. Wright estimates that this invisible subsurface construction constitutes roughly 60 percent of the effort invested in building Machu Picchu.

One unexpected discovery at this excavation of construction fill was made by Peruvian archaeologist Elba Torres. She found a gold bracelet that had been left as an offering before the placement of the thick stone fill layer (Wright and Valencia Zegarra 2000: 43). This bracelet, the only known example of a gold object from Machu Picchu, was taken to the Cusco Regional Museum for display (Figure 6.10). More important than the gold object is the new evidence on the massive and comprehensive modification of the ridge at Machu Picchu, which helps us understand why the site has remained intact for so long, resisting innumerable seasons of heavy rain, earthquakes, and other forces that could have led to the site's collapse and destruction. The sound subsurface foundations created by the Inca builders provided a level and well-drained surface that has successfully supported the heavy granite architecture and, more recently, accommodated the not inconsiderable flow of tourists (see Chapter 7).

Scientific Insights into Ritual Life at Machu Picchu

As illustrated in the foregoing sections, modern science has permitted many insights into the everyday world of Machu Picchu and its residents. It has also begun to provide us with a window on the less accessible, but equally important, realm of cosmology and religious rituals that was so central to life at Machu Picchu. Here we focus on three examples of recent advances in this area.

During Bingham's 1912 excavations, he encountered an anomalous cache of more than thirty obsidian pebbles near the main gateway into Machu Picchu. The origin and meaning of these small subangular objects was puzzling because of the absence of recent volcanic activity in the area and the uniqueness of the find. In an effort to make sense of the pebbles, Bingham (1930: 200) mentions the suggestion of a colleague at the Sheffield Scientific School that their source might be extraterrestrial, possibly the result of a meteorite shower. Fortunately, as already noted, much progress has been made over the past three decades in the chemical characterization of obsidian using such techniques as instrumental neutron activation and x-ray fluorescence. These procedures can be used to precisely characterize the trace element composition of obsidian artifacts like the Machu Picchu pebbles, and this data, in turn, can be employed to link the artifacts with the unique composition of the obsidian source from which they were obtained.

Research on the obsidian pebbles from Machu Picchu was initiated at the Lawrence Berkeley Laboratory and continued more recently at the University of Missouri Research Reactor. To date, four obsidian pebbles from the Gateway cache have been analyzed using x-ray fluorescence, and in all instances they have proved to come from the Chivay obsidian source in Arequipa's Colca Valley (Burger, Chavez, and Chavez 2000: 347; Glascock and Burger, unpublished data). This result was surprising because the Alca obsidian source is closer and more convenient to Cuzco populations and, by extension, to the residents of Machu Picchu. As already mentioned, none of the obsidian utilized in the making

of tools used at Machu Picchu had been derived from the Chivay obsidian source.

Why, then, had the dozens of obsidian pebbles been carried some 250 miles to Machu Picchu from the high-altitude obsidian flow near the modern town of Chivay? In order to answer this question, it is important to recall that the obsidian pebbles from Machu Picchu are unmodified and show no evidence of having been used as tools. In fact, measuring less than an inch in diameter, the pebbles are too small to serve as raw material for cutting tools. Their placement together near a crucial location at the site, the main Gateway, further indicates that they were a ritual cache or offering. Such ceremonial offerings of precious or symbolically charged materials at special spots were common in Inca times and continue to be made in traditional highland communities.

But why would small obsidian pebbles have been selected, and why was volcanic glass from the Chivay source selected for the offering? A closer look at the pebbles and their source is necessary to begin considering this issue. Jay Ague, a geologist at Yale specializing in petrology, examined the pebbles and concluded that judging from their rounded facets, these small pieces of obsidian had been shaped by the eroding forces of water. Given the local geology, the obsidian pebbles had probably been collected from the banks of the Colca River at roughly 12,500 feet above sea level near the foot of the volcanic deposit in which the primary obsidian deposits are located, at over 15,700 feet above sea level. Because volcanic glass is brittle, it is quickly ground to dust by intense river action and, consequently, obsidian appears in the riverbed only immediately adjacent to the Chivay source (Burger et al. 1998b). Because only a short hike from the river (less than an hour) would have been required to procure large obsidian blocks over 1 foot on a side, it is reasonable to conclude that the selection of the small water-worn obsidian pebbles was intentional. Given this background, the simple explanation that the obsidian pebble cache was left by visitors from the Colca Canyon or some nearby area who journeyed to Machu Picchu and placed an offering of precious items from their region as they entered into the royal palace complex (Burger, Chavez, and Chavez 2000: 347) seems, at best, a partial answer to the question posed (Figure 6.11).

It is likely that a set of symbolic meanings lay behind the obsidian cache — meanings related to the special character of pebbles and the Chivay area itself. The Colca Canyon in general, and the Chivay area specifically, is one of the most actively volcanic zones in the Central Andes. In recent times, ash and smoke have risen from Mt. Sabancaya, a peak near Chivay. The Incas, like many of their highland ancestors, worshipped high mountains and considered them to be the source of supernatural forces (*apus*) and, consequently, they made offerings on or near important mountain peaks, including those near Chivay. In a related belief, the Incas viewed mountain peaks as sources of water and fertility (Reinhard 1985). Thus, it is possible that the obsidian pebbles left at Machu Picchu drew their multivalent symbolic force from their natural associations in the Colca Valley with high mountain peaks, the power of the underworld as manifested by active volcanoes, and the rushing water of the powerful river that shaped this group of unusual translucent stones.

A second example of the way in which scientific analysis may provide unexpected insights into ceremonial behavior is instructive because it illustrates how unexpected laboratory results may draw attention to previously ignored passages in the works of Spanish chroniclers, such as Bernabé Cobo, in order to make sense of the newly available findings. As mentioned earlier in this chapter, the faunal analysis of zooarchaeologist George Miller revealed that the most common animal offerings in the Machu Picchu graves were of elderly alpacas, almost always more than four years of age. This anomalous finding led Miller (2003) to return to the historical records, where he encountered references to Inca herds consisting exclusively of old or retired camelids (Cobo 1964). These animals were known as *aporucos*. He also found that these special animals, usually male, were required as offerings on particular ceremonial occasions. We do not know whether the symbolic links of aporucos to breeding, maleness, maturity, or some combination of these and other qualities led them to be considered desirable offerings at the graveside ceremonies at Machu Picchu, but their inclusion may have been result of Inca religious belief rather than simple socioeconomic considerations.

The third and final illustration of the way in which

modern science has offered powerful new perspectives on ritual behavior shifts attention away from the laboratory to the new field research that has occurred since Bingham's time. It has long been known that the role of celestial observation was central to the ceremonial cycles and belief systems of the Incas and other cultures of the prehispanic world. Several of the architectural features, such as the Intihuatana (Hitching Post of the Sun) and Torreón (Temple of the Sun), were interpreted by Bingham and others as linked to the worship of the sun and its observation. There was, however, little consensus on exactly what was being observed by the Incas and what techniques were being employed to achieve these ends. In many early studies of archaeoastronomy, sweeping claims were made using Western notions of the sky and how it should be studied. These hypotheses, often untested or impossible to test, led to skepticism among many scholars about astronomical interpretations. Fortunately, recent research by ethnographers, archaeologists, and astronomers has made for a much clearer and more rigorous understanding of what astronomical patterns were being observed and how the Incas went about making those observations (Aveni 1981; Bauer and Dearborn 1995). From the perspective of archaeological practice, the introduction of powerful computing tools and more sophisticated surveying devices made it possible to assess the significance of the orientation of buildings or other features thought to be involved in Inca astronomical activities. As part of this intellectual renewal in archaeoastronomy, a field collaboration was initiated at Machu Picchu between astronomer Raymond White, astrophysicist David Dearborn, and archaeologist Katharina Schreiber. Their research during the 1980s demonstrated that the Incas at Machu Picchu made observations of the June and December solstices and other celestial phenomena (Dearborn and Schreiber 1986: 17) (see Chapter 3). In their work, a high degree of agreement was necessary between the observed orientations of observation points and the position where computer simulations determined the phenomenon in question should have occurred.

According to the Spanish chronicles, both the June and December solstices were major observances in the religious calendar of the Inca royalty. The June celebration, known as Inti Raymi, was a cause for pilgrimages to

SCIENTIFIC INSIGHTS INTO DAILY LIFE

6.11 Volcanic formations in the Chivay area of the Colca Valley along the western Andean slopes of Arequipa. River pebbles from the foot of this deposit were left as an offering near the Main Gateway at Machu Picchu. Photo by Richard L. Burger.

Cuzco and was celebrated throughout the empire. In fact, it continues to be widely celebrated today at archaeological sites in the Cuzco heartland (see Chapter 7). The December celebration, known as Capac Raymi, was of special importance to the Inca elite, marked by a feast that culminated on the day of the solstice with the initiation of noble boys into adulthood by piercing their ears, thus allowing them to wear ornamental ear spools

that were the visual markers of the Inca elite (*orejones*). The findings at Machu Picchu are significant not only because they give us a clearer idea of how and where celestial observations were being made, subjects that are ambiguously alluded to in the historical documents, but also because they imply the presence of astronomically informed specialists among the populace at Machu Picchu. Also, the existence of observatories for both the

June and December solstices suggests that observations and associated rituals were being carried out at Machu Picchu throughout the year, including the rainy season when royal visits would have been unlikely.

The application of scientific techniques to better understand the archaeology of Machu Picchu is still in its infancy. Nevertheless, it has already yielded many exciting results. Each new finding raises additional questions that serve to stimulate research in the laboratory and in the field. These, in turn, force investigators to return to the ambiguous and often incomplete historical records with a new perspective and allow these materials to be used in a more critical and productive manner. The interplay between these multiple lines of evidence along with expertise drawn from many disciplines builds upon the seminal efforts of the 1912 Yale Peruvian Expedition and its groundbreaking interdisciplinary research.

While much of the mystery of Machu Picchu has been dispelled by recent breakthroughs, much remains to be learned. The work reported here represents the beginning of a long process of scientific rediscovery rather than its conclusion. One can only begin to imagine what new advances will be achieved in the next ninety years given the rapid pace of scientific developments and their incorporation into archaeological practice.

7.1 Cuzco residents view the Inti Raymi celebrations from the terraces of the Inca site of Sacsahuaman. The participants dressed as Inca soldiers are preparing to enter the site's central plaza to join in the re-created ceremonies marking the winter solstice. June 24, 1966. Photo by Richard L. Burger.

VII Contemporary Significance of Machu Picchu

Jorge A. Flores Ochoa
Translated by Richard L. Burger

Machu Picchu evokes many different kinds of emotions. Some have ancient roots, others are the result of developments over the past twenty to thirty years, as it has transformed within the framework of national and international tourism. Gradually, Machu Picchu has become a multivocal symbol. It has become identified in a profound way with Peru in general and with Cuzco more specifically. Almost all Cuzqueños (residents of Cuzco) who travel outside the country tell stories of meeting people who, merely knowing that one is Peruvian, ask about Machu Picchu. It is also commonly the case that people who are uncertain about the location of Peru will identify it as the country in which Machu Picchu is located.

The image of Machu Picchu pervades the brochures that promote tourism to Peru. Some countries in South America sell tours with connections to Machu Picchu without clarifying that it is located in another country. In books for travelers, the classic illustrations of Inca constructions at Machu Picchu with a backdrop of Huayna Picchu's profile are never lacking.

Professional meetings such as congresses, seminars, and scientific and cultural courses in fields covering the gamut of knowledge from chemistry to history as well as

law, economy, education, business administration, hotel management, and fashion all publicize their meetings by way of posters, brochures, and other types of advertising featuring photographs, drawings, and simplified images of Machu Picchu. As a result, Machu Picchu has become synonymous with Peru and Cuzco, just as the pyramids have come to symbolize Egypt; the Parthenon, Greece; the Great Wall, China; the Eiffel Tower, Paris; Big Ben, London; the Statue of Liberty, New York; the Taj Mahal, India; and so forth.

These associations are the result of the growth of tourism as a contemporary phenomenon. In considering the meanings of Machu Picchu, I do not examine the processes set in motion by conventional tourism but focus instead on other processes, particularly the traditional and popular use of archaeological remains. I consider the ecological importance of Machu Picchu, which derives from its natural characteristic as one of the most extensive and highest mountain systems in the world. I also touch on the development of mystical tourism at Machu Picchu and, finally, the transformation of the site into a symbol of local, regional, and even national identity.

Popular Use of Archaeological Sites

As has often been observed by professional social scientists, for the inhabitants of the southern Andean region there exists a deep relationship between peasants and the archaeological remains in their surroundings. Ruins are sacred spaces that are used for a variety of activities specific to contemporary life.

In Cuzco, for example, archaeological sites are considered the work of the Incas. This appreciation is shared by peasants and urban residents, those who have been educated and those who do not speak Spanish and may not be able to read and write. Their perception is the result of their ignorance of technical information such as archaeological chronology. Also, a popular myth that has spread throughout the region is that all archaeological remains are of Incan origin, no matter what their form and size. Peasants frequently reiterate that archaeological remains were made by the Incas ("Fueron hechos por los incas"), are from the time of the Incas ("Son del tiempo de los Incas"), or everything is the work of the Incas, who are our ancestors ("Todo es obra de los incas que son nuestros antepasados").

Rural farmers perpetuate the myth, explaining that the Incas, a people of great strength and knowledge ("Incas eran gente de gran poder y conocimiento"), created the architectural structures of large dimension with high-walled rooms, the walls utilizing finely polished stones of considerable dimensions, the dozens of terraces that cover the slopes of the mountains, the canals that cross valleys and are still transporting water. According to these natives, with only the force of their thought, the Incas were able to make the stones place themselves one on top of the other, forming beautiful and imposing structures that we can appreciate today. They also utilized whips in order to make the stones align themselves into walls. The terraces that continue to be cultivated were likewise the work of the Incas. These farmers add that the fertile soil that covers them and that permits excellent agricultural productivity even today was brought by the Incas from faraway places, including distant Amazonian valleys.

In the southern Andes, archaeological sites are used as ceremonial spaces that are transformed into sacred zones. These are appropriate places for carrying out rites of thanks in August, which are the most important in the annual cycle. August signals the beginning of the Andean year and the initiation of the time to carry out ceremonies of propitiation. For the peasants and city residents, it is the time that is dedicated to making offerings to Pachamama (Mother Earth), the principal Andean divinity. People believe that the harvesting of the crops in June leaves Mother Earth exhausted, and that a period of repose or cooling then begins. In order to start the new agricultural cycle, it is necessary to make offerings that contribute to the recuperation of warmth.

These ceremonies involve feasting. The banquet offered to the Earth consists of a variety of dishes. Their selection follows diverse criteria imposed by a variety of people, from specialists to the offerants themselves, given that each one "knows" what the divinity enjoys. The feast demands many hours of careful preparation, sometimes even the entire night. The result is a packet prepared with the selected foods. All this is done in the home of the offerant. After midnight or at dawn, the participants travel to archaeological ruins in the vicinity. They prepare a bonfire in which they deposit the packet so that it can be consumed by the fire. The divinity consumes the offering by inhaling the smoke that rises from the fire. The residents of Cuzco carry out this incineration at Sacsahuaman, Kenko, Teteqaqa, or Tambomachay, which are archaeological sites near the center of the city. Different activities occur in different archaeological sites depending on the region. For example, some sites are used for dancing at carnivals, such as happens at Pisac, when the compounds at this archaeological site are reserved for use by the rural communities of the district.

Over the past fifty years, another use of archaeological sites has become more common. The best example is from the city of Cuzco, and its best-known antecedent dates back to the 1920s. At that time, the confrontation between the Incas and the Spanish was staged at the archaeological site of Sacsahuaman, with the Spanish attacking the "fortress" occupied by the Incas. This recalls a historical episode from the sixteenth century when Manco Inca laid siege to Cuzco in a war of resistance against the Spanish invasion.

In 1934, on the occasion of the celebration of the fourth centennial of the Spanish founding of Cuzco, various activities were organized by a commission in

Lima. In commemoration of the Spanish invasion, the main events staged were theatrical representations of the Incas. The activities were organized by Luis E. Valcarcel, a scholar known for his ethnohistoric investigations and who had also carried out excavations at Sacsahuaman (Berta Bermudez, personal communication). On that occasion, the program announced that on 31 May 1934, the following would be presented:

A great evocative drama at the fortress of Sacsahuaman, with a
parade of the fourteen Incas of Tawantinsuyu. A great Quechua
drama will be represented, especially written for said function,
involving the placement of powerful floodlights in order to illuminate
the entire esplanade (Diario El Sol, May 23, Cuzco).

On the evening of Sunday, June 3, another activity was presented, with the following program:

The Festival of the Appearance of the Moon, at the fortress of
Sajsaywaman; and the evocation of the culminating events
of the Inca Empire by dramatic groups from Cuzco and Urubamba (Diario El Sol, May 23, Cuzco).

The celebration culminated on June 24, with a great ceremony in which archaeological activities were combined with theatrical representations, described in the program as :

The opening of the rediscovered and restored ruins of Sajsaywaman
with the representation of the "Inti Raymi" (Diario El Sol, May 23, Cuzco).

In 1944, ten years later, and every year afterward on June 24th, the Inca ceremony of the Inti Raymi was staged at the ruins of Sacsahuaman (Figure 7.1). The production of this ceremony was based on the descriptions found in historical sources from the sixteenth and seventeenth centuries, especially one by the Inca Garcilaso de la Vega (Flores Ochoa 2000). As part of the ceremony, offerings were made to the god Punchao, the sacred name taken by the Sun, or Inti. As indicated by Inca Garcilaso

de la Vega, the Inca plaza of Hawkaypata, now converted to the main plaza (Plaza Mayor) of Cuzco, was the original location of this ceremony on the June solstice.

On June 24 the Inti Raymi served as a source of inspiration, giving birth to a cycle of similar modern representations at diverse places in Cuzco and other parts of Peru. These presentations all take place at archaeological sites. At the end of the theatrical event, offerings are made to the Andean divinities in the same space in accordance with modern Andean religious rituals.

Returning to the use of "ruins" for traditional ceremonies, it is likely that those peasants who possessed parcels of agricultural land at the hacienda Cutija, where the citadel of Machu Picchu is found, had similar ceremonies as part of Andean farming calendrical rituals. The same rituals were performed by neighboring haciendas, such as Collpani, Mandor, Cedrobamba, Pampacahuay, and other smaller ones, which were occupied by settlers on the properties of Cuzco's residents.

Machu Picchu as Part of the System of Mountains
The year 2002 was declared the International Year of Mountains, or "IYM 2002." Its stated objectives: "The International Year of Mountains 2002 fosters the conservation and sustainable development of mountain regions, thus assuring the welfare of mountain communities and those in the lowlands" (Declaration of IYM's Objectives).

At the Earth Summit in Rio de Janeiro, Brazil, state leaders subscribed to Agenda 21, Chapter 13, which deals with "Managing Fragile Ecosystems: Sustainable Mountain Development"; it is known as the Mountain Agenda. The Food and Agriculture Organization (FAO), an organization of the United Nations, is responsible for coordinating this agenda and committing the states and nonprofit organizations to put it into action. In 1995, the Mountain Institute of Virginia brought together in Lima, Peru, more than 120 nonprofit organizations from 40 countries. They agreed to prioritize actions related to the Mountain Agenda, and to create a center to share information and knowledge.

The same institution conducted a workshop in April 1998 with the theme "Sacred Mountains and Environmental Conservation." Jane Pratt, its president, wrote:

111

7.2 Special recognition of the importance of mountain systems in the contemporary world encouraged the Peruvian government to extend legal protection to Machu Picchu and the surrounding landscape. These have now been incorporated into the Historic Sanctuary of Machu Picchu, a reserve that covers over 80,000 acres. Photo by Paul Duda.

"Inspirational to all, mountains are sacred to over one billion people. In mountain regions throughout the world, traditional cultures and conservation have evolved together over the ages. Sustainable natural resource management is driven by beliefs and behaviors of human communities, and local cultures are strengthened by their intimate connections to the natural environment that sustains them. . . . The Inca culture of Latin America believed mountains to be sacred, and offered human sacrifices on an exceptional basis. There is evidence that this practice was, in some cases, intended to propitiate the mountains gods, and in other cases was done in exchange for taking precious resources." (Mountain Institute 1998).

The recognition of the importance of mountain systems is well established in the contemporary world. It was confirmed by the decision of the Peruvian government to extend legal protection to Machu Picchu (Figure 7.2). This commitment is highlighted by: the decision in 1964, which includes Machu Picchu within the Protection of Cultural Patrimony; that of 1981, when Machu Picchu was declared a natural and cultural area; and that of 1999, which created the Historic Sanctuary of Machu Picchu. As defined, this sanctuary covers 80,535 acres, which include various archaeological remains, such as the Inca Road (Hatun Ñan), which leads to Machu Picchu and which is traveled by thousands of tourists each year.

The sanctuary is, in addition, a center for the biodiversity typical of the cloud forest regions, with a valuable and interesting variety of microclimates and ecological habitats that support plant and animal life (Figure 7.3). Currently, 401 species of birds, 10 species of reptiles, 10 species of amphibians, 13 species of fish, 300 species of diurnal butterflies, and 400 species of nocturnal butterflies have been documented in this location (Galiano 2000). The vegetation is too bountiful and varied to enumerate here. Perhaps it is enough to indicate that in the cloud forests of other latitudes, an average of 50 species of trees has been found per hectare. In contrast, in the Historic Sanctuary of Machu Picchu counts have reached 90 species of trees per hectare. Over 200 species of orchids have been identified in the sanctuary, which represent 12 percent of the 1,625 species of orchids known from Peru (Galiano 2000: 28). It is believed that a

careful and exhaustive study in the sanctuary could yield a count of as many as 400 species of orchids (Galiano 2000: 29).

To the biotic diversity of the Historic Sanctuary of Machu Picchu it is necessary to add nine life zones. These comprise the lands permanently covered with snow; glacial lakes (*lagunas*); regions covered with shrubs; primary and secondary forests; and high-altitude wetlands (*pajonales*) (Galiano 2000: 30). Many investigators have proposed that the Incas chose this spot to erect ceremonial centers such as Machu Picchu and the neighboring sites of Wiñaywayna, Phuyupatamarca, and Sayaqmarca, which form part of the Historic Sanctuary, because of its numerous life zones and remarkable biodiversity.

As a sanctuary, the zone is governed by legislation and by authorities who have as their mission the conservation, maintenance, and care of that which makes this protected area culturally and naturally unique. Despite their efforts, however, contrasting interests, especially in relation to tourist activity, have led to conflicts that have resulted in inadequate maintenance and care of the sanctuary.

Sacrality, Mysticism, and Tourism

Modern world travelers are no longer interested in visiting ten countries in fifteen days. Most tourists prefer to know more about fewer places. They spend consecutive days in a single location, learning something about its culture and people. In order to satisfy this interest, other forms of tourism have developed, including what has been referred to as environmental or ecological tourism, or "ecotourism"; there is also cultural historical tourism, especially a variant focusing on religious, esoteric, or spiritual matters. Recently, travel agents have begun to offer what is known as living or participatory tourism.

Mystical tourism in the Andes appeared in large part as an answer to the steep drop in tourist activity over the past quarter century. Tourism in Peru represents under 0.1 percent of world tourist activity, and constitutes something less than 5 percent of that in South America, which in 1989 was around 8 million tourists (Aguilar, Hinojosa, and Milla 1992: 16). Because of the terrorism of the 1980s and 1990s in Peru, the number of visitors diminished dramatically. Yet, even on this reduced scale, tourism has great economic repercussions in a depressed area such as Cuzco, which does not possess industries and other productive activities besides agriculture and herding. Thus, the national government and local business people are justified in their concerted efforts to address this crisis.

The experiences of other countries that have succeeded in attracting visitors with environmental tourism, nature tourism, and ecotourism, as well esoteric or mystical tourism, has motivated a change in Peru's tourist offerings. Nepal and Tibet are examples: known as centers of spirituality, they attract a steady stream of visitors. This kind of tourism has the additional advantage that it does not need to be massive. Small groups move around with greater facility and have a less negative impact on the natural environment. It is more profitable because of the high prices tourists pay for these excursions, and typical clients are well educated and have more economic resources.

In order to create parameters for mystical tourism at Machu Picchu, the travel industry drew upon the knowledge of anthropologists from Cuzco who specialized in the study of Andean religion and who, in the 1980s, were the only professionals who showed serious interest in its study. They held informational workshops, after which they began to publicize "Andean religion." It was converted into a new "commodity" and offered to the world market in the style that studies of tourism have referred to as "culture by the kilo" (Greenwood 1991). Official documents of the Peruvian government began to incorporate language such as: "It is known that Cuzco is the first point to visit for the non-traditional tourist who can come with a 'work program' based on his or her psychic or spiritual experiences. . . . Thus, Cuzco and the citadel of Machpiqchu, symbol of the Planetary Field (*Chakra planetario*) will receive in the 1990's the seekers of the mystical, magical and mysterious" (Longato 1991: 25).

The Office of Tourist Promotion (FOPTUR), a dependency of the Peruvian government, disseminated information about this kind of tourism to inspire travel agencies. These businesses then began to offer: "PERU MYSTIC TOURS; PERU . . . Country of mystical paradises.

Come to discover the vibrations of magical and millennial Cuzco."

Help in developing this kind of tourism in Peru came from outside the country. Beginning in the decade of the 1940s one group of mystics, the Great Universal Fraternity, announced the emergence of a new center of spirituality called the "Dynamic Tellurgical Center of the Planet." The center was said to be close to Cuzco, having shifted from Katmandu. In 1974, according to one advertisement, the Dalai Lama of Tibet was said to have announced that "The magnetic center of the earth is directed towards the Peruvian Andes and leaves our Himalayas." Whether or not these affirmations are true, the belief was widespread that the new magnetic zone comprised the great space that began at Lake Titicaca and extended along the length of the valley formed by the Vilcanota River, also known as the Urubamba, until it reached Machu Picchu, where the greatest sacrality and energetic charge would be.

Within a short time, the different archaeological sites began to be used for ceremonies specific to Andean mysticism, dedicated to tourists. Kenko, Tambomachay, Lanlakuyuq, Laqo, Kuslluchayuq, Ollantaytambo, and especially Machu Picchu were considered the centers of magnetism and spirituality. Many of these were rebaptized with names — such as Cave of the Monkeys and Temple of the Moon — calculated to attract tourists.

Advertisements claimed that at these sites one could renew one's energy and come into contact with the purest spirituality by way of meditation and exposure to the sacred space. These places were said to exemplify "universal principles," as touted in the following advertisement:

METAPHYSICAL TOURS TO PERU IN 1993
(*pre-announcement*)

When one goes to Machu Picchu it is to meet oneself. Every ritual initiation is a profound immersion into yourself. It is a process where emotions, feelings, remembrances, and passion are liberated and released so you have full control of your life and discover who you truly are. A trip to Machu Picchu offers the possibility of an initiation into the magical mystical earth, the inheritance of all humanity.

7.3 Orchids at Machu Picchu. Photo by Paul Duda.

In this way, mystical tourism was formalized. The search for the spirits of the Andes was rapidly converted into an important attraction (Flores Ochoa 1996). Mystical tourism had informal antecedents in the tourist guides who noticed that many tourists were interested in mysticism, esoteric knowledge, meditation, and even the search for extraterrestrial life. They began to offer as an extra attraction special ceremonies, especially at Machu Picchu. They searched for spots with a certain level of privacy in order to prepare sacred packets in the presence of tourists, who they asked to make wishes that they wanted fulfilled. These guides promised to burn the packets in special places that only they knew. The tourists also joined together in circles in order to medi-

7.4 Tourists from throughout the world travel to Machu Picchu on a spiritual quest that typically involves "traditional" Andean ceremonies, meditation, and prayer. The visitors shown here are drawing upon the purported energetic forces radiating from the Sacred Rock in the northern extreme of the Machu Picchu palace complex. August 2001. Photo by Richard L. Burger.

tate and to attract the energy of the sacred place (Figure 7.4). Another ceremony required placing hands on the Intihuatana in order to receive the energy radiating from it. In other instances, guides had tourists lie outstretched on the large flat stones in order to absorb the force that emanated from them.

On one typical tour, the first day was a trip to Cuzco. In the afternoon, a visit was scheduled to Sacsahuaman to "see the sacred portals." The next day was spent at Kenko "in front of an important figure in stone that expresses the theme of the sacred and mysterious cult." Special exercises were recommended in order to transmute energy and raise the mental, emotional, and physical level of the visitor. One announcement on this tour declared: "Profound meditation will be achieved by way of very special exercises that prepare one for the

Supreme State that will be achieved (after bathing at Agua Calientes [Hot Springs]), a place where the Inca and his court magnetized their bodies by submerging them in the special energies of the thermal baths, whose waters come from the depths of the Andes." The tour guides announced the possibility of entering into contact with "superior beings coming from other galaxies" as either an alternative to or a supplement to the tours, depending on visitors' tastes and requests. Apparently, extraterrestrials selected the Machu Picchu region in order to enter into contact with humans. Numerous books have been published that support this tourist offering, asserting a relationship between the Incas and beings from other galaxies. Some even claim that Machu Picchu is the result of the constructive labors of these extraterrestrial beings.

Nor is the influence of "New Age" currents alien to this kind of tourist promotion. An example is actress Shirley MacLaine's account, in her book and the film adapted from it, *Out on a Limb*, of her contact with "brothers from space" during her mystical experience in the Andes.

Conferences were also organized around the theme of extraterrestrial contact at Machu Picchu:

Into the Fifth Dimension/UFO Conference
There are various mysterious phenomena in Peru that stimulate the imagination into thinking about how the extraterrestrials have been part of the earth's history since antiquity. This pilgrimage will take us to view the figures and lines of Nasca, that can only be seen from the air. Some people speculate that the lines were part of a landing strip for the U.F.O.'s. We'll explore the ruins of Cuzco where there are examples of extraordinary work with huge stones of 300 tons, that many feel were put into place with the knowledge that was brought from other planets. We'll have conference time in Cuzco and Machu Picchu where we'll have the opportunity to make contact as others have done there in the past (SON OF THE SUN. UNIVERSAL BROTHER/SISTERHOOD. October 1990).

The mystical commodity sold to tourists features Machu Picchu as the center of attraction. The guided visit to it provides teachings that reveal "secrets" known only by the initiated and that remain invisible to those who do not have the eyes to see them. At night, in the ruins of Machu Picchu, ceremonies are carried out by guides that are considered of central importance to the mystical tourist. They select special sites such as the Intihuatana, the Main Temple, or the Temple of the Moon. The Temple of the Moon, located in the lower part of Machu Picchu and reachable by the road to Huayna Picchu, is rarely visited by common tourists.

The ceremony conducted for these particular visitors exhibits variations according to the specialists who direct the tour, the interests of the group itself, and, of course, the amount that is paid. Coca is chewed and divination is carried out using its leaves, prayers are offered, meditation is engaged in, and spiritual work is done in groups or individually. At the culminating moment a higher state of consciousness is reached when the participants have extranormal sensations, communicate with the past, see supernatural beings, and even perceive the presence of the Incas. The experience ends with the curing of physical maladies and the elimination of uncertainty and lack of faith in order to find spiritual peace, the goal of their journey to Machu Picchu.

The interest in Andean mysticism has resulted in the prolific production of books and brochures that highlight the sacred, energetic, and mystical features of Machu Picchu. Often these are the product of sheer imagination, with influences coming from Asian philosophical practices, although ties with extraterrestrials and references to lost continents such as Atlantis also abound in these publications. It has been said that Andean mysticism is Orientalism wearing a poncho.

The demand for accurate information about Machu Picchu has reached the academic world. To this end, archaeologists, historians, and anthropologists have produced serious works based on years of research. Yet, some publications combine authentic scientific information with fantasy and invention. Lay readers can be misled because they do not have the background necessary to differentiate between the scientific and the imagined.

Machu Picchu as a Symbol of Identity

In the 1990s, the government of President Alberto Fujimori authorized the construction of a cable car system to ascend to Machu Picchu from the river below. The actions that occurred following that decision demonstrate that the Machu Picchu archaeological site was considered one of the principal symbols of Cuzco regional identity. The perceived threat to the sanctity of Machu Picchu led the Cuzqueños to confront the authoritarian Fujimori government from 1990 to 2000. The opposition of the population materialized in the form of general strikes that paralyzed the city and region of Cuzco, marches to Machu Picchu involving hundreds of students, the organizing of support from the national and international scientific community, and the support of the media and, above all, of the Cuzco community, which identified with the fate of Machu Picchu and were concerned for its conservation. This opposition forced the government to reconsider its intentions. This was significant politically, because the suspension

7.5 Residents of Cuzco protesting the government policy favoring the private sector and the modification of the site's infrastructure in favor of more visitors and greater profit. Photo by Jorge Flores Ochoa.

7.6 Protest against government policy concerning Machu Picchu. The placard, in English translation, says "Machu Picchu: Don't Sell It, Defend It." Photo by Jorge Flores Ochoa.

of the plans for the cable car at Machu Picchu was one of the first defeats suffered by the authoritarian and corrupt regime of Fujimori (Figures 7.5 and 7.6).

Machu Picchu, with its architectonic structures existing in harmony with the environment, has no rival in Peru. It is an expression of what human labor is capable of producing. It is also a symbol of human creativity, an example of the balance between culture and nature that modern society seeks. The exceptional quality of workmanship at Machu Picchu, from which its sacredness emanates, has transformed it into a destination of national and international pilgrimage. After traveling the "sacred route," many travelers return to Machu Picchu as pilgrims.

The Cuzqueños consider themselves fortunate to have received this legacy, the work of mythical and royal ancestors. They seek to conserve it in its "purest" state in order to maintain the character of the Inca past as well as that acquired in the modern world. Whatever the orientation and motivation of visitors might be, they will have the possibility of feeling the "energy" that Machu Picchu possesses. It could be one reason that led Inca Yupanqui (Pachacuti) to construct his "royal estate" there, designing it for religious meditation (Rowe 1990).

Given that Machu Picchu has been converted into a "sanctuary," it should be treated as such. It should not be disturbed by modern constructions of questionable quality and use, such as has occurred since the highway was constructed sixty years ago. At that time, it was claimed that the road was needed to provide "facilities and commodities" for tourists. Access would take less time and visitors would be able to spend more hours visiting the monument. The road would improve the service, given that the visitors would no longer have to walk uphill; with its construction, tourists would exchange horses and mules for comfortable seats in "modern" minibuses.

The building of the highway was enthusiastically supported and defended by progressives and modernists in the 1940s. During the same period, the building of the hotel next to the archaeological center was begun. Since that time, the hotel has been transforming, continually growing in small increments. The most recent refurbishment and expansion was in 2001. It was carried out at a time when support for the need to eradicate the

hotel in its current location was gaining ground because it clearly was inconsistent with the nature of the archaeological monument. The proximity of the hotel disturbed the integrity of the Inca citadel, breaking its harmonic relationship with the landscape, which is one of its principal attractions.

Today the highway is objected to and criticized for good reason because it alters the landscape, disturbs the surroundings, and requires motorized vehicles, which contaminate the natural environment. Given these antecedents, the proposed cable car was, for the residents of Cuzco, equally damaging and disturbing. Only a distorted modernist ideology could consider large structures of cement and metal towers with thick cables crossing the open air a symbol of progress.

The proposal to install the cable car was justified as being consistent with a broader modernist or progressive ideology of economic development. As a government project, bidding for its construction and administration was sought from and conceded to investors in the tourist industry. The request for bids consisted of a brief announcement published in what seemed like a surreptitious manner. The contract was won by the only company that presented a bid. This procedure favored a business consortium that maneuvered in a strategic manner to control the Historic Sanctuary of Machu Picchu by way of companies linked together. These included an airline; hotels in Lima, Cuzco, and Machu Picchu; and the Cuzco–Machu Picchu railroad, which is the only way to reach the archaeological center. With possession of the cable car they would close the circle, creating a monopoly.

The station from which the cable car would ascend to and descend from the archaeological center would also function as a crafts center and place for the sale of handicrafts, and for a concentration of restaurants. Visitors would neither need nor have time to wander through the town of Aguas Calientes or Machu Picchu Pueblo, utilizing their restaurants, hotels, and other services. The economic interests of small local business people and the owners of the minibuses would certainly be affected. It is worth noting that the minibus service merits more stringent controls because of the evident contamination and the disturbance to the landscape it creates. This problem will generate future study and debate, and we should not rule out that the climb to Machu Picchu should be on foot, which is the way one traditionally arrives at sanctuaries.

Public opinion objected to the conditions and even the legality of the bid procedure. Also, there were obvious links with people in President Fujimori's inner circle. The contract that was adjudicated demonstrates how the government gave an advantage to the concessionary company and set aside the pubic interest, an interest that should be the main concern of the government.

It is self-evident that the installation of a cable car would alter any landscape. Manifesting remarkable ingenuity and cynicism, although lacking in candor, one of the impresarios of the Machu Picchu cable car endeavor offered to paint the gray cables green in order not to alter the landscape. Proponents repeated the arguments of sixty years before: all tourists would ascend to the site in less time, they would travel in greater comfort, they would have more time to spend in the archaeological center, and, consequently, this change would increase the flow of visitors. Of course, tourists would use the time they had saved in traveling to the site by taking advantage of the services provided by the same company that was administering the cable car.

More convenient access to Machu Picchu will be the theme of discussions in the near future. Because of the unique character of the site and its singular relation with the natural environment, these discussions merit adequate treatment. Developers cannot abuse the rights of traditional users — the descendants of Machu Picchu's builders — who want to use the sacred sites of their cultural heritage and who have the right to enjoy them in their natural and cultural context as exceptional places, thereby conserving them for the enjoyment of future generations.

The cable car was designed to satisfy the interests of business managers who neither thought about the future of the monument nor took into account the modern criteria of sustained and sustainable development. The technicians and official bureaucrats were insensitive to these matters and were, unfortunately, charged with making the decisions about authorizing proposals of this type. They ignored the legitimate interests of the region's population, which demanded the right to pre-

sent its opinion and to have its point of view respected. The technicians and officials were not the only ones to be convinced by the alleged advantages of the plan. It was in the interest of the business managers that tourists be able to ascend to the archaeological complex in five, ten, or fifteen minutes. By doing this, they would be able to circulate 400 travelers per hour on the cable cars, totaling 3,200 visitors every eight hours, ultimately reaching a total of 1,168,000 per year. This statistic would double and perhaps even triple if Machu Picchu remained open twenty-four hours a day through the installation of sound and light systems, as has been proposed. It must be kept in mind that studies by the United Nations Educational, Scientific, and Cultural Organization (UNESCO) and special consultants calculate that Machu Picchu should not received more than 2,200 visitors per day. Irreparable damage will be sustained if the number is increased beyond that without controls.

Setting aside the constraints established by these studies, the business consortium in question did not present environmental impact studies. It tried to compensate for this after receiving the concession from the government by hiring the services of consulting firms to be paid by the very same company that would be benefited.

The possible installation of the cable car at Machu Picchu became a public scandal. By investing $8 million, the company stood to obtain profits of $250 million. This was not, however, the main problem. The main problem was that a monopoly was being created, and that Machu Picchu was being threatened by damage from intensive use to precisely those features of the natural environment that attract visitors to the site.

The cable car operation would have extended over almost 2 miles, and the installation of the intermediate support towers would have destroyed the last remains of the primary forest that still exists along the left bank of the Urubamba River. The station terminal would have dramatically altered an Inca cemetery and other archaeological remains, damaging the natural vegetation and wild life in the surrounding environment that serve to define the fundamental characteristics of the site. The arrival station in the upper zone would have required deep excavations to anchor its foundations. These excavations would have endangered the stability of a mountain characterized by geological faults and debris slides.

The insensitivity of the Fujimori government to these concerns produced massive public protests. At the core of the resistance were professors and students from the anthropology, archaeology, and history programs of the social science faculty at the National University of San Antonio Abad of Cuzco. Their activism found support in diverse unionized and professional institutions such as the Regional Assembly, which brings together the professional societies of the city; the Departmental Federation of Workers of Cuzco; and the Departmental Federation of Cuzco Peasants.

In 1999, the first large general strike was called to protest and impede the construction of the cable car at Machu Picchu. For the first time in the history of Cuzco, of Peru, possibly of the Americas and, perhaps, even of the world, a social mobilization of this kind was realized for the defense of an archaeological patrimony. The city of Cuzco was totally paralyzed by the strike. The unions, professional societies, and citizens in general marched together with the students in the streets, expressing their rejection of the government's intentions. The protest was repeated at a later date, with the added request that the Hydroelectric Center of Machu Picchu, destroyed by a landslide, be reconstructed. The similarity of the name of this facility to the archaeological site helped motivate and activate the Cuzqueño population.

Later in 1999, still another protest took place. The professors and students of the University of Cuzco decided to organize a long walk to Machu Picchu as a sacrifice in protest. The route of the railroad was selected because of the difficulties that walking on the cross ties of the rails presented. The protest began at mile 55, arriving at Machu Picchu in less than eight hours. Close to three hundred students participated. They received a warm reception at Machu Picchu from the residents of Aguas Calientes and Machu Picchu Pueblo, who provided the students with food and lodging. The students ascended to the monument where they held rallies. The print and television media submitted to political pressure, remaining silent about the march, which, nonetheless, was publicized beyond the borders of the country (Figure 7.7).

In 2000, the march to Machu Picchu was repeated. This time almost five hundred students took part. In ad-

dition to those studying anthropology, archaeology, and history were students from communication sciences, biology, law, and tourism. The march received the support of the new university administration. The weakening of the government regime was clear. Fujimori was obliged to announce the suspension of the cable car construction, using the argument that it was necessary to carry out environmental impact studies.

An information network was established in which Peruvians residing abroad, especially in Paris, collaborated with sympathetic people from different countries. They sent messages by email to the Peruvian government. A statement was composed, to which the international scientific community adhered. The most active in this network were the archaeologists, anthropologists, and historians who denounced to the world the absurdity of the Peruvian government's position. They contributed to creating a current of public opinion against the alteration of Machu Picchu.

In turn, UNESCO sent a commission to Peru to investigate what was happening at Machu Picchu. The "Report of the Mission to the Historic Sanctuary of Machu Picchu (Perú) from October 18–25, 1999" was examined at the Twenty-third Session of the World Heritage Committee at the Convention Concerning the Protection of the World Cultural and Natural Heritage of UNESCO, held from November 29 to December 4, 1999, in Marakesh, Morocco. The report was approved in its totality. According to the delegate from Zimbabwe, the document, for the first time, was written in a form that presented the theme with clarity, permitting officials to form a definitive opinion about the Machu Picchu complex and not only in reference to the construction of the cable car. Point 8 of the report declares that the Peruvian government must not introduce new means of access to Machu Picchu, and it must not permit new construction. In this way, the support needed to preserve the sanctity of Machu Picchu was achieved.

Without doubt, the force of the defense of the archaeological monument and the protest against the cable car rested upon the importance that Machu Picchu held in the collective mentality. It was a symbol of regional identity and it had been threatened by the arbitrary actions of the national government.

During the Peruvian national elections of 2001,

7.7 Students and professors from the University of Cuzco march along the railroad tracks from Cuzco to Machu Picchu in pilgrimage to the site and as an expression of the symbolic importance of this extraordinary site. Photo by Jorge Flores Ochoa.

Machu Picchu was a theme in the presidential debate. When only the two contenders, Alejandro Toledo and Alan Garcia, remained in the debate, the rector of the National University of San Antonio Abad of Cuzco asked them to present their views with respect to the construction of the cable car and the inviolability of Machu Picchu. Both responded by promising to respect Machu Picchu and not to permit the installation of the cable car or the building of any new structures.

During the electoral campaign Alejandro Toledo made known his desire to take the oath as president in front of the Apu Machu Picchu in gratitude to Pachamama (Mother Earth). Fulfilling his debate promise on July 29, 2001, he chose this unique archaeological monument as the site of public ceremony. His intention was clear. By utilizing a symbol of Peruvian-

ness, to which the Andean population is sensitive, Toledo identified with its meaning, which extends from Incaism to indigenism and contemporary Andeanism. The act was part ceremony, part spectacle. Presidents of foreign countries attended, along with cabinet members, congress members, diplomats, fellow party members, and friends of the elected president. The ceremony, televised internationally, showed only portions of the Andean ritual because the religious ceremony was intentionally minimized. The president participated in the ritual only minimally, avoiding contact with the Andean religious specialists. His wife, however, participated in the ceremony actively and visibly. The important preparation of the sacred packet or offering was carried out far from the television cameras, and it was incinerated at another time and place.

The presence of Peru's new president served to confirm the sacredness of Machu Picchu and the symbolic importance it possesses for the Andean population. Similarly, there is value and importance in the decision by Cuzco University professors and students to walk each year to Machu Picchu not as protesters but as a pilgrims, ascending to the monument on foot in order to show that this is the way one should arrive at this sacred place.

Catalogue

Lucy C. Salazar and Richard L. Burger

The material remains from Machu Picchu and other Inca archaeological sites provide a unique vision of the world in which they lived. Produced by craft specialists, part-time artisans, household servants, and simple farmers, these objects also embody the cosmology and socio-economic organization of Tahuantinsuyu. Despite the fascination Inca items hold, they have rarely been the focus of museum exhibitions or illustrated volumes. Even the contents of the famous collection recovered by the 1912 Yale Peruvian Expedition to Machu Picchu remains little known, and has rarely been illustrated outside of the expedition's pioneering publications (Bingham 1913b, 1930; Eaton 1916).

The catalogue section of this book illustrates the most memorable objects recovered at Machu Picchu in 1912, as well as historic items from the Yale Peruvian Scientific Expeditions; these items have Yale Peabody Museum (YPM) catalogue numbers. In addition to showing the most significant and visually appealing objects, this section offers an overview of the tools and items used in everyday life at Machu Picchu. The specimens from the Yale Peabody Museum were photographed by William Sacco. The materials from Machu Picchu are supple-

mented by other objects from the Yale Peabody Museum, many of which were acquired by Bingham in Cuzco during his time in Peru.

At Machu Picchu, the royal family and their guests would have dressed in fine clothing and precious metal jewelry; even their plates and cups would have been made of gold and silver. When Machu Picchu was abandoned, the elite took these valuable objects with them to Cuzco, thus making it impossible for Bingham and later archaeologists to encounter them during their excavations at Pachacuti's royal estate. In order to provide the reader with some idea of this unrepresented class of elite materials, objects are illustrated from museum collections in the United States and France.

Finally, the remarkable cultural tradition of Tahuantinsuyu did not disappear with the Spanish conquest. On the contrary, it continued to develop during the following centuries, sometimes incorporating and transforming elements of European artistic traditions into distinctively Andean art forms. Examples of these post-Conquest items are included here to illustrate this complex melding of cultural traditions.

1

Memorabilia

Cat. No. 1
Kodak No. 3A Folding Pocket Camera
Cat. No. YPM 260816 (*right*)
Height: 10.6 in. (27.0 cm)
Width: 5.5 in. (14.0 cm)

Hiram Bingham III was committed to documenting the Yale Peruvian Scientific Expeditions through a systematic program of field photography. The principal tool was the Kodak No. 3A Folding Pocket Camera, provided to the expedition at no cost by Kodak's founder, George Eastman. This camera was relatively small and resilient and could utilize either roll film or glass plates, but Bingham opted for the former. It produced 3.25″ by 5.5″ black and white negatives. Focusing by way of a waist-level finder on top of the lens mount was more approximate than with ground glass but did not require a focusing "dark cloth" (Edward Ranney, personal communication). The film was developed in the field and printed after Bingham returned home to New Haven, Connecticut. Bingham provided the members of the expeditions with cameras and with instructions on their use.

The expedition camera was stamped with the inscription "YALE PERUVIAN EXPEDITION NO. 1." Its case was embossed with the Spanish expedition name "COMISION CIENTIFICA YALE Y N.G.S." This camera was used by Bingham himself during the 1912 and/or 1914/1915 expedition. Bingham's special dedication to documenting the investigations through the use of photography is evident from the Yale Peabody's archives, which include detailed photographic logs indicating the hour of the day and the exposure of the thousands of pictures taken during the Yale Peruvian Scientific Expeditions.

Panoram Kodak No. 4
Cat. No. YPM 264294 (*left*)
Height: 10.1 in. (25.7 cm)
Width: 4.7 in. (12.0 cm)

In addition to standard cameras, the members of the Yale Peruvian Scientific Expedition employed special cameras designed to take panoramic photographs. Such cameras were ideal for recording landscape and archaeological sites. Each roll of film produced four

3.5″ by 12″ negatives. The panoramic coverage was achieved by a lens that moved through a large field of vision at the time of making an exposure. When using this camera, as with the Kodak No. 3A, Bingham and his colleagues always employed a wooden tripod. The panoramic camera is engraved with "YALE PERUVIAN EXPEDITION NO. 2."

Cat. No. 2
Expedition Trunk
Cat. No. YPM 264293
Height: 9.8 in. (25 cm)
Length: 24.6 in. (62.5 cm)
Width: 13.8 in. (35 cm)

The provisioning of the 1911 and 1912 expeditions was a formidable challenge that required considerable dedication and organizational skill. Bingham took a personal interest in these matters and carefully oversaw the acquisition and distribution of field equipment. Metal trunks, such as this one used in 1911 by expedition naturalist Harry Foote, were essential in order to safeguard project supplies and personal belongings during the lengthy sea voyage via the Panama Canal and arduous trips by mule and horse through the southern highlands of Peru.

Inca Pottery

The ceramics produced in Tahuantinsuyu were technically sophisticated and although somewhat austere, many have an aesthetic elegance that cannot be denied. They were fired in an oxidizing atmosphere, and most of the decoration was accomplished through cream, dark red, and black painting before firing. The potter's wheel was unknown, and hand modeling and molds were employed to obtain the desired shapes. Similarly, vitreous finishing or glazing was alien to Inca technology, but fine surface finishes were accom-

3

4

plished by pebble polishing. The ceramic forms and geometric motifs favored on classic Inca pottery identified the ceramics with Tahuantinsuyu, and variations in these reflected the multiplicity of ethnic and geographical identities within the empire.

Aryballos

The Inca state sponsored the production of pottery characterized by a limited range of distinctive forms and designs, and this pottery served as symbols of Tahuantinsuyu and those involved in its administration. One of the most common and distinctive Inca forms was the handled jar with pointed conical base, low-set vertical strap handles, rim nubbins, a central lug, and a long flaring neck. Bingham (1915c) drew upon his knowledge of ancient Greek pottery and referred to this classic Inca form as an *aryballus*, and this term, al-

beit with various spellings, is still commonly used despite the great differences between the Inca and Greek vessels. The placement of the handles and central lug made it feasible for people to carry these large and awkward vessels on the back by running a rope through the handles and around the lug (Bingham 1930: 124, fig. 79). This practice is depicted in the modeled provincial Inca pottery of Peru's north coast (Matos 2000: 108). The conical pointed base of the aryballos allowed the large vessels to be set into the earth for greater stability and reduced the danger of breakage.

Large aryballi were used for the fermentation, storage, and transportation of corn beer (*chicha* or *asua*), as well as other goods, and thus aryballi played a key role in public festivals and rituals. The easily recognizable Inca form and the associated geometric motifs would

have constituted a visual reminder that the corn beer being dispensed was a function of the generosity of the Inca state. The large aryballi were a common feature at the public feasts held at Machu Picchu and other Inca royal estates, where such feasting was a common activity. Bingham (1930: 127) estimated that 28 percent of the vessels recovered at Machu Picchu were aryballi, and that at least 150 of these were huge vessels. The great capacity of the very large aryballi indicates that they were designed to hold enough corn beer to accommodate large groups rather than a single household or individual.

Medium-sized and small aryballi served as liquid containers to be used in other contexts. Small aryballi, for example, could have been used to hold chicha for a pair of drinkers, and they were a common feature in the burial caves at Machu Picchu. Outside of the Cuzco heartland, potters produced provincial imitations of the classic aryballos or created aryballi that combined local and Cuzco Inca features. The Incas made gifts of classic Inca-style goods, such as textiles and pottery, to their allies and the leaders of subjugated ethnic groups, and the utilization of these goods was controlled by the Inca state. The kind of Inca pottery an individual used reflected his or her eth-

5

nic, social, and political identity in a conspicuous and relatively unambiguous manner. The diversity of aryballi illustrated in this book demonstrates the multi-ethnic character of Tahuantinsuyu and, more specifically, the diversity of the population residing at Machu Picchu.

Cat. No. 3
Aryballos
Cat. No. YPM 17478
Late Horizon, Inca
Machu Picchu, Cave 29/76
Height: approx. 25.6 in. (65 cm)
Rim Diameter: approx. 6.7 in. (17.0 cm)
Max. Diameter: approx. 31.5 in. (80.0 cm)

This large classic Inca Cuzco-style aryballos has a central vertical panel of nested diamonds flanked by two vertical bands filled with red cross-hatching. The two bands flanking the central panel are filled with rows of black pendant triangles. The painted red neck is filled with rows of black diamonds. The vessel was repaired in two places during Inca times, and in one of these spots a lead plug held in place by resin or tar is still visible. Due to breakage, the upper section of the vessel's neck is missing. Judging from where it was found, it is likely that this aryballos once held corn beer for grave-side rituals at Machu Picchu.

Cat No. 4
Aryballos
Cat. No. YPM 17479
Late Horizon, Inca
Machu Picchu
Height: 26.5 in. (67.2 cm)
Rim Diameter: 3.9 in. (10.0 cm)
Max. Diameter: 23.6 in. (60.0 cm)

This large Cuzco Inca aryballos is decorated with a central horizontal band filled with dark red concentric diamond patterns. The neck and the modeled appliqué feline lug are painted dark red, contrasting with the orange color of this classic Inca vessel. In addition to the reworking of the neck to compensate for breakage are several holes in the vessel chamber filled with lead plugs held in place by resinous material. This repair technique occurs on several vessels from the Machu Picchu collection.

Cat. No. 5
Aryballos
Cat. No. YPM 17477
Late Horizon, Inca
Machu Picchu
Height: 31.5 in. (80.0 cm)
Rim Diameter: 6.5 in. (16.5 cm)
Max. Diameter: 23.6 in. (60.0 cm)

This large Inca aryballos was probably used to hold *chicha* during the feasts at Machu Picchu. Its polished surface has oxidized to an orange color. A horizontal band consists of a black and white double-fret band bordered in red on the sides. The central appliqué lug is modeled into a stylized feline head, and the neck is painted black. At some time during Machu Picchu's occupation, the upper section of the vessel was broken and in order to continue using this huge aryballos, the top of the neck was removed and a new horizontal rim was created by abrasion. Repairs such as this one are relatively common (see, e.g., YPM 17479), a fact that suggests that these vessels were highly valued. The

7

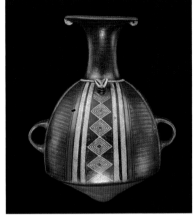

9

vertical central panel filled with white diamonds. The central band is flanked by bands of black triangles. The appliqué lug is modeled as a stylized zoomorphic head, and the "ear" nubbins on the rim are pierced.

Cat. No. 9
Aryballos
Cat. No. YPM 17471
Late Horizon, Inca
Cuzco
Height: 11.6 in. (29.6 cm)
Rim Diameter: 4.7 in. (12.0 cm)
Max. Diameter: 10.0 in. (25.4 cm)

A classic Cuzco-style aryballos of medium size, this orange-buff slipped vessel is beautifully painted and well polished. Its chamber is decorated with a central panel filled with nested diamonds flanked by horizontal bands of solid black triangles. Pairs of cream-colored vertical bands filled with red fine-line cross-hatching run along side of the central decorative band. The neck is painted red and covered with rows of solid black diamonds. The central lug is shown as a stylized feline head with upright ears.

Cat. No. 10
Aryballos
Cat. No. YPM 17476
Late Horizon, Inca
Machu Picchu
Height: 20.0 in. (50.7 cm)
Rim Diameter: 7.6 in. (19.4 cm)
Max. Diameter: 18.7 in. (47.5 cm)

This classic Inca Cuzco-style aryballos is decorated with black and red painting on its central chamber. The front of the vessel features three vertical bands with double-crosses and broken lines separated by red bands. The central panel is flanked by two wide bands filled with typical examples of a pattern possibly inspired by Inca knotted string records, *quipus* (see Cat. No. 180, YPM 19236).

difficulty of producing pottery of this size using traditional techniques has been well documented among contemporary highland groups (Ravines and Villiger 1989).

Cat. No. 6
Aryballos
Cat. No. YPM 194269
Late Horizon, Inca
Machu Picchu
Height: 36.6 in. (93.0 cm)
Max. Diameter: 23.6 in. (60.0 cm)

This massive aryballos would have been appropriate to ferment, store, and serve *chicha*, but it could have been used as a storage vessel for other products (Morris and Thompson 1985). It is completely covered with red slip and lacks the geometric painting commonly associated with this class of vessels at Machu Picchu. Heavily reconstructed from the fragments recovered at the royal estate, the vessel shape is slightly irregular, probably as a result of firing the vessel at too high a temperature. The central lug of the aryballos is shaped into a very stylized feline face with large eyes represented by diagonal incisions and modeled ears. The conical base is flattened at its lower extreme. This feature, like the others already described, suggests that the vessel was not local.

Cat. No. 7
Aryballos
Cat. No. YPM 18631
Late Horizon, Inca
Machu Picchu
Height: 22.0 in. (56.0 cm)
Rim Diameter: 4.7 in. (12.0 cm)
Max. Diameter: 23.2 in. (59.0 cm)

This large aryballos is covered with a cream-colored slip. The central lug is modeled as a feline's head and painted brown, in contrast to the rest of the vessel. As in the case of YPM 17477, the upper part of the neck was cut and abraded so that it could be reutilized after the uppermost section was damaged. This vessel is not in a classic Cuzco Inca style and was probably brought from outside the Cuzco heartland, perhaps from the Lake Titicaca Basin.

Cat. No. 8
Aryballos
Cat. No. YPM 16954
Late Horizon, Inca
Machu Picchu
Height: 8.1 in. (20.5 cm)
Rim Diameter: 2.5 in. (6.5 cm)
Max. Diameter: 5.1 in. (13.0 cm)

This Cuzco Inca-style small aryballos is slipped brown and highly polished. The chamber is painted red and features a

12

Cat. No. 12
Aryballos
Cat. No. YPM 16415
Late Horizon, Inca
Machu Picchu, Cave 6A
Height: 8.6 in. (21.9 cm)
Rim Diameter: 3.0 in. (7.7 cm)
Max. Diameter: 6.8 in. (17.3 cm)
Publication: Bingham 1930: 121, figs. 7a, 7b, 7c

Small provincial versions of the aryballos were produced throughout Tahuantinsuyu, and they varied from the classic Cuzco vessels in their form and decoration. This distinctive provincial aryballos was probably brought from the Lake Titicaca region. Unlike the classic Cuzco aryballos, the tapered base on this vessel is flattened and the appliqué lug is a simple protuberance rather than the feline or stylized zoomorphic head. While Cuzco aryballi have an orange tone as a result of oxidation firing, this vessel has a cream color because it was slipped with a fine wash of kaolin clay. Its main decoration, a crosshatched central horizontal band of repeating diamonds filled with pinwheels, is alien to Cuzco but common farther to the south. The neck is adorned with alternating horizontal lines of red and black. The scale of small aryballi such as this one suggests that they were designed for personal use, a fact that helps to explain why they were common grave goods in the Machu Picchu cave burials. This piece had been placed in the interment of a young woman approximately 18–20 years old (Verano 2003).

The central lug, modeled as a stylized feline head, is painted black, as is the neck of the vessel. The upper back of the chamber is painted with a horizontal band filled with vertical undulating lines.

Cat. No. 11
Aryballos
Cat. No. YPM 16909
Late Horizon, Inca
Cuzco
Height: 7.5 in. (19.0 cm)
Rim Diameter: 2.6 in. (6.7 cm)
Max. Diameter: 6.3 in. (16.0 cm)

This small aryballos is made of finely painted and carefully polished orangeware. A triangular portion of the chamber's front is painted dark red and contrasts with the cream colored central nubbin. A white band filled with a pendant *quipu* design runs along the lower extreme of the dark red zone; it resembles a necklace or garment fringe. The handles and back of the aryballos are painted dark red, as is the neck, which is encircled by horizontal white lines. The central lug is shown as a simplified zoomorphic head with its eyes and mouth represented by straight incisions.

Cat. No. 13
Aryballos
Cat. No. YPM 05462
Late Horizon, Inca
Cuzco
Height: 6.7 in. (17.0 cm)
Rim Diameter: 2.0 in. (5.2 cm)
Max. Diameter: 4.6 in. (11.8 cm)

This small, highly polished red aryballos is covered with polychrome painting in red, black, cream, and orange. It features repetitive and densely packed geometric motifs. The neck has four rows of truncated diamonds filled with vertical lines. On the main chamber, bands of stacked inverted triangles, painted red and white, alternate with bands of double triangles filled with nested squares or rectangles. Horizontal orange bands divide the geometric bands, and vertical orange bands frame the heavily decorated central zone of the main chamber. The central lug is a simple protuberance encircled by a line of circle-dot elements. Decoration on the back of the chamber is limited to a band of fine black cross-hatching. Elaborate decoration such as that found on this vessel was rare in the Cuzco area, but it has been found on the pottery in the Lake Titicaca area.

Cat. No. 14
Aryballos
Cat. No. YPM 17589
Late Horizon, Provincial Inca
Machu Picchu
Height: 6.5 in. (16.5 cm)
Rim Diameter: 2.4 in. (6.0 cm)
Max. Diameter: 5.1 in. (13.0 cm)

This small provincial Inca-style aryballos has an overall red slip. The stylized human face with its coffee-bean eyes and mouth and pendulous nose was modeled using an appliqué technique. The vertical bands applied to the vessel neck represent braids, and it is possible that a female is being depicted. The back of the neck presents rows of black diamonds separated with white lines. The potter did not include pierced "ears" on the vessel rim, and the style of vessel suggests that it may have been produced in Peru's central highlands.

Cat. No. 15
Aryballos

13

Cat. No. YPM 16964
Late Horizon, Provincial Inca
Machu Picchu
Height: 7.9 in. (20.0 cm)
Max. Diameter: 6.3 in. (16.0 cm)

This small polychrome aryballos follows many of the common conventions of Cuzco Inca vessels, but its unusual form raises the possibility of a provincial origin. The central register has alternating double-X motifs with blocks of parallel horizontal lines. This section is flanked with vertical bands of red zigzag lines. On both sides of these are vertical registers painted with the full *quipu* motif, in classic Inca fashion. Unfortunately, the central lug has been broken off and the neck rim is heavily damaged from wear. The handles on the vessel have an unusually low placement, but what really sets this piece apart is the flattened shoulder of the chamber; traces of pigment suggest that this area was originally painted white. Aryballi with flattened shoulders are known from the Lambayeque drainage on the far north coast of Peru (Hyerdahl et al. 1995: 92, fig. 51). Another nonstandard feature of the vessel is that the upper section of its back was painted red and outlined with parallel black lines.

14

Cat. No. 16
Aryballos
Cat. No. YPM 16958
Late Horizon, Provincial Inca
Machu Picchu
Height: 7.9 in. (20 cm)
Rim Diameter: 2.4 in. (6 cm)
Max. Diameter: 6.1 in. (15.5 cm)

Provincial versions of Inca aryballos frequently look like coarser versions of the classic style. In the case of this small aryballos from Machu Picchu, the short neck and flat tapered conical base, as well as the rustic appearance, suggest a provincial manufacture. The entire vessel was covered with dark red slip and polished to a low luster. The central lug is a zoomorphic circular face with round eyes and a straight mouth. It has relatively large pierced "ear" nubbins that could have been decorated with cordage.

Cat. No. 17
Aryballos
Cat. No. YPM 16967
Late Horizon, Provincial Inca
Machu Picchu
Height: 8.5 in. (21.5 cm)
Rim Diameter: 2.2 in. (5.5 cm)
Max. Diameter: 8.9 in. (22.5)

18

the warm waters off the Ecuadorian shores, were highly valued in the Lake Titicaca region where this aryballos was produced. The modeled shells appear on a heavily painted background of geometric designs, some of which use a diagonal pattern similar to that in the "key" motif of Inca textiles, to create an overarching pattern symbolizing a fishing net. Conceptually, this net is "holding" the precious spondylus shells. The elaborate polychrome painting includes other elements alien to the Cuzco drainage including tabbed hemispherical forms, hour-glass forms with concentric circles, and a zigzag band of small black squares. Another unusual feature of this aryballos is the presence of two modeled feline lugs rather than a single central lug; unfortunately, one of these is no longer present. Despite these rare stylistic elements, this vessel reflects many of the imperial decorative and shape conventions and constitutes one of the most beautiful examples of provincial Inca ceramics to have survived the Spanish conquest.

This small aryballos has common Inca features but they are executed in a rustic and unconventional fashion, suggesting that it was produced outside of the Cuzco heartland. The vessel has an oxidized orange color and is painted in red, black, and white. The decoration consists of a single narrow vertical band filled with double crosses flanked by panels filled with full *quipu* motifs. The thickness of the painted lines is unusually wide, and the pendant cords of the quipu motifs lack the diagonal orientation of standard Cuzco Inca pottery. The central lug is sculpted in the shape of an oval zoomorphic head with circular eyes, a straight mouth, and a V-shaped incision on the forehead. The neck of the aryballos was repaired in antiquity by abrading the neck to form a usable rim.

Cat. No. 18
Aryballos Decorated with Modeled Spondylus Shells
Musée de l' Homme
Cat. No. 94.105.1, Photo KIDO
Late Horizon, Provincial Inca
Department of La Paz, Lake Titicaca Region
Height: 18.1 in. (46.0 cm)
Diameter: 24.4 in. (62.0 cm)
Publication: Fauvet-Berthelot and Lavallee 1987: 181, fig. 594

This unique aryballos, collected by M. de Sartiges in the Lake Titicaca area, was published for the first time in 1902. Its neck and handles were broken in antiquity. The front of the aryballos chamber features representations of red spiney oyster shells modeled using an appliqué technique. These shells, considered to be a sacred food (*mullu*) consumed by the gods and imported from

Cat. No. 19
Aryballos
Cat. No. YPM 16941
Late Horizon, Inca
Machu Picchu
Height: 7.9 in. (20.0 cm)
Rim Diameter: 2.4 in. (6.1 cm)
Max. Diameter: 5.5 in. (14.0 cm)

The neck and rim of this medium-sized aryballos are painted red, and a horizontal band with nested diamonds in black, red, and white decorate the front of the chamber. A white and black band encircles the neck. The central lug is shown as a simplified animal head with circular eyes and a straight mouth. The vessel has pierced rim nubbins.

Cat. No. 20
Wide-Mouth Aryballos
Cat. No. YPM 194271

Late Horizon, Inca
Machu Picchu, Cave 29/76
Height: 30.3 in. (77.0 cm)
Rim Diameter: 21.3 in. (54.0 cm)
Max. Diameter: 31.5 in. (80.0 cm)

To produce corn beer (*chicha*) for state ceremonies and feasts, it was necessary to boil the maize and water for many hours and then allow the mixture to settle before transferring it to a jar with a constricted neck for fermentation and storage. The wide-mouth jar seen here bears a strong resemblance to the cooking pots in which chicha is currently prepared in the Peruvian highlands (Ravines and Villiger 1989) in its size and form. The wide-mouth jar shares its pointed conical base, its vertical strap handles, and its central appliqué lug with the classic Inca aryballos form. Despite its mundane purpose, the cooking pot is decorated with the standard polychrome painted motifs of the Inca state, most notably panels filled with the *quipu* motif. On the back of the vessel are traces of a band beneath the rim filled with groups of simple curvilinear lines. The uneven coloration of this restored vessel is due to the differential impact of moisture and elements on its shattered fragments.

Bottles and Jars
Bottles and small jars were among the finest vessels produced by Inca potters. Frequently decorated with classic Cuzco Inca-style polychrome decoration, these serving vessels for liquids were often made of carefully selected clays and decorated with detailed polychrome painting.

Cat. No. 21
Bottle
Cat. No. YPM 16927
Late Horizon, Inca
Cuzco
Height: 6.2 in. (15.7 cm)

21

Rim Diameter: 1.4 in. (3.6 cm)
Max. Diameter: 5.7 in. (14.5 cm)
Related objects: Purin 1990: 193, fig. 244

This small Cuzco Inca-style polychrome bottle is a finely crafted example of Inca elite pottery. It features an elongated red slipped neck that was decorated with a cream-colored band filled with a line of five black birds in profile. The front of the squat bottle chamber was slipped red and divided into three panels. The central panel features a central lug painted in black and cream. Below it are rows of alternating rectilinear S-motifs and concentric diamonds with a central dot. The arrangement of these motifs in a repeating checkerboard fashion is reminiscent of the simpler *tocapu* (Inca geometric designs arrayed in rows of squares or rectangles) textiles or tocapu-like decorations on wooden drinking vessels

(*qeros*). The central vertical panel is flanked by red panels filled with rows of pendant black triangles. Alongside these panels are narrow vertical bands of finely painted red chevrons on a cream background. The back of the bottle has a band of black cross-hatching below the neck.

Cat. No. 22
Bottle with Stirrup Spout
Cat. No. YPM 16452
Late Horizon, Chimu Inca
Machu Picchu
Height: 8.8 in. (22.4 cm)
Rim Diameter: 1.2 in. (3.1 cm)
Max. Diameter: 5.5 in. (14 cm)
Publication: Bingham 1930: 165, fig. 115A; Eaton 1916: plate IV, no. 1
Related objects: Schjellerup 1985: 20, plate 41

22

23

Bottles with stirrup spouts were never characteristic of the Cuzco region; the only area of the Andes where they were still common during Inca times was the coastal region once dominated by the Chimu state. The shape of the monochrome vessel, including the cylindrical spout, and stylized modeled bird on the stirrup is typical of the Chimu style. Vessels such as this one were produced using a two-piece mold, but traces of the seams were obliterated on the vessel exterior. The workmanship on this piece is coarse, and the bottle is unusually heavy. Moreover, rather than the polished black-ware that usually characterizes Chimu pottery, the surface is an uneven reddish brown as a result of being fired in an oxidizing atmosphere. It is possible that this vessel was brought to Machu Picchu from a rural area along the north coast of what now is Peru; alternatively, it could have been produced in the Cuzco area by a retainer trying to emulate the style of his or her homeland. Although the bottle is in good condition, the wear on its base indicates that it was repeatedly used before its interment in a burial cave southeast of the palace complex of Machu Picchu (Bingham 1930: 164).

Cat. No. 23
Jar with Everted Rim
Cat. No. YPM 16491
Late Horizon, Inca
Machu Picchu, Cave 59
Height: 5.1 in. (12.9 cm)
Rim Diameter: 3.0 in. (7.7 cm)
Max. Diameter: 5.5 in. (14.0 cm)
Publication: Bingham 1930: 163, fig. 112; Salazar 2001a: fig. 8

Burial 59 was one of the most interesting burials discovered by the 1912 expedition. An adult female who, judging from the accompanying grave goods, may have been a healer or sorceress (see Salazar 2001a for fuller discussion) was buried with the small classic Cuzco Inca-style jar shown here. The jar was filled with a host of disparate items, such as a rodent's cranium, bits of silver, twisted rawhide, seeds, and human teeth (Eaton 1916).

The pottery vessel has a natural orange color, and it was decorated with polychrome painting. The rim is flat, everted, and painted black, and its interior is painted red. Its globular body has a central panel design of two vertical rows of double-cross motifs with broken lines framed by bands of zigzag designs. Two *quipu* pattern designs divided by

bands of a basketry motif complete the body decoration. When it was originally produced the jar had a vertical loop handle, but at some time in antiquity the handle was broken off. The junctures where the handle had been attached were carefully reworked by abrasion so that the vessel could continue to be used.

Cat. No. 24
Jar with Everted Rim
Cat. No. YPM 16576
Late Horizon, Provincial Inca
Machu Picchu, Caves 68, 71, 73
Height: 5.5 in. (14.0 cm)
Rim Diameter: 3.9 in. (10.0 cm)
Max. Diameter: 5.5 in. (14.0 cm)
Publication: Bingham 1930: 168, fig. 119b

The form and decoration of this vessel from Machu Picchu does not fit the conventions of jars produced in the Cuzco heartland. The neck is barely constricted, and it is much shorter than typical Cuzco Inca jars. The jar had a broken vertical strap handle, which has been restored. In decorating the vessel, only two colors were used — red and black — and no distinction was made between the neck and the chamber. The entire chamber was divided into three zones. A narrow central zone was simply painted red and left without any of the detailed geometric designs typical of decorated Inca jars. The two broader flanking zones were filled with rows of irregularly shaped hatched diamonds. A double curved black line defines the lower limit of the decoration. The source for this piece is unknown, but it may have been brought from what is now the far south coast of Peru or the neighboring highlands.

Cat. No. 25
Face-Necked Jar
Cat. No. YPM 16438
Late Horizon, Inca

25

Machu Picchu, Cave 26
Height: 2.3 in. (5.9 cm)
Rim Diameter: 1.5 in. (3.8 cm)
Max. Diameter: 4.7 in. (12.0 cm)
Publication: Bingham 1930: 123, fig. 75

This small orange jar in Cuzco Inca style is one of a matching pair found in Burial Cave 26. A red anthropomorphic face is painted on the jar's neck, with the eyes, mouth, and teeth shown in black on a white background. Only the nose is augmented with appliqué modeling. A white horizontal band framed in black extends around the body; it is filled with a half *quipu* design in red and black. Bingham plausibly interpreted the suspended circles in this motif as pendants of a necklace. The solid handle has two black bands and a small perforation; the latter would have allowed the vessel to be hung by a cord. The 1912 Expedition to Machu Picchu

encountered other fragmented face-necked jars (Bingham 1930: 167), but none as well preserved and attractive as this one.

Cat. No. 26
Short-Necked Jar
Cat. No. YPM 16940
Late Horizon, Inca
Machu Picchu
Height: 5.5 in. (14.0 cm)
Rim Diameter: 1.7 in. (4.3 cm)
Max. Diameter: 5.1 in. (13.0 cm)

A small jar decorated in the classic Cuzco Inca style, this piece was apparently highly valued by its owners since it was repaired three times without being discarded. Originally it had a strap handle, but after being broken, the remnant was reworked into a small ornamental lug on the back of the vessel. A hole was apparently punched in the

side of the vessel, but it was plugged with resin and an unidentified material. Finally, the vessel lip was abraded and polished to hide damage to the original vessel rim.

Despite these post-production modifications, the Cuzco Inca-style painted decoration can still be appreciated. The detailed black painting on this vessel is unusually fine. As is so often the case, a central panel features two bands with double-cross and broken-line designs separated by three bands. On each side of these are two panels filled with zigzag lines. Two broad zones decorated with the full *quipu* pattern appear on each side of the centrally located decoration. The short jar neck has eight vertical bands of chevron designs.

Cat. No. 27
Short-Necked Jar
Cat. No. YPM 16952
Late Horizon, Inca
Machu Picchu
Height: 4.7 in. (12.0 cm)
Rim Diameter: 1.3 in. (3.4 cm)
Max. Diameter: 5.5 in. (14.0 cm)

This specimen is a short-necked jar with a high horizontal loop handle decorated with polychrome painting. The vessel is made of oxidized orange-ware that was completely covered with cream-colored slip. The main decoration on the chamber is a horizontal red band outlined with black lines and filled with pendant necklace-like *quipu* elements. The handle is painted with alternating solid black stripes and red double-X designs that contrast with the cream-colored background. Like YPM 16438, the handle is perforated with a small circular hole. The black jar neck was broken in antiquity and was reworked in Inca times by abrading the edges to a smooth horizontal rim so that the vessel would continue to be serviceable.

28

30

Cat. No. 28
Short-Necked Jar
Cat. No. YPM 16953
Late Horizon, Inca
Machu Picchu
Height: 6.3 in. (15.9 cm)
Rim Diameter: 1.8 in. (4.7 cm)
Max. Diameter: 5.5 in. (14.0 cm)

As already noted, many of the burial ceramics were produced and buried in pairs; YPM 16953 and YPM 16952 constitute an example of a matching pair of short-necked jars. They are decorated in the same manner, and on initial inspection they appear to be almost identical. Close comparison shows that there are small differences in body shape. Originally, YPM 16953 had a slightly greater height, judging from the intact handle and chamber. In contrast to YPM 16952, the black concave curved neck of this piece is intact and the original lip was painted red.

Cat. No. 29
Short-Necked Jar
Cat. No. YPM 16955
Late Horizon, Inca
Machu Picchu
Height: 5.1 in. (13.0 cm)
Rim Diameter: 2.4 in. (6.0 cm)

Max. Diameter: 5.7 in. (14.5 cm)

The body of this small ceramic jar is painted dark red, but the edges of the rim and the vertical looped strap handle are painted black. The chamber of this Cuzco Inca jar is squat, and its neck was short and everted. The interior of the handle and the vessel remain a light orange color, resulting from the firing of the vessel.

Cat. No. 30
Short-Necked Jar
Cat. No. YPM 16598
Late Horizon, Chimu Inca
Machu Picchu, Cave 52
Height: 6.5 in. (16.4 cm)
Rim Diameter: 1.5 in. (3.8 cm)
Max. Diameter: 6.7 in. (17.0 cm)
Publication: Bingham 1930: 161, fig. 111

This black monochrome bottle represents a hunch-backed adult male. The neck of the vessel has been sculpted as a face and the chamber doubles as his body. Arms and hands are represented in low relief through modeled appliqué bands on the upper chamber. The back has a single high vertical strap handle and a slight protuberance that gives the bottle the overall look of a hunchback.

Judging from the chronicles and the drawings of Guaman Poma and other colonial depictions of court life, hunchbacks were favored as servants by the Inca royalty and were conspicuously present in the palaces of the Coya and Sapa Inca (e.g., Guaman Poma 1980: 98, 112).

Unlike classic Inca pottery, the vessel was shaped using a mold rather than with coils and fired in a reducing rather than an oxidizing atmosphere. The production and style of vessel derives from the Chimu pottery tradition of Peru's north coast, but the closest analogues to this pot occur at sites near Lima. It is likely that this piece was brought to Machu Picchu by a retainer from Peru's central coast.

Cat. No. 31
Short-Necked Jar
Cat. No. YPM 16951
Late Horizon, Inca
Machu Picchu
Height: 6.8 in. (17.3 cm)
Rim Diameter: 2.6 in. (6.7 cm)
Max. Diameter: 4.7 in. (12.0 cm)

This is a rustic short-necked polychrome jar with a vertical loop handle. The entire vessel is covered unevenly with a dark red slip, and the quality of the polishing is uneven. One unusual feature of this vessel is the grooved nubbin placed in the front of the vessel as on an aryballos. The main decoration is a large horizontal panel defined by a white band and filled with a black and white zigzag motif. Despite the unexceptional quality of the jar, it was valued enough to warrant repairing a hole by using a lead plug.

Cat. No. 32
Short-Necked Jar
Cat. No. YPM 16939
Late Horizon, Chimu Inca
Machu Picchu
Height: 5.5 in. (14.0 cm)

Rim Diameter: 1.5 in. (3.8 cm)
Max. Diameter: 4.3 in. (11.0 cm)
Related object: Schjellerup 1985: 21

This monochrome brown jar was not
made in the Cuzco Inca style. Unlike
Cuzco Inca jars, it has flattened sides
and a handle that extends from bottle
chamber to middle of the neck. In cross
section the handle is circular rather
than wafer-shaped, the color of the ware
is brown rather than orange, and the
vessel is coarse and heavy. A firing
cloud, due to uneven circulation of oxy-
gen during firing, is visible on the lower
edge and bridge of the jar. In addition
to differences in form and ware from
classic Inca bottles, it was produced using a two-piece mold. This technique
was popular on the north coast of Peru
but not in the Inca heartland. The only
decorative element is a low relief band
that encircles the lower bottle neck,
perhaps emulating a piece of cord. This
was created using press-molding rather
than an appliqué technique. The vessel
is related in style to the handled bottles
of Chimu pottery (Schjellerup 1985: 9)
and it is probable that this bottle was
brought to Machu Picchu from the distant Pacific coast, perhaps from what today is the north central coast of Peru.

Cat. No. 33
Short-Necked Jar
Cat. No. YPM 16892
Late Horizon, Provincial Inca
Cuzco
Height: 4.1 in. (10.5 cm)
Rim Diameter: 2.7 in. (6.8 cm)
Max. Diameter: 4.7 in. (12.0 cm)

This classic Cuzco Inca-style small jar
with a horizontal loop handle is decorated with polychrome painting. The
short neck is painted white, but black
lines delineate the edge of the jar lip
and the bottom of the neck. The vessel
chamber is painted with a wide red
zigzag band from which hang *quipu*

33

motifs on a painted white background.
The center of the vessel chamber is decorated with a large motif of nested diamonds with a red core. Two black birds
shown in profile appear above the red
band and constitute a rare case of figurative representation. The looped handle was broken in antiquity but has
been reconstructed. Judging from the
rough underside of the jar, the vessel
was used extensively.

Cat. No. 34
Short-Necked Jar with Looped Handle
Cat. No. YPM 16963
Late Horizon, Inca
Machu Picchu
Height: 4.5 in. (11.5 cm)
Rim Diameter: 2.2 in. (5.7 cm)
Max. Diameter: 5.7 in. (14.5 cm)

This plain short-necked jar is fired to a
light tan color but the chamber, neck,
high looped handle, and interior rim
are painted with dark red slip. In addition, the strap handle is decorated with
alternating black X and broken-line motifs, and small white dots. This decoration is difficult to see because it is ob-
scured by the thick, uneven red slip.
The back of the chamber neck and base
were left unslipped, revealing the light
color of the ware. The uneven applica-

34

tion of the paint, its unusual color, and
the overall decorative scheme suggest a
provincial source for this piece, perhaps
the Lake Titicaca area.

Cat. No. 35
Jar with Horizontal Looped Handle
Cat. No. YPM 16965
Late Horizon, Inca
Machu Picchu
Height: 5.3 in. (13.5 cm)
Rim Diameter: 1.5 in. (3.8 cm)
Max. Diameter: 5.5 in. (14.0 cm)

This polished red jar has a long concave
curved neck and a horizontal looped
handle. Although its surface is fire-
blackened, the chamber reveals traces
of a horizontal band filled with red diamonds. The horizontal handle is perforated and decorated with a double-cross
and broken-line design.

Cat. No. 36
Jar with Tubular Spout
Cat. No. YPM 16890
Late Horizon, Inca
Peru
Height: 4.0 in. (10.2 cm)
Rim Diameter: 2.9 in. (7.5 cm)
Max. Diameter: 4.0 in. (10.2 cm)

This unusual small jar has a narrow
tubular spout on the upper side of its

vertical strap handle. The entire vessel is covered with orange slip and polished. A rectangular horizontal band on the upper chamber is decorated with alternating crosses and broken-line designs, and the interior of the rim is painted red. Tubular spouts, as seen on this vessel, were not common in the Cuzco region, so, despite the classic Inca style of the decoration, this vessel may have been produced outside of the Inca heartland. This particular form was popular, for example, in the region occupied by the Cañari ethnic group of Ecuador.

Cat. No. 37
Jar with Tubular Spout
Cat. No. YPM 17593
Late Horizon, Inca
Machu Picchu
Height: 4.3 in. (11.0 cm)
Rim Diameter: 2.9 in. (7.5 cm)
Max. Diameter: 4.7 in. (12.0 cm)

YPM 17593 is an unusual small jar. It was fired to a light orange color and it was carefully finished to an even matte surface. Only the lip of the vessel is painted with red slip. Unlike Cuzco Inca-style vessels, it has a handle that is circular in cross section rather than the standard strap handle. Moreover, unlike YPM 16890 the handle connects the

37

38

chamber with the rim with a distinctive peak protruding above the level of the rim. The tubular spout, attached to the opposite side of the vessel, has a similar peak rising slightly above the vessel mouth. Like the other jar with tubular spout shown here (YPM 16890), this piece probably came from outside the Cuzco region, perhaps from southern Ecuador.

Cat. No. 38
Pair of Two-Handled Jars
Cat. No. YPM 16439 A
Late Horizon, Inca
Machu Picchu, Cave 52
Height: 5.9 in. (15.0 cm)
Rim Diameter: 4.5 in. (11.5 cm)
Max. Diameter: 4.4 in. (11.3 cm)
Cat. No. YPM 16439 B
Late Horizon, Inca
Machu Picchu, Cave 52
Height: 6.0 in. (15.2 cm)
Rim Diameter: 4.3 in. (11.0 cm)
Max. Diameter: 4.4 in. (11.3 cm)

This pair of small polychrome jars conforms to the conventions of classic Cuzco Inca style. They are made of fully oxidized orange-ware and are carefully polished. The chambers of these matching vessels are decorated with narrow horizontal bands that encircle the vessels. These bands are painted cream color and filled with alternating black double crosses and groups of parallel red vertical lines. The handles are adorned with the same motifs but painted only in black. The neck of each jar is covered with cream-colored paint, which contrasts with the jar lip, painted black, and the jar interior, painted dark red. These small jars, found together in Cave 52, reflect the Inca custom of producing and using serving vessels in matching pairs, probably symbolizing social customs of reciprocity in food consumption. Although the two vessels are almost identical, one is slightly taller and more graceful in appearance; the pair was probably produced by the same potter.

Cat. No. 39
Two-Handled Jar
Cat. No. YPM 16419
Late Horizon, Inca
Machu Picchu, Cave 37
Height: 8.8 in. (22.3 cm)
Rim Diameter: 6.7 in. (17.0 cm)

40

This small jar, acquired by Bingham in Cuzco, represents a particularly elaborate example of Inca ceramic artistry. The red-slipped vessel chamber is decorated using polychrome painting with four vertical panels, each of which is filled with a design of stacked hexagons and concentric squares. The neck, like the chamber, is painted with red, black, and cream-colored pigments. It was divided into two horizontal registers adorned with a red and white zigzag band flanked by concentric squares. Beneath each of the decorated registers on the neck is a narrow orange band whose color reflects the tone of the oxidized ware from which this vessel was made. The handles of the vessel were modeled in the form of undulating spotted snakes representing the mythical *amarus*. These creatures were associated with water and the underworld in Inca mythology, and their representation on the vessel suggests its use in ceremonial activities.

Bowls

Handled bowls were a common form in the Cuzco heartland, constituting approximately 16 percent of the vessels recovered in both the architectural complex of Machu Picchu and the adjacent burial caves (Bingham 1930: 156). These serving vessels would have been appropriate for stews and porridges and, as serving vessels, they were heavily decorated with many of the same Inca motifs that were painted on other such vessels.

Cat. No. 41
Two-Handled Bowl
Cat. No. YPM 16423
Late Horizon, Inca
Machu Picchu, Cave 60
Height: 2.6 in. (6.6 cm)
Rim Diameter: 5.0 in. (12.6 cm)
Max. Diameter: 6.5 in. (16.5 cm)

Max. Diameter: 7.3 in. (18.6 cm)
Publication: Bingham 1930: 169, fig. 120d
Related objects: Matos 2000: 131, 132

This medium-size jar has the standard Cuzco Inca form and one of its most characteristic kinds of decoration. The vessel is divided into sections of contrasting or opposing colors, a pattern of decoration known among Quechua speakers today as *missa* (Matos 2000: 134). Such a convention would seem inextricably linked to the dual vision that pervades traditional Andean ideology and social structure. This principle resulted in communities being divided into upper (*hanan*) and lower (*hurin*) sections or moities, a practice that continues to survive in some areas of the highlands. On this jar, the contrasting colors utilized are red and cream. It has been suggested based on ethnographic analogy that red was associated with blood and male forces, while the white was associated with ice and female aspects (Matos 2000: 154). This jar itself was divided both vertically and horizontally into four zones, a pattern of quadrapartition reminiscent of the division of Tahuantinsuyu. If the vessel is seen frontally from one side, the neck and the upper part of the body is red and the lower half cream; seen from the other side, this pattern is reversed. The strap handles and the interior lip are painted red. Wear on the base of this jar indicates that the vessel was heavily utilized before its inclusion in the burial cave.

Cat. No. 40
Two-Handled Jar
Cat. No. YPM 16887
Late Horizon, Inca
Cuzco
Height: 6.0 in. (15.3 cm)
Rim Diameter: 4.5 in. (11.5 cm)
Max. Diameter: 5.5 in. (14.0 cm)
Related objects: Matos 2000: 127, 136

41

crosshatched red diamonds. A narrow cream-colored band outlined in black runs below the everted rim of the vessel. The horizontal strap handles are painted with alternating double-cross and broken-line motifs. This bowl, larger than most of the serving bowls encountered in the burial caves, would have been appropriate for serving several individuals. The flat bottom of the bowl displays heavy wear.

Cat. No. 44
Two-Handled Bowl
Cat. No. YPM 16441
Late Horizon, Inca
Machu Picchu, Cave 3
Height: 4.6 in. (11.8 cm)
Rim Diameter: 4.5 in. (11.4 cm)
Max. Diameter: 7.1 in. (18.0 cm)
Publication: Bingham 1930: 159, fig. 109c

YPM 16441 is a reddish orange two-handled bowl made in the Cuzco Inca style. It is adorned with a horizontal white band outlined in black and filled with finely crosshatched black diamonds that encircle the chamber. Alternating black double-cross and line motifs decorate the horizontal strap handles. The vessel lip is covered with black paint, but the interior of the rim is painted with a band of dark red. As in many of the burial objects, the flat base shows considerable wear.

Cat. No. 45
Modeled Feline Handle from a Two-Handled Bowl
YPM No. 191355
Late Horizon, Inca
Machu Picchu
Height: 3.1 in. (7.8 cm)
Width: 2.6 in. (6.7 cm)
Publication: Bingham 1930: 177, fig. 136
Related objects: Morris and von Hagen 1993: 169, fig. 156

This modeled feline was encountered

Publication: Bingham 1930: 157, fig. 108c

YPM 16423 is a small two-handled bowl made in classic Cuzco Inca style. Fired to an orange buff, it was finished with great care and decorated with unusually fine geometric painting. Similar decorative panels appear on the front and back of the vessel. Each panel has two vertical bands filled with alternating double crosses and horizontal lines. These panels are separated by solid red bands and flanked on each side by two bands of the *quipu* motif. The horizontal strap handles and rim are painted black, and a cream-colored band runs beneath the rim above the chamber decoration. The wear on the base confirms that this serving vessel was used prior to its inclusion in Cave 60.

Cat. No. 42
Two-Handled Bowl
Cat. No. 16440
Late Horizon, Inca
Machu Picchu, Cave 37
Height: 3.9 in. (10.0 cm)
Rim Diameter: 6.4 in. (16.2 cm)
Max. Diameter: 8.3 in. (21.0 cm)

This classic Cuzco Inca-style bowl has the orange color characteristic of state pottery from the imperial heartland,

and, in accordance with Cuzco Inca stylistic conventions, it was carefully polished and painted with black, red, and white paint. The main decoration was a narrow white rectangular band outlined in black and filled with finely detailed crosshatched red diamonds. The same decoration appears on both sides of the chamber. In addition, a thin white band encircles the vessel immediately below the everted black and red flat lip of the pot. The plain horizontal strap handles were attached to the chamber at a slight angle, as is the case on most two-handled bowls.

Cat. No. 43
Two-Handled Bowl
Cat. No. YPM 16454
Late Horizon, Inca
Machu Picchu, Cave 37
Height: 5.1 in. (13.0 cm)
Rim Diameter: 9.5 in. (24.0 cm)
Max. Diameter: 11.8 in. (30.0 cm)
Publication: Eaton 1916: plate XII, no. 6

This large orange buff two-handled bowl conforms to the conventions of the Cuzco Inca style. Fired orange in an oxidation atmosphere, the exterior was decorated on both sides with a similar geometric design: a cream-colored horizontal band outlined with black lines and filled with finely detailed

amid the architecture of Machu Picchu. Judging from similar Inca vessels,
this fragment comes from a handle on
an elaborate two-handled bowl. On
such vessels, the ceramic feline was
shown grasping the rim of the bowl with
its paws; the body of the animal would
have been held by the user of the vessel.
This handle is carefully sculpted with
the feline's snout and upright ears
shown realistically, and the canines and
other teeth are depicted with care. The
eye and the nostrils are shown using incision. The surface of this fragment
from Machu Picchu is heavily eroded,
but Bingham (1930: 169) believed that it
came from a polychrome ceremonial
bowl. Based on what can be observed at
present, most of the handle fragment
was painted black but the teeth and
eyes were colored white.

Cat. No. 46
Two-Handled Bowl
Cat. No. YPM 16458
Late Horizon, Provincial Inca
Machu Picchu, Cave 104
Height: 3.7 in. (9.5 cm)
Rim Diameter: 4.5 in. (11.5 cm)
Max. Diameter: 4.5 in. (11.5 cm)

YPM 16458 is an unusually small two-
handled bowl. It does not conform to
the Cuzco Inca style in its shape or decoration: its bottom is rounded rather
than flat, its rim flares sharply outward,
and the strap handles attach to the rim.
The entire vessel is slipped red, and
sloppy black designs are painted over
much of the bowl. As on standard Inca
two-handled bowls, the same decoration is painted on both sides of the
chamber, but the design is composed of
two wavy lines enclosing a horizontal
row of black dots. Another line of black
dots is painted on the exterior immediately below the rim. The interior of the
rim is decorated with a line of vertical
straight black lines. The bottom of the
vessel displays substantial wear. This

47

unusual piece was brought from outside
the Cuzco heartland, perhaps from the
Arequipa area of southwestern Peru.

Plates
Among the serving vessels, plates are
among the most popular and highly
decorated ceramics found at Machu
Picchu and other Inca sites in the
Cuzco heartland. Small and shallow,
they seem designed for small portions
of solid food, such as toasted corn kernels or other delicacies. Many plates
had solid handles modeled in the form
of birds or other creatures. Like the aryballos, Inca plates were common
throughout Tahuantinsuyu and so provide a useful index of imperial expansion and influence. The form and decoration of Inca plates varied according to
location and ethnic affiliation. Consequently, plate styles provide insights
into the interregional linkages of the
populations living at places such as
Machu Picchu.

Cat. No. 47
*Pair of Plates with Anthropomorphic
Handles*
Cat. No. YPM 16429 A
Late Horizon, Inca
Machu Picchu, Cave 61
Height: 1.3 in. (3.2 cm)

Rim Diameter: 6.5 in. (16.5 cm)
Max. Diameter: 8.5 in. (21.5 cm)
Cat. No. YPM 16429 B
Late Horizon, Inca
Machu Picchu, Cave 61
Height: 1.3 in. (3.3 cm)
Rim Diameter: 6.5 in. (16.4 cm)
Max. Diameter: 8.7 in. (22.0 cm)
Publication: Bingham 1930; Eaton 1916;
Salazar 2001b

Two nearly identical plates with handles modeled as human heads were recovered from Burial Cave 61. As is always the case in "matching" sets of
vessels, one is always a bit larger than
the other. These plates were among the
most remarkable items the 1912 Yale Expedition recovered. Despite their rarity,
the style of this pair of plates is classic
Cuzco Inca. The interior of each plate
is filled with a cross consisting of two
bands, one of which runs from the handle to the two nubbins. This band is red
and filled with five large nested diamonds detailed in black. A second
band, running perpendicular to the
central one, is filled with rows of pendant black triangles. The crossed bands
are outlined with parallel black lines,
and the four zones in the interstices of
the cross are painted with a cream-color
pigment. Each of the handles is mod-

48

49

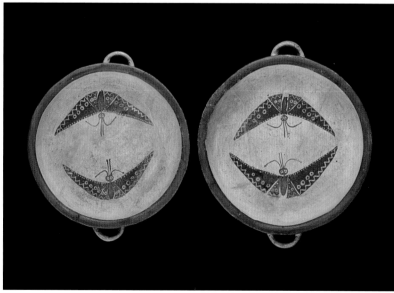

50

eled as a human neck ending in an adult male head. The neck and face of each head are painted red; the hair, ears and pupils are colored black; and the eyes, mouth, and crown are painted white. The quality of the modeling was excellent, and care is taken to show details such as the facial muscles and nostrils. The ears are perforated so that ear ornaments of perishable material could be added.

Although the form and decoration of the plates link them to Cuzco, the individuals shown on the handles wear upright white headdresses or crowns that were not worn in the Cuzco highlands in Inca times. These unusual headdresses may signal an exotic origin for the men represented; in many respects, this headwear is reminiscent of that worn by people from the tropical forests of the Amazonian lowlands. The matching plates were found in Cave 61 near the head of a 30- to 40-year-old woman.

Cat. No. 48
Plate with Bird Handle
Cat. No. YPM 16950
Late Horizon, Inca
Machu Picchu
Height: 1.8 in. (4.5 cm)
Rim Diameter: 6.7 in. (17.1 cm)
Max. Diameter: 10.4 in. (26.5 cm)

This classic Cuzco Inca-style plate, made from the characteristic orangeware, was decorated with black, white and red polychrome painting. The main decoration of the interior is a central band running from the bird's head handle to the grooved nubbins. The band is a wide red stripe outlined with black lines on which there are three sets of four concentric white squares. Around the rim of the plate are two bands: one filled with a line of stylized alpacas, with their hair hanging to the ground, and the other filled with pendant black triangles alternating with white dots. The modeling of the duck-like bird with its red beak, black head and neck, and white horizontal markings is particularly attractive. The nubbins at the other extreme of the plate represent tail feathers.

Cat. No. 49
Pair of Kaolin Plates
Cat. No. YPM 16459 A
Late Horizon, Inca
Machu Picchu, Cave 6A
Height: 0.8 in. (2.0 cm)
Rim Diameter: 4.7 in. (12.0 cm)
Cat. No. YPM 16459 B
Late Horizon, Inca
Machu Picchu, Cave 6A
Height: 1.2 in. (3.0 cm)
Rim Diameter: 5.0 in. (12.6 cm)
Publication: Bingham 1930: 165, fig. 115f

These two matching plates, found together in Cave 6A, constitute a set of serving vessels. Their shape and style is alien to the Cuzco region, being much smaller and lacking both handle and nubbins. The white clay from which they are made is rare in the Central Andes and is widely utilized in only a few regions, most notably the Titicaca Basin, the Callejon de Huaylas, and Cajamarca. These pieces, together with the white provincial-style aryballos (YPM 16415) found in the same grave, appear to be from the Titicaca Basin. The decoration on the interior of the plates is not typically Inca in its layout or design elements. The entire plate, including the flattened lip, is covered with a black geometric design, possibly inspired by the texture of a fiber basket. As is the case on Inca plates in general, whether Cuzco Inca style or not, the underside of the vessels was left undecorated.

Cat. No. 50
Pair of Plates with Butterfly Motif
Cat. No. YPM 16426 A
Late Horizon, Inca
Machu Picchu, Cave 37

Height: 1.0 in. (2.5 cm)
Rim Diameter: 4.5 in. (11.5 cm)
Max. Diameter: 5.2 in. (13.3 cm)
Cat. No. YPM 16426 B
Late Horizon, Inca
Machu Picchu, Cave 37
Height: 1.0 in. (2.5 cm)
Rim Diameter: 4.8 in. (12.3 cm)
Max. Diameter: 5.7 in. (14.5 cm)
Publication: Bingham 1930: 171, fig. 123

These matching plates from a burial of three adult females, displaying a provincial Inca style rather than the Cuzco Inca style, are some of the most beautiful examples of ceramic art from Machu Picchu. Each plate is very small and made of white kaolin ceramic rather than orange oxidized ware. Rather than the projecting solid handle and nubbins found on Cuzco Inca plates, these vessels have small horizontal strap handles attached to their sides. The plates also have straight rather than convex curved sides, and their lips are flattened. Even their broad and nearly flat base is exotic in style. The decoration on each of these plates consists of two butterflies detailed in black, red, and white. The circles, spots, and zigzag markings are painted in white to contrast with the black and red wings of the butterflies. Careful attention was given to representing the eyes and antennae of the insects. The flat rim of each plate is painted dark red to contrast with the overall cream color of the vessels. Given the style of these pieces, their source is probably somewhere in the Titicaca Basin.

Cat. No. 51
Pair of Plates with Alpaca Design
Cat. No. YPM 16428
Late Horizon, Inca
Machu Picchu, Cave 52
Height: 1.4 in. (3.6 cm)
Rim Diameter: 4.9 in. (12.4 cm)
Max. Diameter: 6.7 in. (17.0 cm)
Publication: Bingham 1930: 134, fig. 89c

Cat. No. 194257
Late Horizon, Inca
Machu Picchu, Cave 52
Height: 1.4 in. (3.5 cm)
Rim Diameter: 5.3 in. (13.4 cm)
Max. Diameter: 7.5 in. (19.0 cm)

These two vessels from Cave 52 are a matched pair, although there is considerable difference in their size and preservation. Each one is a small, deep plate with dark brown designs on a thin cream-colored slip. The center of each plate was left undecorated and is ringed by two bands of stylized alpacas, flanked by parallel dark lines. A line of dark pendant triangles is painted beneath the rim of each plate. The handle on each plate is modeled in the form of a long, narrow, black and white tufted bird head, perhaps representing a duck. The incised nubbins and rim are painted black, and this dark band extends onto the outer surface of the rim.

Cat. No. 52
Light Brown Plate with Bird Handle
Cat. No. YPM 194261
Late Horizon, Inca
Machu Picchu, Cave 37
Height: 2.2 in. (5.5 cm)
Rim Diameter: 5.5 in. (14.0 cm)
Max. Diameter: 7.1 in. (18.0 cm)

This plate with a short bird-shaped handle is unusual because it lacks any painted decoration and is missing nubbins. It forms a matching pair with YPM 16449. The plate is carefully modeled and polished, and its simple but elegant design makes it one of the most attractive pieces the 1912 expedition recovered. Its interior is a light tan, perhaps owing to a light clay slip, but its underside has the characteristic orange color of Inca-style pottery. The head of the bird has a protruding round eye with a central punctation to mark the pupil. The curved neck, pointed beak, mouth, and rounded head are all carefully

51

53

55

sculpted, and the plate is remarkably light. It was found in a burial of three females — the same burial with the unique pair of butterfly plates. The matching pair strongly resembles a third plate (YPM 19259) found at Machu Picchu.

Cat. No. 53
Light Brown Plate with Bird Handle
Cat. No. YPM 16449
Late Horizon, Inca
Machu Picchu, Cave 37
Height: 1.6 in. (4.0 cm)
Rim Diameter: 5.3 in. (13.5 cm)
Max. Diameter: 7.1 in. (18.0 cm)
Previous publication: Bingham 1930: 134, fig. 89d

This small cream-colored plate with a narrow bird handle is the other half of a matching pair with YPM 194261. The main thing that sets them apart is a small difference in their size. This could be a function of handcrafting, but probably it was intentional.

Cat. No. 54
Plate with Bird Handle
Cat. No. YPM 16448
Late Horizon, Inca
Machu Picchu, Room 50A
Height: 1.2 in. (3.0 cm)
Rim Diameter: 5.3 in. (13.4 cm)
Max. Diameter: 7.1 in. (18.0 cm)
Publication: Bingham 1930: 137, fig. 94a

This small orange-ware plate features a broad red band filled with concentric black diamonds running across its interior. At the extremes of the band is a solid handle painted black and small black incised nubbins that correspond to the tail feathers of the bird. The bird handle on this plate is unusual because it employs appliqué as well as simple modeling. The head of the bird is modeled, the beak incised, and the crest and eyes are shaped from fine coils of clay added onto the solid handle. Although

56

it shares features with the Cuzco Inca style, this piece appears to be a provincial Inca product, perhaps from the Lake Titicaca drainage.

Cat. No. 55
Polychrome Plate with Stylized Bird Motif
Cat. No. YPM 16938
Late Horizon, Inca
Machu Picchu, Cave 59
Height: 0.8 in. (2.0 cm)
Rim Diameter: 5.1 in. (13.0 cm)
Max. Diameter: 5.5 in. (14.0 cm)
Publication: Bingham 1930: 172, fig. 123a

This small painted plate is covered with red slip and heavily painted with polychrome decoration. It has nubbins on both extremes rather than the usual combination of a handle and nubbins. In the center of the plate is a highly stylized compound bird motif consisting of a red and black hatched rectangle, representing the bird body, from which extend white bird heads from two opposing corners and white tail feathers from the other corners. The result is an attractive but difficult-to-read stylized image of a bird. Three circular bands adorn the sides of the plate. The middle band has alternating white dots and black diagonal lines. The other two

bands are filled with white and black triangles and black diagonal lines. The nubbins are painted white and incised with deep circular punctations. Based on the size, shape, and decoration of this plate, it is likely that it was brought from the Lake Titicaca drainage.

Cat. No. 56
Plate
Cat. No. YPM 16447
Late Horizon, Inca
Machu Picchu, Cave 61
Height: 2.2 in. (5.5 cm)
Rim Diameter: 6.5 in. (16.4 cm)
Max. Diameter: 9.2 in. (23.5 cm)

This large polished orange plate with beveled rim is decorated with a broad band filled with a white and red double-fret design. A narrow band of pendant black triangles is painted around the rim. The flattened loop handle is adorned with the double-cross and line design.

Cat. No. 57
Plate
Cat. No. YPM 16427
Late Horizon, Inca
Machu Picchu, Ingenuity Group
Height: 1.4 in. (3.5 cm)
Rim Diameter: 6.3 in. (16.0 cm)
Max. Diameter: 8.3 in. (21.0 cm)
Publication: Bingham 1930: 137, fig. 93

This plate is covered with cream-colored slip, and its interior is decorated with four parallel horizontal bands extending from the solid handle to the nubbins. The bands are filled with wavy red lines outlined with black lines. The most distinctive feature of this plate is its solid flattened mushroom-like modeled handle.

Cooking Pots, or *Ollas*, with Pedestals

Many of the Inca cooking pots (*ollas*) at Machu Picchu and elsewhere in the Cuzco heartland featured pedestals with expanded bases for stability. This form allowed the pots to be placed within a fire or on hot stones in order to heat stew or other food. The relatively small size of these pots suggests that they were designed to cook food for an individual or a small family. The lateral handle attached to the side of the pot allowed manipulation during heating. Although these vessels are not painted, they are decorated with appliqué modeling. Ceramic lids with strap handles were used to cover the pots during cooking.

Cat. No. 58
Pedestal Olla
Cat. No. YPM 16418
Late Horizon, Inca
Machu Picchu, Cave 69
Height: 7.8 in. (19.8 cm)
Rim Diameter: 8.2 in. (20.8 cm)
Max. Diameter: 10.2 in. (25.9 cm)
Previous publication: Bingham 1930: 151, fig. 104

This dark brown, fire-blackened pedestal cooking pot has a single handle that attaches at a diagonal angle to the body of the cooking pot. Its pedestal is relatively broad and short. The chamber has an appliqué decoration of an undulating serpent with rounded in-

59

61

cised punctations on the body. As with small and medium-sized aryballi, small-pedestal cooking vessels were often found in the Machu Picchu graves.

Cat. No. 59
Pedestal Olla
Cat. No. YPM 16451
Late Horizon, Inca
Machu Picchu, Cave 26
Height: 3.9 in. (10.0 cm)
Rim Diameter: 4.5 in. (11.5 cm)
Max. Diameter: 6.3 in. (16.0 cm)
Publication: Bingham 1930: 153, fig. 106e

This typical small-pedestal olla from Machu Picchu is a natural orange color from oxidation firing, but it is darkened from use in cooking. Only the lip of the vessel is painted red. The chamber is decorated with an appliqué serpent whose body is covered with round punctations and whose extremes are incised with straight lines. Found in a burial cave, the small size of this vessel suggests that it was designed for individual use. This vessel has an unusually high looped strap handle and its pedestal is particularly short.

Cooking Pot Lids
Cooking at high elevations presents special challenges particularly because of

the lower atmospheric pressure. Water evaporates at a lower temperature, and the Inca potters realized that lids were crucial in keeping moisture and heat within the pots to ensure adequate cooking. As a consequence, ceramic lids were produced for the pedestal ollas, which were the primary cooking vessel on a household level. The monochrome color and low luster of these lids matches the pots that they originally covered and, as would be expected, the upper visible surface of the lid was more carefully finished than the underside. The handles of the lids would have facilitated their manipulation, particularly during cooking. There is considerable variety in the form of these lids and their handles in the Machu Picchu assemblage.

Cat. No. 60
Cat. No. YPM 16464
Late Horizon, Inca
Machu Picchu, Cave 37
Height: 2.2 in. (5.5 cm)
Diameter: 4.4 in. (11.3 cm)

This reddish brown olla lid has a convex form and a high flattened handle. Several parts of this handle are discolored, possibly as a result of exposure to cooking fires.

Cat. No. YPM 16466
Late Horizon, Inca
Machu Picchu, Cave 37
Height: 1.6 in. (4.0 cm)
Rim Diameter: 5.7 in. (14.5 cm)

This example of an olla lid has a concave form and a low handle that is circular in cross section. It shows traces of a faint red slip and a small scorched patch on the underside.

Cat. No. 61
Brazier
Cat. No. YPM 16481
Late Horizon, Inca
Machu Picchu, Cave 94
Height: 6.1 in. (15.5 cm)
Rim Diameter: 2.5 in. (6.3 cm)
Max. Diameter: 7.5 in. (19.0 cm)
Publication: Bingham 1930: 173, fig. 125
Related objects: Heyerdahl et al. 1995: 98, plate 64

This dark reddish brazier with a loop handle on top is supported by three solid rounded feet. The mouth is wide and placed at the extreme end of the vessel. Three openings or vent holes were left in the top of the brazier. Judging from its form, this vessel was used to heat or cook something, and the lower portions of the chamber and base appear to be blackened by fire. Bingham speculated that braziers such as this one could have been used by metallurgists for reheating or annealing bronze objects (Bingham 1930: 174), but there is no direct evidence to support this interpretation. Although these vessels were rare at most Inca sites, Bingham found evidence for at least thirty-seven of them at Machu Picchu.

Ceramic Beakers, or Qeros
The consumption of corn beer (*chicha*) was essential at all state and religious rituals, and probably at some domestic activities as well. As a consequence, the

Incas produced distinctive drinking vessels (*qeros*) that were important bearers of Inca identity and style (Cummins 2002; Flores Ochoa et al. 1998). The most common drinking vessel was a simple beaker-like cup with straight or concave sides. Such ritual drinking vessels were usually made of wood, and the Inca term *qero* technically refers to these, but similar vessels were made of precious metals and pottery. The ceramic versions of the *qero* were probably less prestigious than equivalent vessels of metal or wood. Bingham (1930: 170) encountered twelve of them at Machu Picchu and acquired others during his stay in Cuzco. Some were relatively simple, while others were painted with classic Inca polychrome designs. The qeros recovered during the Machu Picchu investigations were found primarily near the most elaborate residential architecture in the west section of the site; only one was encountered in a grave.

Cat. No. 62
Ceramic Qero
Cat. No. YPM 16450
Late Horizon, Inca
Machu Picchu
Height: 3.3 in. (8.5 cm)
Rim Diameter: 3.3 in. (8.3 cm)
Max. Diameter: 3.3 in. (8.5 cm)
Publication: Bingham 1930: 171, fig. 121a

This small *qero* is a dark bluff color and has a flat bottom and concave curved sides that flare out at both top and bottom. A combination of a half diamond and half *quipu* design painted in black decorate the interior of the flaring rim.

Cat. No. 63
Ceramic Qero
Cat. No. YPM 16432
Late Horizon, Inca
Machu Picchu
Height: 2.8 in. (7.0 cm)
Rim Diameter: 18.5 in. (47.0 cm)

62

This small ceramic drinking vessel has classic concave walls that are slipped white on both the interior and exterior. Its rim is painted black. On the upper interior of the qero, the potter painted a motif in black on opposing sides; the design, which consists of three vertical lines ending in solid circles, is derived from the *quipu* motif.

Cat. No. 64
Ceramic Qero
Cat. No. YPM 16926
Late Horizon, Inca
Ollantaytambo
Height: 6.0 in. (15.2 cm)
Rim Diameter: 5.5 in. (14.0 cm)
Related objects: Donnan 1992: 110, fig. 214; Flores Ochoa et al. 1998: 12–13, 23

This large polychrome drinking vessel from the Inca royal estate at Ollantaytambo has concave sides and a flaring rim. A narrow recessed band encircles the interior of the back rim above a red painted zone. On the exterior, a band with black pendant triangles encircles the lip and the base. The main motif consists of a wide black and white zigzag band flanked by two groups of narrow horizontal white bands filled with red cross-hatching. Small rectangles each filled with an X are located in the interstices of the zigzag band.

64

Cat. No. 65
Ceramic Qero
Cat. No. YPM 18556
Late Horizon, Inca
Ollantaytambo
Height: 4.1 in. (10.8 cm)
Rim Diameter: 2.5 in. (6.4 cm)
Related objects: Flores Ochoa et al. 1998: 12–13, 23

Like YPM 16926, this polychrome *qero* with a flaring rim comes from the royal estate at Ollantaytambo. Inside the black painted rim of the cup is a distinctive recessed or beveled band. Below this is a red painted zone. The exterior is decorated with a hatched horizontal zigzag band surrounded by a dark field filled with orange-brown diamonds. A pair of white bands encircles the upper and lower sections of the vessel, and a narrow zigzag band encircles the base. Immediately under the rim is a band of pendant triangles followed by a band of parallel zigzag lines.

Cat. No. 66
Cup with Feline Handle
Cat. No. YPM 16930
Late Horizon, Inca
Cuzco
Height: 2.9 in. (7.3 cm)
Rim Diameter: 3.7 in. (9.5 cm)
Max. Diameter: 4.7 in. (12.0 cm)

66

stimulant. It played a crucial role in religious rituals as well as in feasts and other state-sponsored activities. The alkaloids within the coca leaf are bitter in flavor, so it was usually chewed in conjunction with ground lime (*cal*), an alkaline substance. Known today as *llipta* in Quechua, this lime "sweetens" the chew and increases its stimulating effects (Plowman 1986: 6). The white powdered lime was kept in tiny ceramic or stone jars with small openings designed to keep the lime dry; the powdery substance was extracted by a thin pin or spatula of metal or organic material. Modern lime containers known as *caleros* resemble the Inca vessels in size and general form, although they are now most frequently crafted from small bottle gourds. A small number of ceramic lime receptacles were discovered at Machu Picchu during the 1912 expedition.

Related objects: Matos 2000: 129; Schindler 2000: 315

YPM 16930 is a very small polychrome cup with a handle in the form of a modeled feline. Made of fine orange-ware, this tiny drinking vessel has an unusual form. It has a prominent basal angle and a rounded bottom, neither of which was common in Inca drinking vessels. Also, the cup constricts near its midsection and then flares outward. The handle is rounded in cross section and extends from the basal angle to the rim. The modeled feline is highly conventionalized, and the only features that can be easily identified are the large upright ears, the shape of the head, and two legs that extend onto the interior of the rim. The body of the feline is entirely covered with black paint, and the forelimbs are painted rather than modeled. On the interior of the rim is a line of small vertical black lines; a black horizontal line separates the upper section of the cup from the lower. The most elaborate decoration is reserved for the lower half of the cup.

Three pairs of human figures depicted frontally adorn this area, separated from one another by solid red bands. The heads of the figures are red but their rounded hats and costume are shown in black; there is faint evidence of costume detail on what would have been the tunics of the figures, and V-like patterns descend from the shoulders on at least two of them.

The representation of human figures was rare on Inca pottery, as was the presence of modeled felines. So it is tempting to speculate that this vessel may have been produced for some special ceremonial use. An analogous cup with a feline handle but with a different painted decoration has been identified by Matos (2000: 128–29) as a ritual vessel.

Small Lime Receptacles
The chewing of the coca leaf (*Erythroxylum* spp.) was widespread among the Inca elite. The leaf was valued for its symbolic significance as well as for its medicinal qualities and its role as a mild

Cat. No. 67
Two Caleros
Cat. No. YPM 18522 (left)
Late Horizon, Inca
Machu Picchu
Height: 1.5 in. (3.8 cm)
Rim Diameter: 0.4 in. (1.0 cm)
Max. Diameter: 2.4 in. (6.0 cm)
Related objects: Schindler 2000: 320

This small ceramic *calero* is slipped red and polished. Its hemispherical body has a round bottom and a nubbin-like handle. The perforated nubbin would have allowed a cord to be passed through the vessel so that it could be hung or worn. The short neck has a very small opening on a thick lip.

Cat. No. YPM 16913 (right)
Late Horizon, Inca
Machu Picchu
Height: 1.8 in. (4.5 cm)
Rim Diameter: 1.0 in. (2.5 cm)
Max. Diameter: 1.8 in. (4.5 cm)

67

Related objects: Schindler 2000: 320

This red-slipped and polished ceramic lime *calero* has a thick lip and small opening. Its undecorated hemispherical body has a perforated nubbin-like handle.

Miniature Ceramic Vessels

The potters of the Tahuantinsuyu, like those of the Huari and Nasca cultures before them, produced miniature ceramic vessels that mirrored full-sized pottery in their form, decoration, and firing. The purpose of these vessels is poorly understood, but there is evidence that they were used in religious rituals. For example, an offering of seventy-five Inca miniature vessels has been reported for Huari Huilca near Huancayo, Peru. Although the site was built as a Middle Horizon temple, the Inca used it for ceremonial offerings, including a cache of miniature vessels representing the full range of Inca vessel forms (Matos 2000: 164). Another similar Inca offering was excavated by Frank Meddens (1994) at the Chiqna Jota site in the Chicha/Soras Valley in the central highlands of Peru.

The Inca-style miniatures shown in this book were acquired by Bingham in Cuzco or unearthed by him at Machu Picchu or other sites. The substitution in offerings of ceramic miniatures for full-sized pottery vessels may parallel the offering of small gold and silver anthropomorphic figurines, small sculptures of camelids in stone and silver, and miniature tunics and other garments; examples of these are shown in this book. It is interesting that miniatures continue to be produced in the Central Andes to this day and are still utilized in ritual activities (e.g., Allen 2000; Meddens 1994: 139–41).

Cat. No. 68
Miniature Aryballos
Cat. No. YPM 16944
Late Horizon, Inca
Machu Picchu
Height: 4.5 in. (11.4 cm)
Rim Diameter: 1.3 in. (3.3 cm)
Max. Diameter: 2.8 in. (7.0 cm)

This miniature aryballos is executed in classic Cuzco style. The neck and front of the vessel are covered with dark red slip, and its neck is painted dark red with white horizontal lines. The eroded chamber shows traces of vertical bands filled with the *quipu* motif, and adjacent are remnants of a vertical band filled with zigzag lines. The central lug is shown as a stylized feline's head. The nubbins on the rim are pierced and could have been decorated with perishable colored cordage.

Cat. No. 69
Two Miniature Wide-Mouth Aryballi
Cat. No. YPM 16949 (*right*)
Late Horizon, Inca
Machu Picchu
Height: 2.6 in. (6.5. cm)
Rim Diameter: 2.2 in. (5.6 cm)
Max. Diameter: 3.5 in. (9.0 cm)

This miniature wide-mouth jar is polished and oxidized to an orange buff

69

color. The middle of the chamber is decorated by a red band framed by triple black lines and with a white band around the exterior rim. The appliqué lug is modeled as an animal head. The form and the typical Inca decorative characteristics parallel those used on the huge Inca corn beer (*chicha*) brewing vessels, such as YPM 194271.

Cat. No. YPM 16860 (*left*)
Late Horizon, Inca
Cuzco
Height: 2.9 in. (7.4 cm)
Rim Diameter: 2.6 in. (6.5 cm)
Max. Diameter: 3.5 in. (9.0 cm)

This miniature version of a wide-mouth aryballos has the characteristic conical base with vertical strap handles in the lower chamber. The exterior is painted red as a base coat. A central vertical panel is filled with bands of black crosses, and the flanking panels have the *quipu* design in black. A tiny appliqué lug is shaped as a small zoomorphic head with punctated eyes and an incised mouth.

Cat. No. 70
Miniature Short-Necked Jar with Strap Handle
Cat. No. YPM 16946
Late Horizon, Inca
Machu Picchu
Height: 2.3 in. (5.8 cm)
Rim Diameter: 1.6 in. (4.0 cm)
Base Diameter: 2.0 in. (5.0 cm)

This miniature jar mimics a bottle in classic Cuzco Inca style. The handle, vessel neck, and rim are painted red. The front of the vessel is decorated with a vertical band filled with black concentric diamonds flanked by two thin vertical bands filled with fine red cross-hatching on cream-colored slip. Two large bands are filled with rows of black pendant triangles on the lower section of the chamber to complete the decoration.

72

Cat. No. 71
Miniature Pedestal Olla with Lid
Cat. No. YPM 16893
Late Horizon, Inca
Choqquequirau
Height: 3.5 in. (8.9 cm)
Max. Diameter: 3.9 in. (10.0 cm)
Diameter (lid): 3.1 in. (8.0 cm)
Related objects: Bingham 1930: 153, fig. 106g

This miniature pedestal olla from the site of Choqquequirau in the Apurimac drainage features a short everted rim, a squat pedestal, and a diagonally attached handle. The tiny cooking pot is covered by a flat discoidal lid with a strap handle. The only adornments on

this monochrome vessel are two round appliqué nubbins on the side of the chamber opposite the handle. Similar decoration was found on full-sized pedestal ollas from Machu Picchu.

Cat. No. 72
Miniature Black-ware Short-Necked Jar
Cat. No. YPM 16435
Late Horizon, Chimu Inca
Machu Picchu, Cave 84
Height: 3.8 in. (9.7 cm)
Rim Diameter: 0.9 in. (2.2 cm)
Max. Diameter: 2.5 in. (6.3 cm)
Related objects: Schjellerup 1985: plate no. 19

This miniature black-ware vessel, found

with the second skeleton in Cave 84 near Machu Picchu's Main City Gate, is exotic in its style and manufacture. Its highly polished black monochrome color was produced by firing in a smudging atmosphere. Its surface color as well as its cylindrical spout and lateral strap handle indicates that this vessel was Chimu Inca in style and probably was brought to Machu Picchu from what is now Peru's north coast.

Ceramic Conopas, or Illas, of Maize Cobs

These miniature sculptures (*illas*) acquired by Bingham in Cuzco portray cobs of corn, or maize. Maize effigies functioned in village-level religious rituals and sometimes were burned and cached as offerings. In some cases, they were wrapped in textiles and adorned with pins and other ornaments in order to petition agricultural divinities and ancestors to help ensure abundant harvests. Maize was not only one of the staple crops of Inca-period peoples (Chapter 6), but also the main ingredient of corn beer (*chicha*) — the social drink of

choice, obligatory at most public occasions, including festivals, weddings, and funerals. It also served as the quintessential libation in Andean civic and religious ceremonies. Although the specimens presented here are ceramic, analogous effigies in stone also are common (e.g., Fauvet-Berthelot and Lavallee 1987, figs. 296, 365; Santillana 2000: 69). The diversity of Inca maize effigies reflects the distinctive morphology of the different varieties of maize cultivated in the ancient (and modern) Andes.

Cat. No. 73
Ceramic Effigies of Maize
Cat. No. YPM 17360 D
Late Horizon, Inca
Cuzco
Length: 1.9 in. (4.8 cm)
Diameter: 1.2 in. (3.0 cm)
Cat. No. YPM 17360 B
Late Horizon, Inca
Cuzco
Length: 2.1 in. (5.3 cm)
Diameter: 1.2 in. (3.0 cm)
Cat. No. YPM 17360 A

Late Horizon, Inca
Cuzco
Length: 2.2 in. (5.5 cm)
Diameter: 1.4 in. (3.6 cm)
Cat. No. YPM 17360 C
Late Horizon, Inca
Cuzco
Length: 2.0 in. (5.0 cm)
Diameter: 0.9 in. (2.3 cm)

These four effigies of maize cobs are remarkably realistic, with individual kernels and different cob forms rendered expertly through modeling and carving. Each specimen is apparently one of a kind, portraying a different type and/or developmental stage of the corn cob. For example, 17360 D depicts a smaller cob, with fewer and much larger, globular kernels, and 17360 A features lenticular-shaped kernels. All the specimens show evidence of fire darkening and charring (e.g., nos. 17360 A, 17360 B), which is consistent with the ethnohistorical descriptions of burning the cob effigies as offerings. Some darkening may have also occurred during the process of firing the clay.

73

75

Cat. No. 74
Ceramic Effigy of Double Maize Cob
Cat. No. YPM 17361
Late Horizon, Inca
Cuzco
Length: 2.0 in. (7.5 cm)
Diameter: 2.0 in. (5.0 cm)

This example of a maize illa, the largest in the Yale Peabody Museum collection, represents an unusual double cob bearing numerous angular-shaped kernels. The Incas believed that extraordinary or monstrous plants or animals had special magical properties, so they were treated with great respect. The dual ear of maize that served as the model for this illa may have been considered to be one such exceptional item.

Ritual Vessels, or Pacchas
The concept of reciprocity permeated Inca cosmology. Consequently, the gift of food and drink to ancestors and supernatural forces played an important role in Inca religious ceremony. Specialized vessels were produced of wood and pottery to make the liquid offerings;

some of these were referred to as *pacchas* by the Incas, and archaeologists have come to apply this term to a broad range of vessels that were fabricated for making offerings of corn beer (*chicha*) to the supernatural world (e.g., Carrión Cachot 1955; Flores Ochoa et al. 1998: 63–64; Matos 2000: 157–59). While classic pacchas often emphasize the movement of the liquid through an elaborate path often ending with its expulsion through a tubular spout, small sculpted receptacles showing animals, plants, farming tools, and other themes were also used as ritual vessels for such offerings.

Cat. No. 75
Paccha Showing a Hand Grasping a Qero
Cat. No. YPM 16962
Late Horizon, Provincial Inca
Machu Picchu
Height: 3.1 in. (7.8 cm)
Rim Diameter: 2.0 in. (5.2 cm)
Max. Diameter: 5.5 in. (14.0 cm)
Related objects: de Lavalle 1988: 98, 99; Purin 1990: 156, 157

This naturalistically modeled pottery vessel depicts a human hand grasping a beaker, or *qero*. The piece is slipped red and has a matte finish. A circular hole or vent was made in the hollow forearm to prevent the piece from exploding during firing. The beaker would have held a small amount of liquid, and, although not practical as a drinking vessel, it was appropriate for use in ritual offerings. The portrayal of a realistic Inca qero on this paccha underlines the symbolic importance of qeros as a key ingredient in Inca ceremony. The realistic sculptural treatment of human anatomy, typical of Chimu Inca pottery from Peru's north coast, contrasted with the emphasis on two-dimensional geometric decoration that typifies Cuzco Inca ceramics. Moreover, monochrome Chimu and Chimu Inca ceramics frequently show disembodied hands or feet using a two-piece mold technology (e.g., Disselhoff 1967: 71), such as that used to produce this object from Machu Picchu. It is likely that this piece was imported to Cuzco from Peru's north coast, since ceramic effigies of this kind were rare in the Inca heartland and do not seem to have been produced in this area.

Cat. No. 76
Effigy Cup of a Llama
Cat. No. YPM 16747
Late Horizon, Chimu Inca
Peru
Height: 5.0 in. (12.7 cm)
Rim Diameter: 2.8 in. (7.0 cm)
Related objects: Donnan 1992: 97, plate 184; Fauvet-Bertholet and Lavallee 1987: 119, plate 336; Matos 2000: 128; Schjellerup 1985: plates 4, 58

This cup is modeled in the form of a llama's head. Its facial features are realistically represented, as is the rope harness on the pack animal. The quality of the modeling, the dark monochrome coloration, and the technique of using a two-piece mold link this vessel to the ceramic tradition of Peru's north coast. The Chimu ceramic style was developed centuries prior to Inca expansion but continued after the Inca conquest. Small naturalistically modeled cups such as this one have been interpreted as vessels used in religious rituals to make offerings of corn beer (*chicha*) (Matos 2000: 156).

Cat. No. 77
Paccha in the Form of Stacked Vessels
Cat No. YPM 16916
Late Horizon, Inca
Cuzco
Height: 3.1 in. (8.0 cm)
Rim Diameter: 5.7 in. (14.6 cm)
Max Diameter: 9.4 in. (24.0 cm)

This unique paccha, acquired by Bingham in Cuzco, joins a two-handled bowl to an Inca plate with a bird handle in order to produce a monstrous yet quintessentially Inca shape for the purposes of religious ritual. To make offerings from this paccha, *chicha* would have been poured from the two-handled bowl, which constitutes the chamber of the paccha, through the conical tube that runs through the modeled bird-head plate handle. The entire vessel is decorated with fine Inca polychrome painting. The two-handled bowl portion is slipped black and then painted with triangles and other geometric forms skirted by lines of fine white dots. The lateral strap handles are slipped black, with rows of red squares outlined in white. The upper section of the vessel, in the form of the plate, is cream-colored with a decorative central band divided into three vertical columns. The central portion is devoted to a checkerboard design, while the flanking columns alternate crest and pinwheel motifs superimposed on alternating red and black rectangles. A band of pendant triangles encircles the plate-like form. The head and damaged

78

tail of the bird are painted black, but the neck of the bird head has fine white spots. The eyes of the bird are indicated by fine incisions.

Cat. No. 78
Paccha in the Form of Stacked Bowls
Cat. No. YPM 16922
Late Horizon, Inca
Cuzco
Height: 6.5 in. (16.5 cm)
Rim Diameter: 2.2 in. (5.6 cm)
Max. Diameter: 3.9 in. (10.0 cm)

This portion of a ceramic *paccha* combines two miniature two-handled bowls with the upper section of an Inca face-necked jar or small aryballos. The anthropomorphic face has long braided hair, suggesting a woman. The upper miniature two-handled bowl has two side panels filled with rows of rectangular geometric motifs, or *tocapus*, whose use appears to have been a royal prerogative. The second and lower two-handled miniature bowl has a central panel decorated with a female figure and side panels filled with insects and tocapus. In both miniature vessels, the back of the upper body has a band with double cross-hatching. This unique piece, acquired by Bingham in Cuzco,

79

jones, or big ears, wore pairs of ears plugs usually made of silver or gold; wood and baked clay were also used.

The only example of this class of Inca material culture recovered by Bingham at Machu Picchu was an isolated terra-cotta ear ornament with punctations on its outer surface. Little care had been given to the surface finishing of this oxidized ceramic object, perhaps because little of it would have been visible to the viewer. Bingham (1930: 210–11) plausibly suggested that the small holes made in the surface had been pierced to hold small feathers, a decorative practice common along Peru's coast (e.g., Rowe 1984: 169, fig. 180, p.171, fig. 183, p. 172, plate 28). It should be noted that the shaft of the Machu Picchu ear ornament is concave, while most published coastal examples have cylindrical shafts.

was produced in classic Inca style. It was probably designed for use as an "offering vessel," and its combination of stacked ceramic vessels resembles that of YPM 16916.

Cat. No. 79
Rattle in the Shape of a Two-Handled Bowl
Cat. No. YPM 16928
Late Horizon, Inca
Cuzco
Height: 3.4 in. (8.6 cm)
Rim Diameter: 3.5 in. (9.0 cm)
Max. Diameter: 5.7 in. (14.5 cm)

This is one of the most unusual objects in the Bingham Collection at the Yale Peabody Museum. Although it is shaped like a miniature Cuzco Inca-style two-handled bowl, the chamber is sealed by a sheet of clay with thirteen ovoid perforations. Trapped inside the chamber are pellets that make a percussive sound when the object is shaken. Although it is reminiscent of a colander or strainer, such a function would not have been practical, and it is inter-

preted as a rattle, perhaps used in special ritual settings. The central panel on the front and back of this vessel has four white bands of diagonally hatched red diamonds outlined in black, separated in two sections by a red horizontal band. A vertical white band with concentric black diamonds filled with red cross-hatching is painted on the the sides of the piece and across the vertical strap handles. The orange color of the ceramic ware is visible on the undamaged base of the rattle.

Ceramic Ear Plug
Cat. No. 80
Cat. No. YPM 18209
Late Horizon, Inca
Machu Picchu
Length: 1.2 in. (3.0 cm)
Diameter: 1.1 in. (2.8 cm)
Publication: Bingham 1930: 210, fig. 180

Ear piercing was a crucial rite of passage for males. The large ear ornaments worn by adults were an important symbol of ethnic identity and social status. The Inca elite, appropriately called *ore-*

Ceramic Whistle, or Ocarina
Cat. No. 81
Cat. No. YPM 18208
Late Horizon, Inca
Machu Picchu, near Main City Gate
Length: 2.7 in. (6.8 cm)

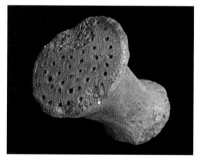

80

81

82

Diameter: 1.2 in. (3.0 cm)
Publication: Bingham 1930: 210, fig. 181
Related objects: Cornejo 2001: 81

Whistles, or *ocarinas*, were popular in Inca times, but their role in daily life is not well understood. This fired ceramic ocarina has a single circular hole on its upper surface and smaller holes at its two extremes. The ocarina has a distinctive barrel-shape form with a thickened midsection, tapered extremes, and flattened ends. It was left undecorated, although the surface is carefully polished to a low luster.

Found during the 1912 investigations in "the house nearest [the] Main City Gate of Machu Picchu" (Bingham 1930: 210), it makes a shrill sound when blown that could have been heard from far away. Bingham speculated that it might have been utilized by the palace's sentry to signal alarm. An ocarina with a

similar form was found at an Inca site in Ovalle, Chile. According to Cornejo (2001: 81), instruments of this kind were utilized by musicians of the Diaguita ethnic group before, during, and after the Inca conquest. Throughout prehispanic America, ocarinas were sometimes used to communicate with the supernatural realm (Olsen 2002: 100–133). This tradition continues: analogous whistles are used by modern shamans in Peru during their rituals of curing, and examples recovered from archaeological sites are particularly valued in modern shamanic practice.

Ceramic Gaming Pieces
Bingham deemed the group of small fired ceramic objects shown here "problematical." They were recovered from the 1912 Machu Picchu excavations, mainly in the Snake Rock region and near the City Gate. Although such ob-

jects are rare, Lardner noted similar pieces previously in Cuzco. Bingham (1930: 209) suggested that these objects might have functioned as counters to facilitate calculations. According to this interpretation, they would have complemented the *quipu*, a device for recording numbers rather than doing calculations. Although Montesinos and other chroniclers have mentioned counting devices, this interpretation of the mysterious small ceramic objects does not explain why each one is unique or why most have symbols on one or more of their facets.

Inca adults were fond of games, and various chroniclers refer to games called *picqana* in Quechua that were played with a die. Rowe (1946: 288) identified the anomalous ceramic objects Bingham found as picqana, although they do not precisely fit the historical descriptions. According to

Father Bernabé Cobo, the picqana game was played by trying to throw specific combinations on the dice. An alternative interpretation of the Machu Picchu specimens is that they could have been thrown for purposes of divination. The Inca divined the future by a host of techniques, making use of diverse items including coca leaves, corn kernels, pebbles, and even pellets of llama dung (Rowe 1946: 303). It is conceivable that the ceramic "dice" found at Machu Picchu could have been used for this purpose. These intriguing objects are made of incised clay fired in an oxidation atmosphere. Although they are smoothed and some are polished, none show evidence of overall pigmented slip or decorative painting. As the descriptions indicate, the objects differ in size, shape, and decoration, and no two specimens are alike.

Cat. No. 82
Late Horizon, Inca
Machu Picchu
Cat. No. YPM 18233
Terra-cotta Object with Horizontal Incisions
Length: 0.4 in. (1.1 cm)
Width: 0.4 in. (1.1 cm)
Height: 0.4 in. (1.0 cm)
Publication: Bingham 1930: 203, fig. 172e

This small object tapers to a flat top. The sides vary in their decoration. Two of the sides have three horizontal lines; the other two sides lack incisions. The base is left plain.

Cat. No. YPM 18228
Terra-cotta Object with X Motif
Length: 0.4 in. (1.1 cm)
Width: 0.4 in. (1.1 cm)
Height: 0.3 in. (0.8 cm)
Publication: Bingham 1930: 203, fig. 172b

This small cone with a truncated top has two broad sides incised with four horizontal lines. The two narrower sides are less well preserved, and they have fewer incisions. The flat base and top are left undecorated.

Cat. No. YPM 18227
Terra-cotta Cube with Cross Motif
Length: 0.7 in. (1.8 cm)
Width: 0.6 in. (1.5 cm)
Height: 0.4 in. (1.1 cm)
Publication: Bingham 1930: 203, fig. 172f

Of its six facets, only one is decorated. This adornment of a cross motif is a deep incision on a smooth matte surface. The other three narrow faces of the die are smoothed to a matte surface but left undecorated, as are the two broader faces of the object.

Cat. No. YPM 18232
Incised Terra-cotta Object
Length: 0.5 in. (1.2 cm)
Width: 0.4 in. (1.1 cm)
Height: 0.4 in. (1.1 cm)

This truncated cone tapered slightly at the undecorated but polished top. Each of its four side faces is unique: one has a single incision, one have two incisions, one has three incisions, and the other has four incisions. The broad bottom is left with a matte finish. The edges of this form are slightly rounded.

Cat. No. YPM 18230
Terra-cotta Quadrilateral with Horizontal Incision
Length: 0.7 in. (1.7 cm)
Width: 0.5 in. (1.4 cm)
Height: 0.3 in. (0.8 cm)

Of the six faces of this squat quadrilateral, only one is decorated. On one of the broad faces is a single horizontal incision bisecting the space.

Cat. No. YPM 18229
Decorated Terra-cotta Quadrilateral
Length: 0.4 in. (1.1 cm)
Width: 0.5 in. (1.2 cm)
Height: 0.3 in. (0.8 cm)
Publication: Bingham 1930: fig. 172d

This squat object has six distinctive faces. An X is incised into its upper surface, while the bottom face is left undecorated. One of the narrow side faces is incised with two horizontal incisions, while the opposing face features three roughly parallel incisions. One of the remaining sides has three parallel horizontal lines crossed by two vertical incisions. The remaining face is bisected by a horizontal incision; the area above the incision is left plain, but the space below it is filled with vertical incisions.

Ceramic Spindle Whorls
Cat. No. 83
Late Horizon, Inca
Machu Picchu
Publication: Bingham 1930: 185, figs. 182, 183
Cat. No. YPM 18195
Diameter: 1.2 in. (3.0 cm)
Cat. No. YPM 18193
Diameter: 1.4 in. (3.6 cm)
Cat. No. YPM 18206
Diameter: 0.8 in. (2.0 cm)
Cat. No. YPM 18202
Diameter: 0.7 in. (1.8 cm)
Cat. No. YPM 17464
Diameter: 0.8 in. (2.1 cm)
Cat. No. YPM 18204
Diameter: 1.0 in. (5.0 cm)
Cat. No. YPM 16968
Diameter: 1.5 in. (3.8 cm)
Cat. No. YPM 17463
Diameter: 1.2 in. (3.0 cm)
Cat. No. YPM 18200
Diameter: 1.3 in. (3.2 cm)
Cat. No. YPM 18203
Diameter: 1.3 in. (3.4 cm)
Cat. No. YPM 18189
Diameter: 1.3 in. (3.2 cm)

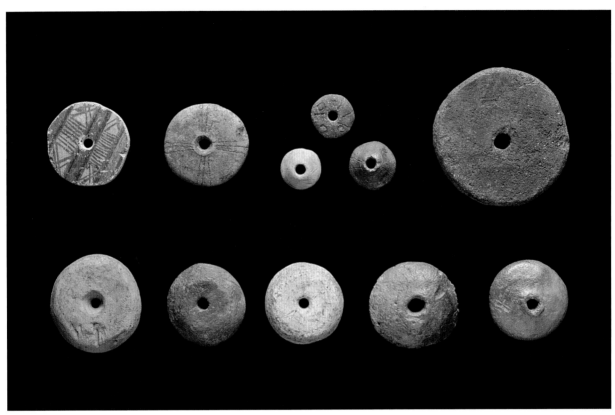

83

In the Central Andes, wool and cotton were spun into thread using a rotating suspended spindle. The spindle consisted of a thin, carved pointed stick. A small circular disk or bead, referred to as a whorl (*piruru* in Quechua), was attached to the spindle in order to help hold the thread and to act as a weight. The circular form of these whorls facilitated the rotational movement of the spindle, thereby producing the thread. Women did most of the spinning. This task could be performed while walking and was done in tandem with other activities such as herding and child rearing. The size of the spindle whorl utilized was a function of the fiber being spun and the desired grade of the resulting thread.

At Machu Picchu, most of the spindle whorls recovered are made of pottery. In many cases, they are modeled from clay to the desired size and weight; these are sometimes decorated with in-cised designs. In some cases the spindle whorls were produced by reworking broken potsherds into a disk shape and then drilling a hole in the center (e.g., YPM 18195, 18204). As expected, the spindle whorls at Machu Picchu vary broadly in size and weight. They also vary in style, consistent with the multi-ethnic composition of Machu Picchu's population. One group of whorls, for example, strongly resembles those used on the central and north coast of Peru (e.g., YPM 18206, 18202, 17464). Some spindle whorls were found in the burial caves, but most were found in the Snake Rock region.

Stone Objects

The Incas produced a wide range of stone objects for utilitarian and ceremonial purposes. Varied types of stone, both local and exotic, were shaped ei-ther through grinding and polishing or by flaking. The special respect for and sensitivity to stone that are so evident in Machu Picchu's architecture are also reflected in the finest Inca portable stone objects.

Schist Pendants
Cat. No. 84
Late Horizon, Inca
Machu Picchu
Cat. No. YPM 18174
Length: 2.3 in. (5.8 cm)
Width: 1.3 in. (3.3 cm)
Publication: Bingham 1930: 205, fig. 173f
Cat. No. YPM 18183
Length: 2.1 in. (5.3 cm)
Width: 1.3 in. (3.2 cm)
Cat. No. YPM 18181
Length: 2.0 in. (5.0 cm)
Width: 1.1 in. (2.7 cm)
Cat. No. YPM 18175

84

Length: 1.6 in. (4.1 cm)
Width: 0.7 in. (1.9 cm)
Publication: Bingham 1930: 205, fig.
173A.
Cat. No. YPM 18179
Length: 1.0 in. (2.6 cm)
Width: 0.5 in. (1.2 cm)
Cat. No. YPM 18176
Length: 0.8 in. (2.1 cm)
Width: 0.6 in. (1.5 cm)
Publication: Bingham 1930: 205, fig.
173d
Cat. No. YPM 18167
Diameter: 1.2 in. (3.1 cm)
Cat. No. YPM 18169
Diameter: 1.1 in. (2.7 cm)
Cat. No. YPM 18168
Diameter: 1.1 in. (2.9 cm)
Publication: Bingham 1930: 210, fig.
176b

Cat. No. YPM 18173
Length: 1.0 in. (2.6 cm)
Width: 0.5 in. (1.4 cm)
Cat. No. YPM 18171
Length: 1.1 in. (2.7 cm)
Width: 0.6 in. (1.6 cm)
Publication: Bingham 1930: 205, fig.
173c
Cat. No. YPM 18177
Length: 0.8 in (1.8 cm)
Width: 0.6 in. (1.6 cm)

Chloritic schist, a green stone sometimes laced with talc, was quarried during the Late Horizon on the lower
slopes of Machu Picchu mountain, less
than a kilometer southeast of the palace
complex. It was located in 1912, and debris from the ancient mining activities
was collected by the Yale Peruvian Sci-

entific Expedition (Bingham 1930: 199;
Bridges 1984: 14–15; Wright et al. 2000:
70, 123). Although it was too soft to be
used for most tools, this distinctive material was easily cut, ground, and polished, and it was shaped into ornaments
and other small objects.

At Machu Picchu, one of the common items made from this distinctive
material were small geometric forms
perforated near their outer edge, as if to
be hung from a cord or necklace. These
are interpreted as pendants. Most of the
twenty-seven flat pendants have simple
geometric forms that are circular, rectangular, or triangular. There are also
rare examples of more complex shapes,
which are paddle-shaped, and anchor-
shaped. The most complex form is a
"dart-shaped" pendant that combines

two triangular shapes. Judging from the availability of the stone and the recovery of blanks and unfinished artifacts, it can be inferred that these pendants and other schist objects were locally produced at Machu Picchu. The pendants were found in different zones and contexts at the site, including the Snake Rock, the Upper City, burial caves, and the terraces separating the upper and lower portions of the palace complex (Bingham 1930: 205, 210).

Schist Miniatures
Some of the most intriguing objects made from the local green chloritic schist were forty-one small cutouts in the form of animals, tools, and other items. Like the flat schist pendants, these were made by cutting out the shape, perhaps using a sharp-edged instrument of chert or some other hard material, grinding down the surface until the object was wafer-thin, and then polishing the surface of the object to a matte or low-luster finish with water and/or a fine abrasive such as sand. The schist miniatures lack perforations and were not designed to be worn. Their function is unknown, and their provenance does little to resolve this question. According to the 1912 field notes of Ellwood Erdis, schist miniatures were recovered from many contexts including burial caves, the Upper City, the area of the City Gate, Snake Rock, the Sacred Plaza, and the East City. They were often found individually and, judging from their occasional presence in graves along with other items used in daily life, they may have been personal possessions. Recent excavations near Snake Rock have encountered additional schist cutouts including one in the form of a bird (Astete 2001: 105). There is no evidence in support of Bingham's interpretation of them as counting tokens, nor were they pre-Inca in date, as Bingham speculated (Bingham 1930: 199). On the contrary, several

of them were found in the burial caves associated with Inca pottery. One plausible but difficult-to-test hypothesis is that these items functioned as charms or amulets for the local population.

Analogous thin miniature cutouts, depicting a broad range of objects (knives and other tools, plants, animals), were unearthed at Túcume on the north coast of Peru. Recovered from the Inca complex known as the Temple of the Sacred Stone, these delicate artifacts were made from silver, gold, and copper sheet rather than stone, and they were deposited in groups as offerings within spondylus shells or in small pits (Hyerdahl et al. 1995: 111–12, plates 84, 85). The ceremonial context of the Túcume cutouts is consistent with our interpretation of the Machu Picchu miniatures as items with a religious or magical function.

Cat. No. 85
Cat. No. YPM 17919
Late Horizon, Inca
Machu Picchu, Cave 100
Length: 1.6 in. (4.0 cm)
Height 0.9 in. (2.4 cm)
Publication: Bingham 1930: 205, fig. 174f; Eaton 1916: plate III, fig. 7

This artifact is a zoomorphic miniature, possibly representing a porcupine. The animal's head contains a perforation representing the eye. Two projections above the head may be quills or the representation of raised ears. The animal stands on two legs, now partly broken. Above the back are five quill-like extensions; the lowermost may be the figure's tail.

Cat. No. YPM 17922
Late Horizon, Inca
Machu Picchu, Cave 103
Length: 1.2 in. (3.0 cm)
Height: 0.9 in. (2.3 cm)
Publication: Bingham 1930: 205, fig. 174d; Eaton 1916: plate III, fig. 12

This dark green chloritic schist object is a zoomorphic miniature of a bird. Extending from a rotund torso are an angular head with a notched beak, a short tail, and a straight tapering leg. On either side of the head is a small hole representing eyes.

Cat. No. YPM 17920
Late Horizon, Inca
Machu Picchu, Cave 100
Length: 1.6 (4.2 cm)
Height: 0.8 in. (2.0 cm)
Publication: Eaton 1916: plate III, fig. 5; Bingham 1930: 205, fig. 174a

This dark green chloritic schist cutout is a zoomorphic miniature, probably representing an anteater. Delicate carving is evident especially in the body features: the animal appears in motion with all four legs and a full tail outstretched. The head ends in a small notch to portray the animal's mouth.

Cat. No. YPM 16671
Late Horizon, Inca
Machu Picchu, Room 35A
Length: 1.2 in. (3.0 cm)
Width: 0.8 in. (2.0 cm)

This thin stone artifact is partly broken, but one edge appears to depict a series of four steps. Step motifs are common in Inca art and appear to have had a religious significance related to the worship of sacred mountains. The carved edge of this miniature is quite thin, while the broken edge is thicker (0.2 in. (0.5 cm)).

Cat. No. YPM 17933
Late Horizon, Inca
Machu Picchu, Cave 101
Length: 2.3 in. (5.9 cm)
Height: 1.3 in. (3.4 cm)
Publication: Bingham 1930: 205, fig. 174c; Salazar 2001a: 124, fig. 11

85

This specimen, a zoomorphic miniature of a llama, is made from dark green chloritic schist. The miniature is thin and flat, with rounded and beveled edges. Simple features are depicted: a large elongated torso, angular front and rear legs, a short tail, and a long neck ending in a very small head with a notched mouth.

Cat. No. YPM 17951
Late Horizon, Inca
Machu Picchu, Upper City
Length: 1.5 in. (3.9 cm)
Width: 0.7 in. (1.7 cm)
Publication: Bingham 1930: 201, fig. 171f

This piece is a thin stone miniature of a projectile point, made from dark green chloritic schist. It features a triangular stem, and two notches separate the stem from the point. The outer edges of the point are quite thin, as if mimicking real points. The faces are left fairly rough.

Cat. No. 86
Schist Miniatures
Cat. No. YPM 17915
Late Horizon, Inca
Machu Picchu, Cave 97
Length: 2.4 in. (6.0 cm)
Width: 1.6 in. (4.0 cm)
Publication: Bingham 1930: 208, fig. 175b; Eaton 1916: plate III, fig. 4

This object takes the form of a special knife, known as a *tumi*. Tumis were usually made of bronze and were distributed widely through the Central Andes and Ecuador in late prehistoric times. Their dissemination beyond Peru's north coast is probably associated with Inca imperial expansion.

Cat. No. YPM 17931
Late Horizon, Inca
Machu Picchu, Cave 101

Length: 1.1 in. (2.7 cm)
Width: 0.9 in. (2.3 cm)
Publication: Bingham 1930: 205, fig. 174b; Eaton 1916: plate III, fig. 9

This object takes the form of an Inca shawl pin, referred to as a *tupu*. The head of the pin is especially thin.

Cat. No. YPM 17939
Late Horizon, Inca
Machu Picchu
Length: 0.5 in. (1.4 cm)
Width: 0.4 in. (1.1 cm)

This object is a miniature of the *tumi* knife form, made of dark green chloritic schist. This version, however, is much more diminutive, and features a long convex blade.

Cat. No. YPM 17916
Late Horizon, Inca
Machu Picchu, Cave 97

Length: 1.6 in. (4.0 cm)
Width: 1.8 in. (4.5 cm)
Publication: Bingham 1930: 208, fig.
175e; Eaton 1916: plate III, fig. 3

This cutout is a thin, dark green chloritic schist miniature of a T-shaped ax head. The main faces are flat. Both ends feature a slightly convex edge.

Cat. No. YPM 17929
Late Horizon, Inca
Machu Picchu, Cave 93
Length: 1.8 in. (4.7 cm)
Width: 0.9 in. (2.2 cm)
Publication: Bingham 1930: 208, fig.
175c; Eaton 1916: plate III, fig. 1

This bow tie–shaped, dark green chloritic schist miniature portrays a doubled-bladed knife or ax. While one side is flat, the other face is slightly convex from removal of thickness near the blade ends, presumably to imitate the sharp edges of a knife. Both ends feature a straight edge.

Cat. No. YPM 17930
Late Horizon, Inca
Machu Picchu, Cave 93
Length: 2.0 in. (5.2 cm)
Width: 0.8 in. (1.9 cm)
Publication: Bingham 1930: 208, fig.
175a; Eaton 1916: plate III, fig. 2

This object is a miniature version of a long knife (*tumi*), or perhaps a spatula, made from dark green chloritic schist. Although the faces are flat, considerable effort was expended to make the convex blade end and upper handle thinner.

Conical Schist Pendants
Cat. No. 87
Late Horizon, Inca
Machu Picchu, unspecified burial cave
Cat. No. YPM 18188
Length: 1.0 in. (2.5 cm)
Diameter: 0.3 in. (0.9 cm)

Publication: Bingham 1930: 210, fig.
178a
Cat. No. YPM 18164
Length: 1.3 in. (3.2 cm)
Diameter: 0.4 in. (1.0 cm)
Cat. No. YPM 18166
Length: 1.5 in. (3.8 cm)
Diameter: 0.3 in. (0.9 cm)
Cat. No. YPM 18165
Length: 1.2 in. (3.1 cm)
Diameter: 0.3 in. (0.7 cm)
Cat. No. YPM 18163
Length: 1.1 in. (2.8 cm)
Diameter: 0.3 in. (0.8 cm)
Cat. No. YPM 18187
Length: 0.7 in. (1.9 cm)
Diameter: 0.3 in. (0.7 cm)
Publication: Bingham 1930: 210, fig.
178b

One unusual group of six cone-shaped pendants made from green chloritic schist were unearthed at Machu Picchu. At least four of these were found together in an unspecified grave containing the bones of a woman; they were interpreted as having been strung as a necklace (Bingham 1930: 195). These distinctive stone artifacts are carefully drilled from opposite sides, and the two fine drillings meet in the middle. After initial production, the exteriors of the pendants were polished to a matte finish, but in most of these, some evidence of the grinding striations remains. On each of the pendants, a horizontal groove extends around the circumference, in some cases connecting the two opposing perforations.

Obsidian Pebbles
Cat. No. 88
Cat. No. YPM 18367–18396
Late Horizon, Inca
Machu Picchu, Room 32A
Max. Width: 0.4–0.9 in. (1.0–2.2 cm)
Publication: Burger et al. 2000: 347

This collection of small river-worn obsidian pebbles was found together in

Room 32A near the Main Gate of Machu Picchu. All the pebbles are opaque black or very dark gray translucent obsidian, shaped irregularly, often with flat and rounded facets resulting from water erosion. They range in size from 0.4 to 0.9 in. (1.0 to 2.2 cm) in maximum width, with an average width of 0.7 in. (1.7 cm). Each pebble is rounded, and some have traces of a light brown patina, especially within the small recesses, which may be additional evidence that they were once waterborne (Jay Ague, personal communication). Others, especially the larger specimens, show a distinctive polish that appears to be intentional. In the most polished examples, very little of the patina remains. In addition, several specimens show flaking scars of recent breaks, but these too have been rounded and polished over.

It is likely that the obsidian pebbles were accorded some symbolic value related to their association with volcanic activity and water (Chapter 6). Trace element analysis of a sample of these pebbles revealed that they were brought from the Chivay Obsidian Source located on the Pacific slopes of the Andes, roughly 250 miles (400 km) west of Machu Picchu. The cache of over thirty small pebbles of obsidian glass encountered by the Yale Peruvian Scientific Expedition probably constituted a ritual offering of some kind.

Hammerstones
Among the Machu Picchu artifacts discovered in 1912 were several dozen stone hammerstones with nicks, abraded surfaces, and discoloration, reflecting their use in shaping building stones and other stone items. These stones were usually river cobbles of great hardness, selected because they were easily held in the hand and could be used for hammering or grinding. Similar tools have been recovered at Sacsahuaman and most other Inca sites.

87

Despite the occasional use of bronze tools for construction activities (Chapter 6), natural hammerstones such as those shown here remained the main tool for heavy-duty masonry activity at Machu Picchu.

Cat. No. 89
Cat. No. YPM 17760
Late Horizon, Inca
Machu Picchu, Room 44A
Length: 3.7 in. (9.4 cm)
Width: 3.0 in. (7.7 cm)
Thickness: 2.2 in. (5.6 cm)

This is a hand grinding stone, made from grainy, dark, dusky red igneous rock. It is roughly trapezoidal with rounded edges. The main work surfaces are located on the narrow and wide ends. Both edges are rounded from grinding and slightly pecked from hammering. The non–work surfaces are smoother and more lustrous.

Cat. No. YPM 18489
Late Horizon, Inca

Machu Picchu
Length: 4.5 in. (11.5 cm)
Width: 3.7 in. (9.4 cm)
Thickness: 2.7 in. (6.9 cm)

This is a large ground-stone implement, made from a dark pink cobble, roughly rectangular. The edges are rounded, especially on the narrow sides, and show peck marks as well as wear from grinding. The narrow sides also bear traces of having been charred, perhaps from use in metalwork or near a fire.

Cat. No. YPM 18490
Late Horizon, Inca
Machu Picchu
Length: 3.5 in. (9.0 cm)
Width: 2.8 in. (7.2 cm)
Thickness: 2.0 in. (5.1 cm)
Publication: Bingham 1930: 214, fig. 196b

This is a roughly rectangular ground-stone implement, made from a dark gray granular stone. The two large flat faces are smooth and slightly polished.

The main work ends are worn convex and rounded from grinding. The side corners also show peck marks from hammering.

Cat. No. YPM 18491
Late Horizon, Inca
Machu Picchu
Length: 4.0 in. (10.1 cm)
Width: 2.5 in. (6.4 cm)
Thickness: 2.2 in. (5.7 cm)

This object is a ground-stone implement, made from dark pink fine-grained stone, roughly cylindrical, with rounded sides. The main work edges have convex surfaces that are rough from use; there are peck marks on either end. Different areas of the specimen, especially on the rounded edges, are darkened, perhaps from general use and handling (hand polish).

Clod-Breakers and Mace Heads
In hand-to-hand combat, the Incas often used clubs of about a meter (39.5 inches) in length hafted with a stone or

metal head. The simplest of the stone mace heads were round, but more complicated ones had tapering or truncated projections around the perimeter, giving them a star shape. These forms had practical advantages, a fact reflected in the head wounds often observed in the skulls found in burials of the Late Horizon. The stone mace heads were produced by pecking and polishing. In addition to their use as weapons (Guaman Poma 1980: 128), the more elaborate star-shaped maces were apparently used as status symbols. In the drawings of Guaman Poma de Ayala (1980: 309), the Inca emperors are often shown holding a club hafted with a star-shaped mace head, perhaps to represent their war-like qualities.

Ring-shaped stones hafted on medium-sized clubs were also used to crush clods of soil as part of the preparation of fields for planting (Guaman Poma 1980: 1062; Rowe 1946: 248). It is difficult to know which stone rings were used in farming rather than warfare or as symbols of status, although some of the coarser examples with substantial wear on their edges were more likely used for the former than the latter purpose. At Machu Picchu, only five ring-stones were recovered by the 1912 expedition, two of which were heavy and coarse, suggesting an agricultural function. The three other examples, which are smaller and have projections, were probably hafted to form star-shaped maces. It may be significant that Erdis (1912) mentions the main terraces of the eastern sector near the southern moat as the provenance of most of the stone rings; one was found in Cave 6A.

Cat. No. 90
Clod-Breaker
Cat. No. YPM 17609
Late Horizon, Inca
Machu Picchu
Diameter: 4.8 in. (12.1 cm)
Thickness: 1.5 in. (3.8 cm)

Related objects: Fauvet-Berthelot and Lavallee 1987: 113, 125, figs. 300, 362

This ring-shaped artifact is made from a light brown granitic stone. The entire piece is rough and shows extensive pitting and chipping administered intentionally to remove material from the rounded edges. A 1-in. (2.3-cm) circular hole has been bored through the center of the stone, to enable hafting of the object to a wooden shaft. Such an object could have been used as the head of a clubbed weapon, but it was probably an agricultural implement for breaking clods.

Cat. No. YPM 17378
Mace Head
Late Horizon, Inca
Cuzco
Diameter: 3.4 in. (8.7 cm)
Height: 1.9 in. (4.8 cm)
Related objects: Fauvet-Berthelot and Lavallee 1987: 139, fig. 406

This ring-shaped object would have been the head of a hafted stone implement, made from a brown, grainy, igneous rock. Roughly oval in plan, the object has rounded convex edges. A central hole, bored from either side, facilitates attachment to a wooden shaft. The object is smooth, with little wear.

Cat. No. 91
Star-shaped Mace Heads
Cat. No. YPM 17367
Late Horizon, Inca
Cuzco
Diameter: 4.0 in. (10.3 cm)
Thickness: 1.4 in. (3.5 cm)
Related objects: Fauvet-Berthelot and Lavallee 1987: 114, fig. 303b

This object is a star-shaped mace head, made of a grainy dark gray stone. The specimen features six blunt prongs that taper sharply at each tip. Two of the points are slightly chipped; the others

show pitting, suggestive of use. The mace head would have been hafted to a club by means of the central hole (width: 1.0 in. (2.4 cm)); the perforation is bored through each side. Grinding striations are uncommon.

Cat. No. YPM 17368
Late Horizon, Inca
Cuzco
Diameter: 5.0 in. (12.7 cm)
Thickness: 1.2 in. (3.0 cm)
Related objects: Fauvet-Berthelot and Lavallee 1987: 114, fig. 303b

This star-shaped mace head, made of a dark grayish brown stone, features seven prongs that taper sharply at each tip. Five of the tips are chipped or damaged, and the others show evidence of pitting; these suggest use. The specimen would have been hafted to a club by means of the central hole (width: 0.8 in. (2.2 cm)); the perforation is bored through each side. The entire artifact has been polished to a matte finish. Grinding striations are common, especially within the hole and topmost surfaces.

Cat. No. 92
Star-Shaped Mace Heads
Cat. No. YPM 17370
Late Horizon, Inca
Cuzco
Diameter: 4.4 in. (11.1 cm)
Thickness: 1.0 in. (2.5 cm)

This ground-stone object is a flat, cross-shaped mace head, made of a dark greenish black stone. The example features four rectangular blunt prongs, with beveled outer edges and rounded corners. The concave notches separating each prong contain slightly rounded, beveled edges. All the prongs show some evidence of use through pitting and chipping damage. The central hole (width 1.0 in. (2.5 cm)) would have facilitated hafting to a club. The entire specimen features a smooth surface with a low luster, and grinding striations are uncommon.

Cat. No. YPM 17383
Late Horizon, Inca
Cuzco
Diameter: 3.1 in. (9.5 cm)
Thickness: 0.6 in. (1.6 cm)

This is a flat, cross-shaped mace head, made of a dark greenish black stone. It features four truncated prongs, with rounded outer edges and corners. The concave notches separating each prong also have rounded edges. All the prongs show some evidence of use through pitting, but chipping damage is especially notable. Bored through either side, the central hole (width: 0.8 in. (2.1 cm)) would have facilitated hafting to a club. The entire specimen features a rather rough, unpolished surface. Small grinding striations are visible.

Cat. No. 93
Unperforated Mace Head
Cat. No. YPM 17369 B
Late Horizon, Inca
Cuzco
Length: 0.3 in. (9.0 cm)
Thickness: 1.0 in. (2.4 cm)

This star-shaped object, made of a light grayish brown stone, has five prongs that taper sharply at each tip. In size and style, the object resembles other mace heads that were hafted to clubs by means of a central perforation. It is possible that this specimen lacks a central hole for hafting because it was in the process of production and left unfinished. The entire artifact, however, has been polished to a dull luster, which suggests that it was complete. It is possible that it was hafted on the shaft using cordage and resin rather than the more common arrangement.

Cat. No. 94
Unperforated Mace Head
Cat. No. YPM 17369 A
Late Horizon, Inca
Cuzco
Diameter: 4.0 in. (10.4 cm)
Thickness: 1.0 in. (2.6 cm)

This is an unusual cross-shaped mace head, made from fine-grained dark brownish gray stone. Each of the four prongs extends away perpendicularly from the center. The prongs are rounded over, and they taper toward the tips; one of the tips is chipped. The entire specimen is ground smooth, and grinding striations are uncommon. As in the case of YPM 17369 B, no central hole was drilled and it was probably hafted using an alternative procedure.

Ax Heads

Ground-stone objects usually identified as ax heads were produced through much of Andean prehistory. Their T-shaped or waisted form was designed to facilitate hafting on top of a wooden handle. Similar artifacts were common in the forested areas of the eastern Andean slopes and tropical lowlands throughout prehistory, a fact that has suggested their importance in the cutting of trees and other woodworking activities. However, such activities probably represent some of the uses to which these versatile tools were put. Significantly, this class of tool was absent in the assemblage recovered by the 1912 Yale Peruvian Scientific Expedition at Machu Picchu.

Cat. No. 95
Ax Heads
Cat. No. YPM 17364
Late Horizon, Inca
Cuzco
Length: 3.4 in. (8.6 cm)
Width: 3.0 in. (7.5 cm)
Thickness: 0.8 in. (2.1 cm)

This example of a T-shaped ax head, made from fine-grained dark gray stone, has a blade that is narrow and tapered to a thin slightly convex edge. The blade is slightly worn and chipped. The outer edges are rounded. The outer projections of the tool facilitated hafting onto a shaft or club. The implement is smooth and polished to a dull luster.

Cat. No. YPM 17377
Late Horizon, Inca
Cuzco
Length: 3.6 in. (9.2 cm)
Width: 3.5 in. (9.0 cm)
Thickness: 1.1 in. (2.9 cm)

This is a T-shaped ax head made from dark gray stone. The main blade portion of the implement is thick and wide. Its two main faces are smoothed and polished. The outer edges are rounded. The upper and lower projections of the tool facilitated hafting onto a large shaft or club. The work edge is flat and blunt, and it is marked with pitting, indicating heavy use.

Cat. No. 96
Ax Head
Cat. No. YPM 17374
Late Horizon, Inca
Cuzco
Length: 4.6 in. (11.7 cm)
Width: 2.4 in. (6.1 cm)
Thickness: 0.9 in. (2.2 cm)

This unusual T-shaped ax head was made from fine-grained brown stone. The ax blade is teardrop-shaped and features a wide convex cutting edge and two small hafting extensions. Chipping scars on the sharp blade edge indicate prehistoric use. The outer edges are rounded; the back edge is beveled. The implement is smooth and polished to a dull luster.

97

Bola Stones

Two finely ground stones with grooves around their centers were recovered during the 1912 Machu Picchu investigations. Bingham found similar ground-stone tools at Choqquequirau and acquired others from collectors in Cuzco. These tools are made from naturally rounded fine-grained stones that were pecked, ground, and polished to achieve the desired waisted form. These distinctive artifacts are believed to be bola stones, an interpretation that is consistent with descriptions of the use of such weapons (known as *riwi* or *aylyo*) in hunting (Guaman Poma 1980: 182). Bolas were also used in warfare to entangle the feet of enemies. According to Rowe (1946: 275), each weapon consisted of two to five bola stones wrapped with rawhide strips and then fastened together in the middle by cords.

Cat. No. 97
Cat. No. YPM 17372 A
Late Horizon, Inca
Cuzco
Length: 2.7 in. (7.0 cm)
Diameter: 2.0 in. (5.2 cm)
Related objects: Fauvet-Berthelot and Lavallee 1987: 115, fig. 317b

This is a bi-conical-shaped stone made from black, iron-bearing material. The object is grooved on the center axis in order to be wrapped, probably using fiber or leather cords, and then attached by cord to the weapon (e.g., Anders 1984: 387, fig. 12.69). One side of the specimen is shorter or more truncated. Both tips show evidence of use, including peck marks and pitting. The artifact is notable for its heavy weight and hardness, which would have enabled powerful blows whether as a weapon or a tool. Most of the object shows a lustrous finish, but in some of

the small natural interstices, iron oxide corrosion has accumulated.

Cat. No. YPM 17381 B
Late Horizon, Inca
Cuzco
Length: 2.5 in. (6.4 cm)
Width: 2.0 in. (5.0 cm)
Thickness: 1.5 in. (3.8 cm)
Related objects: Fauvet-Berthelot and Lavallee 1987: 139, fig. 412

Like other bola stones made of the dense iron-bearing material, this ovoid specimen is unusually heavy and polished to a dull black finish. However, a slightly flattened profile and very shallow central groove distinguishes it from the others. Small natural holes show iron-oxide corrosion. The ends do not show much evidence of wear.

Cat. No. YPM 17381 A
Late Horizon, Inca

Cuzco
Length: 2.2 in. (5.7 cm)
Diameter: 1.9 in. (4.9 cm)
Related objects: Fauvet-Berthelot and
Lavallee 1987: 139, fig. 412

This specimen is made from dense
iron-bearing material, perhaps
hematite. Like other bola stones, this
specimen contains a notched groove
along the center to facilitate tying. The
entire object is smooth and polished to
a dull black luster. The ends do not
demonstrate much evidence of use.

Cat. No. YPM 17372 B
Late Horizon, Inca
Cuzco
Length: 2.7 in. (6.8 cm)
Diameter: 1.9 in. (4.8 cm)
Related objects: Fauvet-Berthelot and
Lavallee 1987: 115, fig. 317b

This ovoid artifact appears to be a small
bola stone or hammer head, made from
a brownish gray rock with many light
brown mineral flecks. The raw material
resembles the stone used to make
camelid effigies. Around the center axis
is a groove that facilitated hafting. It is
smooth and polished to a dull luster.
One of ends shows light pecking wear
from use.

Cat. No. YPM 191369
Late Horizon, Inca
Machu Picchu
Length: 2.9 in. (7.3 cm)
Diameter: 2.2 in. (5.7 cm)
Related objects: Fauvet-Berthelot and
Lavallee 1987: 115, figs. 316, 317a

This stone object is roughly spherical
and made from gray igneous rock. A
shallow groove, located along the center axis, enabled the attachment of
cords. Each hemispherical side served
as a hammering end and shows evidence of pitting. One side has been
ground slightly flat.

Cat. No. YPM 17372 C
Late Horizon, Inca
Cuzco
Length: 2.8 in. (7.0 cm)
Diameter: 2.7 in. (6.9 cm)
Related objects: Fauvet-Berthelot and
Lavallee 1987: 115, figs. 316, 317a

This artifact is made from a fine-
grained dark gray igneous rock. The
work ends are separated on the central
axis by a groove, about 0.2 in. (0.6 cm)
deep and 0.3 in. (0.7 cm) wide, notched
to facilitate hafting. The entire head, including the groove, is smooth with a
somewhat lustrous black finish. Extensive pitting is evident on either peen
end, revealing a lighter gray raw material underneath.

Small Ground-Stone Vessels
Inca mastery of stone carving extended
to portable objects and included the
production of types of objects rarely
shown. For example, Inca artisans produced small polished cups and bowls of
soft sedimentary stone. Owing to their
fragility, archaeologists typically recovered these objects in fragmentary form,
as was the case at Machu Picchu, where
the 1912 expedition encountered the
fragments of two such vessels (Bridges
1984: 50). The function of this class of
objects is unknown.

Cat. No. 98
Polished Ground-Stone Cups
Cat. No. YPM 17435
Late Horizon, Inca
Cuzco
Height: 2.0 in. (5.1 cm)
Diameter: 1.8 in. (4.5 cm)

This vessel, made from fine-grained
black stone with natural white streaks, is
a small cylindrical cup with vertical
side walls, flat base, and a slightly
everted rim. The exterior surface and
the base are extremely smooth and polished to a high luster. The interior is

rounded and left rough.

Cat. No. YPM 17412
Late Horizon, Inca
Cuzco
Height: 1.5 in. (3.9 cm)
Diameter: 1.6 in. (4.2 cm)

This small ground-stone vessel, made of
fine-grained black stone, has the form
of a cup with straight walls that taper
slightly toward the flat base. The lip is
beveled horizontally. The interior surface is slightly rough and has rounded
edges. The exterior surfaces, including
the base, are polished to a medium luster and extremely smooth.

Cat. No. 99
Polished Small Bowls
Cat. No. YPM 17358
Late Horizon, Inca
Cuzco
Height: 1.5 in. (3.9 cm)
Diameter: 2.3 in. (5.8 cm)

This object is a small vessel, ground
from dark brown stone with large mica
inclusions. It has the form of an open
bowl with slightly convex sides that taper toward a flattened base. The lip,
basal angle, and interior surface are
rounded. The upper edges of the vessel
along the interior and exterior have
been darkened, probably from the
burning of ritual offerings, such as
llama fat or blood.

Cat. No. YPM 17434
Late Horizon, Inca
Cuzco
Height: 1.3 in. (3.2 cm)
Diameter: 2.2 in. (5.7 cm)

This small stone vessel, made from
black grainy stone, takes the form of a
bowl with convex walls, a rounded lip
and basal edge, and a rounded interior
surface. The vessel rests on a flat base
and is smoothed to a dull luster.

Ground-Stone Mortars

The Inca produced carved stone mortars in which they ground herbs, spices, and other condiments with stone pestles. In preparing their cuisine, the Incas used several kinds of chili pepper, each with a distinctive flavor and strength, as well as a wide range of wild herbs used to flavor food, such as the mint-like muña (*Minthstachys setosa*) and paiko (*Chenopodium ambrosioides*) (Coe 1994: 225). The portable mortars used to prepare these and other condiments were typically made of hard, fine-grained stone. At Machu Picchu, the Yale Peruvian Expedition encountered portable mortars in many parts of the site, including the Stairway of the Fountains, the Snake Rock area, the Ingenuity Group, and on the terraces (Bingham 1930: 213, 217). Bingham acquired other examples of portable mortars during his time in Cuzco.

The finest examples of portable mortars were made by shaping a stone block using hammer blows and then polishing it using a graded series of abrasives, such as river sand mixed with water. Simpler mortars were carved by pecking a central cavity in a naturally shaped water-worn stone. Pestles were usually shaped from water-worn stones and were designed to fit the mortar with which they were paired. The examples shown here demonstrate that there is considerable variability in form, material, and finishing of Inca mortars and pestles. Although some were decorated, most were left plain. Nevertheless, they achieve a degree of beauty as a result of the skill of carving, the visual and textural qualities of the stone utilized, and the elegance of their design.

While many of the mortars were primarily related to food preparation, some fulfilled other functions such as the preparation of medicinal plants or activities related to metalworking. Most mortars were not, however, utilized in the bulk milling of grain. This task was usually carried out on large, flat slabs that served as a platform for a flat stone with a rounded base that was rocked back and forth. Because the rocking utilizes the weight of the stone, this otherwise laborious activity was often the responsibility of children or the elderly (Rowe 1946: 221).

Cat. No. 100
Circular Mortar
Cat. No. YPM 17458
Late Horizon, Inca
Cuzco
Diameter: 11.0 in. (28.0 cm)
Height: 2.4 in. (6.0 cm)
Depth: 1.0 in. (2.5 cm)
Related objects: Bingham 1930: 217, fig. 199d

This round mortar is made of black basalt with whitish brown inclusions. The mortar features a flattened base, outer walls that taper slightly toward the base, and a beveled rim. The interior surface is rather shallow and flat, measuring only 1.0 in. (2.5 cm) below the rim. The surfaces of the base, the sides, and the interior have been smoothed and polished. The chips along the rim probably resulted from use.

Cat. No. 101
Mortar with Lateral Handles
Cat. No. YPM 17450
Late Horizon, Inca
Cuzco
Length: 12.0 in. (30.5 cm)
Diameter: 8.3 in. (21.0 cm)
Height: 3.0 in. (7.7 cm)
Depth: 2.1 in. (5.3 cm)
Related objects: Anton 1962, fig. 157b; Lumbreras 1975: 284–85, fig. 300; Sawyer 1975: 168, fig. 260

This object is a shallow mortar, made of dark gray stone, with loop handles, flat base, and convex rim. The outer walls taper slightly toward the base, and the rim is rounded along the exterior. The interior surface is conical in profile and slopes gradually toward the center. Large horizontal handles, measuring 2.9 in. (7.4 cm), are located just below the exterior rim. The entire mortar, including the base, exterior, and interior, exhibits a smooth polished surface.

Cat. No. 102
Mortar with Nubbin Handles
Cat. No. YPM 21656
Late Horizon, Inca
Machu Picchu, near Snake Rock
Diameter: 12.2 in. (31.0 cm)
Height: 6.1 in. (15.4 cm)
Depth: 2.8 in. (7.2 cm)
Publication: Bingham 1930: 213, fig. 186

This is a circular mortar with nubbin handles carved from grayish brown rock. The mortar has a flat base, a fairly shallow interior basin, slightly beveled and rounded rim, and convex outer walls. There is a raised band slightly above the base. The mortar is distinguished by two low nubbins, located on opposite ends, which facilitate lifting. The exterior of the mortar has a rough and grainy surface.

Cat. No. 103
Mortar
Cat. No. YPM 17623
Late Horizon, Inca
Machu Picchu
Diameter: 8.7 in. (22.0 cm)
Height: 3.1 in. (7.8 cm)
Depth: 1.8 in. (4.6 cm)
Publication: Bingham 1930: 217, fig. 199c

This circular mortar is made from dark brown stone, possibly granite. The specimen has slightly convex side walls that taper slightly toward a flat base as well as a very shallow interior work surface, which is polished smooth and to a dull luster. The interior walls and base remain fairly rough.

103

105

concave work surface, and a beveled rim (0.5 in. (1.2 cm) wide). The entire piece, including the flat base, is smoothed to a matte finish. Microscopic inspection suggests that it was utilized for metalwork.

Cat. No. 106
Rectangular Mortar
Cat. No. YPM 17444
Late Horizon, Inca
Cuzco
Length: 10.3 in. (26.1 cm)
Width: 9.4 in. (23.8 cm)
Thickness: 1.8 in. (4.5 cm)

Inca artisans shaped this exquisite platter from fine black stone. The object is rectangular and shallow, with a flat base, vertical side walls, a beveled rim, and a flat interior work surface. Traces of circular grinding work appear in the center of the mortar. On one edge is a pouring lip that could have been used to eliminate excess metal, so it is possible that this object also was used for making large, thin metal sheets or ingots.

Cat. No. 107
Stone Receptacle with Pedestal Base
Cat. No. YPM 17452
Late Horizon, Inca
Cuzco
Height: 15.0 in. (38.1 cm)
Diameter: 6.1 in. (15.5 cm)
Depth: 1.7 in. (4.3 cm)

This unusual ground-stone object consists of a large bowl-like vessel supported by a long cylindrical shaft resting on a circular pedestal base. It is made of dark greenish black igneous rock. The bowl has a beveled lip and a flattened base, with sides tapering very slightly. The base of the bowl connects to a long cylindrical stem that ends as a flat, circular pedestal on which the vessel stands. Except for the basal surface, the entire piece is polished smooth. The

Cat. No. 104
Circular Mortar
Cat. No. YPM 17424
Late Horizon, Inca
Cuzco
Diameter: 8.2 in. (21.0 cm)
Height: 1.8 in. (4.7 cm)
Depth: 0.8 in. (2.1 cm)

This object is a circular, platter-like mortar made from black rock. The mortar has a flat and shallow interior basin, slightly beveled rim, and walls that taper slightly toward a flat base. The vessel's base, sides, and interior have a smooth polished surface. The piece dis-

plays considerable evidence of wear from use.

Cat. No. 105
Ovoid Mortar
Cat. No. YPM 17445
Late Horizon, Inca
Cuzco
Height: 2.0 in. (5.1 cm)
Length: 13.1 in. (33.3 cm)
Depth: 1.7 in. (4.3 cm)

This object is an oval stone platter, made from dark gray igneous stone with light-colored quartzitic streaks. The vessel features vertical side walls, a slightly

size and the simple but elegant form suggest that the vessel functioned as a special receptacle, perhaps for ritual offerings or other ceremonial acts.

Decorated Mortars and Stone Bowls

Inca mortars, like other Inca art, rarely depicted naturalistic images of plants, animals, the supernatural, or historical figures. Composite or monstrous beings, so common in other artistic styles from the Central Andes, were rare, and figurative representations were mainly restricted to a small number of animals shown using essential generic shapes. On Inca mortars, the feline and the serpent are the most commonly represented creatures, probably because of the mythical associations of these animals. The feline representations, which lack pelage markings, likely symbolized the puma or other wild felines found in the Andean highlands. The puma was closely associated with the Inca emperor, the Sapa Inca, and the Inca capital city of Cuzco was said to have been designed in the form of a puma.

Cat. No. 108
Mortar with Carved Snakes
Cat. No. YPM 17443
Late Horizon, Inca
Cuzco
Height: 3.8 in. (9.6 cm)
Diameter: 10.6 in. (27.0 cm)
Depth: 1.7 in. (4.3 cm)
Related objects: Jones 1964, fig. 18; Laurencich 2000: 221, fig. 225; Townsend 1992: 357, fig. 14; Willey 1974, fig. 434

This remarkable object is a circular receptacle or basin, made from grainy, dark greenish gray igneous rock. The vessel takes the form of a simple vertical-sided bowl, with a horizontal lip (0.6 in. (1.6 cm) thick), a flat base, and two horizontal strap handles on the exterior. The sculpted detail on the piece depicts ten sinuous serpentine figures in

108

relief. Ending in slightly thickened triangular heads, the figures portray snakes; eight of them appear to emerge from the underside, wind up the sides, and stop atop the lip. A large, rough hole on the base may be evidence that the vessel was once attached to a pedestal base, the depression may represent a cave or entrance into the underworld from which these creatures emerge. Two bicephalous snakes are located on either side of the broken handles, which are now missing; curiously, these snakes are rendered smaller than the other figures. The sculpted basin alludes to Inca beliefs concerning the close connection between serpents, water, the underworld, and agricultural fertility.

Cat. No. 109
Stone Bowl with Feline Handle
Cat. No. YPM 17446
Late Horizon, Inca
Cuzco
Height: 4.0 in. (10.1 cm)
Length: 9.0 in. (23.0 cm)
Diameter: 6.3 in. (16.0 cm)
Depth: 2.9 in. (7.4 cm)

Related objects: Jones 1964, fig. 19; Purin 1990: 183, fig. 232; Willey 1974, fig. 434

This vessel, a squat and spherical incurving bowl, was made of very dark gray igneous stone, possibly basalt. It has a flat base, convex exterior walls, and a horizontally beveled rim. On opposite sides, just below the exterior lip, were thick rectangular handles, each with a slight circular depression in the middle, probably to facilitate gripping with thumbs. On top of one of the handles is a modeled figure that resembles a feline reclining on its right side. The front and hind legs, represented in pairs, extend away from the animal's body. The head is rendered as a thickened protuberance and is detailed with an ax-shaped nose, circular eyes, and curving ears separated by a notched cleft. A deep groove separates the dorsal side of the body from the rectangular handle. The opposite damaged handle was once adorned with a similar figure, traces of which are still evident, including the raised impressions of the legs. Frequent and rough grinding striations

110

These objects, known in Quechua as *conopas* or *illas*, were utilized in ceremonies to ensure the health and fertility of the animals in question. In many cases, a cylindrical depression was carved into the back of the effigy for the placement of items favored in ritual offerings such as animal fat, maize kernels, coca leaves, and seashells. These Inca ritual tools were described by the Spanish chroniclers and in the writings of Catholic priests involved in the campaigns to extirpate idolatry (Flores Ochoa et al. 1998: 196–97). Perhaps because of the enormous economic importance of camelid herding in the high pasturelands of Peru and Bolivia, the most common ritual effigies were of alpacas and llamas, although other animals, such as birds, were sometimes represented. Ritual paraphernalia of this kind was not encountered at Machu Picchu during Bingham's 1912 excavations, but camelid conopas similar to the ones shown here were recovered in the recent excavations directed by Fernando Astete (personal communication 2003).

suggest that this figure was obliterated after its original production.

Cat. No. 110
Mortar with Recumbent Feline
Cat. No. YPM 17451
Late Horizon, Inca
Cuzco
Height: 4.0 in. (10.3 cm)
Length: 11.0 in. (28.0 cm)
Width: 9.8 in. (25.0 cm)
Depth: 2.1 in. (5.3 cm)

This stone effigy mortar, acquired by Bingham in Cuzco, was made of dark black stone flecked with a grayish white mineral. The specimen shows convex exterior walls and elaborate modeling along the base. The exterior surfaces are rough, while the interior is smooth from polishing and wear. The mortar depicts a feline lying on its right side, with its short legs extending away from the torso. A thick raised band, perhaps representing a rope, emerges from the back to wrap around the head; this may explain the feline's seemingly idle and vulnerable pose. The artisan empha-

sized facial features, particularly the large horizontal mouth, the eyes, and the upturned ear lobes separated by a cleft. No tail is represented.

Zoomorphic Ceremonial Containers and Effigies
Highly polished effigies of camelids and other animals were the most common naturalistic stone carvings produced by Inca artists. As in the case of the decorated stone mortars, animals were represented in a highly stylized manner as if to convey the essence of the animal without the distraction provided by individual details. The stone utilized for these images was carefully selected, and the color and grain of the stone often relate to the physical appearance of the animal being represented. The smooth polished surface and curved contours of these representations is reminiscent of water-worn stone and sometimes suggests natural rather than manufactured objects.

Cat. No. 111
Alpaca Conopa
Cat. No. YPM 17417
Late Horizon, Inca
Cuzco
Length: 8.0 in. (20.4 cm)
Width: 3.1 in. (8.0 cm)
Height: 7.3 in. (18.7 cm)
Related objects: Anders 1984: 379; Anton 1962, fig. 157a; Disselhoff 1967: 52; Fauvet-Berthelot and Lavallee 1987: 121, fig. 352; Jones 1964, figs. 24, 25; LaFarge 1981: 153; Laurencich 2000: 221, fig. 224; Lumbreras 1975: 287, fig. 301; Morris and Von Hagen 1993: 172, fig. 160; Stierlin 1984: 196, fig. 198

This large stone *conopa* has the form of an alpaca. The specimen is made of light brown grainy stone with white streaks. The alpaca is standing with its

112

neck extending upward and its mouth open — as if breathing heavily. Emphasis is given to the orderly folds of camelid hair draped around the neck, depicted by eight diagonal incisions. Subtle modeling, in the form of low relief, hints at the presence of short legs and a tail. More elaborate detail is reserved for the face, which features slightly upturned ears, a mouth agape, and distinctive protuberances for the nostrils and eyes. Most of the surface has a dull rough finish, except the legs and hair folds, which show evidence of polishing. On the back of the figurine is a small circular depression that opens into a cavity 1.0 in. (2.5 cm) deep and about 1.4–1.6 in. (3.5–4.0 cm) wide. Parts of the torso, especially the left side, are blackened due to burning.

Cat. No. 112
Alpaca Conopa
Cat. No. YPM 16910
Late Horizon, Inca
Cuzco
Length: 4.7 in. (11.9 cm)
Width: 2.1 in. (5.4 cm)
Height: 3.5 in. (8.9 cm)

This small effigy of an alpaca is sculpted from hard black stone with white diagonal streaks. In form and style it is very similar to other alpaca *conopas* acquired by Bingham. As in the other conopas, the animal is shown with orderly hair folds draped around the neck, a short tail, and an open mouth; a small cavity is on the animal's back. This specimen contains a distinctive white streak that runs across the entire animal from tail to the head via the back and abdomen, giving the impression of natural hair coloring. Emphasis is given especially to the tail, which ends as a dangling rounded tip, and the portion of hair covering the alpaca's eyes, which is shorn across straight and wraps around to connect to a fold of neck hair. The hole measures 1.4 in. (3.5 cm) deep and 0.9 in. (2.3 cm) wide at the opening; it is somewhat wider within the vessel cavity. The entire piece is smoothed and polished to a low luster, except on the flat base.

Cat. No. 113
Alpaca Conopa
Cat. No. YPM 17352

Late Horizon, Inca
Cuzco
Length: 5.1 in. (12.9 cm)
Width: 2.1 in. (5.3 cm)
Height: 3.3 in. (8.4 cm)
Depth: 1.2 in. (3.0 cm)

This third example of an alpaca *conopa* is sculpted from highly polished black stone. Like Cat. No. 112, the effigy figurine shows six folds of hair falling from the neck and a distinctive shorn portion of hair wrapping over the eyes. The figure also has an open mouth, two ear protuberances, and a short, curving tail with a rounded tip. The hole measures 1.3 in. (3.2 cm) deep and 1.3 in. (3.1 cm) wide at the opening and is somewhat wider within the vessel cavity. The specimen rests on a flat base. According to Spanish chroniclers, black alpacas were required as offerings on special ceremonial occasions.

Cat. No. 114
Llama Conopa
Cat. No. YPM 17359
Late Horizon, Inca
Cuzco
Height: 0.8 in. (2.0 cm)
Length: 1.9 in. (4.8 cm)
Diameter: 1.5 in. (3.8 cm)

This miniature *conopa* carved from light green stone with irregular black and white streaks depicts a llama. The bulging, perhaps pregnant, torso of the animal serves to accommodate the round, concave, bowl-like depression. Modeled raised areas represent the four legs and tail; extending away from the bowl is the llama's head. The entire specimen is smooth and polished to a medium luster. The hollow depression is slightly darkened, perhaps from the burning of llama fat offerings. Since conopas were used in fertility rituals, it is not surprising that pregnant llamas may have been portrayed.

113

Cat. No. 115
Bird Effigy
Cat. No. YPM 17393
Late Horizon, Inca
Cuzco
Length: 4.9 in. (12.4 cm)
Width: 3.1 in. (8.0 cm)
Height: 3.8 in. (9.6 cm)

This *illa* of light brown stone with thin dusky red stripes is sculpted in the form of a sitting or resting bird. The stylized sculpture features subtle modeling, particularly on the head, chest, and wings. The bird is represented as healthy, with a rotund chest and heavy midsection. The base of the sculpture is slightly raised, perhaps to represent the skinfold of a resting bird or the edge of a stylized nest. The hemispherical head contains two raised eyes, located on either side of a downward-pointing and tapering beak. The wings, meanwhile, occupy rounded sides extending away from sloping, flat portions of the back. Two simple grooves at the wing tips define a triangular tail.

The craftsman selected the stone intentionally and used its variable col-

oration to highlight features of the effigy. Wide natural stripes accentuate the curvatures of the wings, feathers, and shoulders; the bulging chest is emphasized by tighter, more narrowly spaced stripes, while above, the head is rendered with very few lines. Like many modern illas, the back of the representation lacks a depression or receptacle.

Cat. No. 116
Bird Effigy
Cat. No. YPM 17396
Late Horizon, Inca
Cuzco
Length: 6.7 in. (17.0 cm)
Width: 3.5 in. (8.8 cm)
Height: 4.2 in. (10.7 cm)

This carving portrays a bird and was made from dark brown stone with many light-colored mineral flecks. Three avian body elements are suggested by simple but careful modeling of the head, wings, and tail. The head protrudes from the torso as a cylindrical element, rounded and thickened along the top edge; no facial features, except the tapering tip of the beak, are detailed. The flat, tear-shaped wings, separated along the back by a large groove, curve gently around the side of the body. Like the head, the tail extends from the body with little superfluous detail. The base is slightly convex and rounded, especially along the outer edges. As in other examples, the stone's

115

natural inclusions — in this case, of densely packed light-brown flecks — represent the natural coloration of the bird's plumage.

Cat. No. 117
Camelid Herd Effigy
Cat. No. YPM 17416
Late Horizon, Inca
Cuzco
Length: 8.0 in. (20.2 cm)
Width: 5.1 in. (13.1 cm)
Height: 3.1 in. (7.9 cm)

This unusual object is a triangular stone sculpture made from fine-grained black stone. The entire specimen is polished to a medium luster, including the flattened base; the narrow tip is slightly broken. Eighteen irregularly shaped nubbins dominate the object and seem to portray a group of grazing camelids, huddled together across a sloping hilltop. The heads and backs of the animals are clearly indicated; some of the heads feature small raised ears. Two pairs of raised bumps along the wide end of the object may represent several others schematically. Like the more common alpaca and llama effigies, portable sculptures such as this one may have been used as religious offerings to ensure the health and abundance of camelid herds. The triangular shape of the illa may symbolize a mountain or, alternatively, an ear of maize.

Anthropomorphic Stone Effigies
The range and significance of portable stone carvings sculpted by Inca artisans is poorly understood. While conopas or illas representing alpacas, llamas, and maize are commonly illustrated, other representations have been overlooked. In addition to effigies representing creatures other than camelids, there are portable sculptures that combine anthropomorphic and other elements in distinctive ways. During his time in

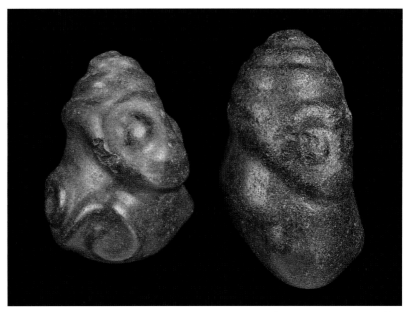

118

Cuzco, Bingham acquired several examples of these carvings from private collections, and a selection of these is shown here. Similar objects are on display at the Museo Inka in Cuzco, where they are referred to as *ch'urukuna*.

Cat. No. 118
Anthropomorphic Effigies
Cat. No. YPM 17418 (*left*)
Late Horizon, Inca
Cuzco
Length: 3.9 in. (10.0 cm)
Width: 4.3 in. (11.0 cm)
Height: 6.5 in. (16.5 cm)

This is a remarkable sculpture shaped from dark brown water-worn stone cobble. The entire sculpture is smooth and polished to a dull luster. It depicts a composite of three different elements. The main representation is of an anthropomorphic head with a distinctive nose, bulbous eyes, and a spiral headdress. On the head's left side is a quadrangular pillow-like representation with two rounded protuberances. On the

other side is an S-shaped volute possibly related to Inca representations of serpents. When laid on its side, the effigy resembles a large marine shell because the spirals of the headdress mimic the form of a conch; the two protuberances resemble conical projections common to shells. The precise function of the sculpture is not clear, although it seems plausible that it functioned in local religious rituals, perhaps as a representation of a household or community divinity. The serpentine and conch-like elements suggest that the image had associations with water and agricultural fertility.

Cat. No. YPM 17421 (*right*)
Late Horizon, Inca
Cuzco
Length: 4.0 in. (10.1 cm)
Width: 4.5 in. (11.5 cm)
Height: 7.8 in. (20.0 cm)

This stone carving is sculpted from dark, grainy, rounded rock. Its main feature is an anthropomorphic oval head, with raised circular eyes and curving tri-

120

grained quadrangular black stone, is decorated with representations in low relief. The entire specimen is polished to a dull luster, particularly the natural flat facets of the stone. The main figure is a highly stylized anthropomorphic face, with an ax-shaped nose, raised circular eyes, and a grooved oval mouth. The head is adorned by a headdress with crown-like projections. Curving grooves depict the shoulders to each side of the head. The back of the object contains a serpent figure, which may be a metaphorical substitution for the main figure's hair.

Stone Architectural Effigy
Cat. No. 120
The Field Museum
Cat. No. 2731
Neg. #A114207d, Photographer John Weinstein
Late Horizon, Inca
Height: 9.0 in. (23.0 cm)
Width: 6.1 in. (15.5 cm)
Related object: Niles 1999: 283, fig. 9.13

The Spanish chroniclers frequently refer to the use of architectural miniatures or models when discussing the ambitious constructions of Inca emperors. According to the historical accounts, models usually were made of clay or perishable materials, but few such models have survived. However, some miniature representations of Inca buildings exist because they were carved in stone. This piece, for example, represents a two-story tower with a flat roof and rectangular windows on the upper floor. Entrance to the building is provided by double-jambed doors on two sides. Additional architectural detail seems to be indicated on one side by graffiti-like depictions of rectangular shapes flanking one of the *hornacinas* and a nested square above it; on another building, roughly square shapes are etched on either side of the doorway. These etched forms may represent

angular nose. No mouth is depicted. The figure wears a conical headdress that coils to a rounded tip. The body of the figure is largely smooth and rounded; two raised bumps may represent stylized breasts or flexed knees or elbows. The sculpture's detail, especially the conical headdress and rounded base, resembles the overall form of a strombus shell. The back of the sculpture appears to be either unworked or roughened from post-production damage. Like YPM No. 17418, which it resembles, this carving may

represent a local deity and may have been utilized in household or village rituals.

Cat. No. 119
Anthropomorphic Effigy
Cat. No. YPM 17420
Late Horizon, Inca
Cuzco
Length: 3.8 in. (9.7 cm)
Width: 4.1 in. (10.3 cm)
Height: 5.2 in. (13.3 cm)

This unique object, made from fine-

niches, outer wall ornamentation, or some other architectural element.

The stone model is particularly valuable because no Inca buildings of this kind have survived intact. The building appears to be related to the style favored in royal architecture by Huayna Capac, since such imposing features are present in that ruler's royal estate at Quispiguanca near Yucay. In fact, the structure in the stone object resembles the gatehouses and portal at Quispiguanca (Niles 1999: 186, plate 1). Towers such as this one are absent in the royal estates of Pachacuti, such as Machu Picchu, and they may represent innovative developments in late Inca architecture. The function of this stone effigy is uncertain. It could have been created as an architectural model or as a ritual effigy of an existing building or special class of buildings with special religious significance.

Cat. No. 121
Stone Model
Cat. No. YPM 17355
Late Horizon, Inca
Cuzco
Length: 3.1 in. (7.9 cm)
Width: 2.8 in. (7.2 cm)
Height: 2.4 in. (6.2 cm)

This unusual object appears to be a miniature representation of an Inca seat or altar. The dark red stone object rests on a flattened base (with a pitted center) and has two main sides. Each side contains a niche-like feature, and they are separated by a curvilinear section of stone. In spirit, if not in detail, this piece is strongly reminiscent of carved stone outcrops at sites such as Qenqo and Machu Picchu.

Ground-Stone Boxes
During the excavations in the Snake Rock sector at Machu Picchu, the Yale Peruvian Scientific Expedition encountered the shattered remains of two

122

finely carved stone boxes. No comparable objects have been found in controlled archaeological excavations before or since the 1912 investigations. There were no lids with the stone receptacles, and it is likely that they lacked covers or utilized ones made of perishable material. The function of these containers is unknown, but given where they were found and the symbols carved on their sides, it is possible that they were used in elite activities associated with religious rituals. Rowe (1946: 248) speculated that they could have been used in ceremonies, perhaps to catch the blood of sacrificed animals. The chips and other evidence of wear on the edges and bottoms of these objects suggest that they were utilized on numerous occasions.

Cat. No. 122
Decorated Stone Box
Cat. No. YPM 16937
Late Horizon, Inca
Machu Picchu, near Snake Rock
Length: 3.7 in. (9.5 cm)
Width: 2.1 in. (5.4 cm)
Height: 1.4 in. (3.6 cm)
Depth: 1.0 in. (2.5 cm)

Publication: Bingham 1930: 216, fig. 198; Hemming 1981: 71

This small rectangular box is made of soft, fine-grained, very dark gray stone. The box features straight side walls (0.2 in. (0.6 cm) thick), a flat base, a horizontal lip, and flat interior surfaces. A low-relief band, produced by carving and incision, is located on the upper exterior register. The band consists of a series of alternating panels bearing the following designs: nested rectangles, a circular spiral with an upper and lower band of parallel lines, and a narrow diagonal band that bisects a zigzag. Horizontal borders frame the entire band of alternating panels. The repetition of distinctive and contrasting geometric motifs within a horizontal band is reminiscent of the decoration on the fine textiles worn by the Inca royal lineages. The surfaces, except for the interior, are smoothed and polished to a medium luster. Grinding striations left from the production process are visible on the interior. This unusual container offers a simple yet exquisite example of Inca aesthetics and craftsmanship.

123

Cat. No. 123
Decorated Stone Box
Cat. No. YPM 16936
Late Horizon, Inca
Machu Picchu, near Snake Rock
Length: 8.0 in. (20.8 cm)
Width: 6.1 in. (15.5 cm)
Height: 2.6 in. (6.5 cm)
Depth: 1.9 in. (4.9 cm)
Publication: Bingham 1930: 216, fig.
197; Hemming 1981: 71

This medium-sized rectangular box is
made of the same soft dark greenish
gray stone as YPM 16937. It was produced in the same style and manner,
perhaps by the same craft specialist.
The box has flat side walls (0.4 in. (1.1
cm) thick), base, and interior surfaces.
The lip edges are beveled horizontally.
A low-relief band, produced by careful
carving and incision, decorates the upper register. Each side of the relief consists of a series of spiral designs fitted between corner motifs. The intermediate
spiral design consists of a central circular spiral, with upper and lower bands
extending in diagonally opposed directions. At the end of each band is a
jagged zigzag. The corner motif consists of a square greco-maze element
and a band of parallel horizontal lines.

On the left corners, the band emerges
from the top of the greco-maze element; on the right corners, the band extends from the lower portion. The open
areas left by the respective corner motifs
accommodate the zigzag projections of
the spiral designs. The exterior side
walls and lip are polished to a medium
luster, but grinding striations are common within the interior and along the
base. On one of the sides is a superficial
curved incision that may be the beginning element of a more complicated volute design. It is possible that the lower
plain register of the box was intended to
have been decorated with similar carving or, alternatively, that this graffito-
like incision was the result of post-
production activity.

Ground-Stone Tools

For most of Andean prehistory, including the period of the Inca empire, the
tools utilized for grinding, crushing, or
hammering were made of ground
stone. The stress generated by these
heavy-duty activities required selection
of hard, resilient raw material that
could withstand the stress generated by
repeated blows against other hard materials without cracking or crumbling.

Usually a stone of appropriate hardness,
size, and form was selected by the
stoneworker, and then its final shape
was produced by pecking with even
harder stone tools, such as a hematite
cobble, and then polished through the
laborious application of abrasives. Despite the increased availability of
bronze, the Inca continued to produce
ground-stone mortars, pestles, clod-
breakers, mace heads, metal working
hammers, and other tools. Some of
these objects, such as the sculpted
ground-stone mortars, were utilized for
religious ceremonies or other elite activities, but most of these ground-stone
objects were used for more mundane
purposes. At Machu Picchu, the 1912
Yale Scientific Expedition recovered
thirty-eight utilitarian ground-stone
tools fashioned mainly from igneous
and metamorphic rocks (Bridges 1994:
38).

Cat. No. 124
Pestle
Cat. No. YPM 18485
Late Horizon, Inca
Machu Picchu, near Snake Rock
Length: 8.1 in. (20.7 cm)
Diameter: 2.8 in. (7.2 cm)
Publication: Bingham 1930: 214, fig. 195
Related objects: Fauvet-Berthelot and
Lavallee 1987: 114, fig. 308

This object is a large conical pestle
made from hard dark gray stone, possibly andesite. The pestle shows polish
from wear on the bottom end as well as
some chipped areas, probably from
grinding use. The top end has been intentionally flattened but does not show
much evidence of intensive use. The
conical handle surface has been polished to a dull luster.

Cat. No. 125
Pestle
Cat. No. YPM 16708
Late Horizon

Machu Picchu, Cave 11a
Length: 11.2 in. (28.5 cm)
Diameter: 3.1 in. (8.0 cm)
Publication: Bingham 1930: 214, fig. 194

This unusual stone object, found in the burial of an adult female at Machu Picchu, was probably a large pestle or grinding stone. Made from greenish gray rock, it is long and roughly conical, tapering slightly toward its tip. The tip is truncated, so it could have been used as a hand-held pestle. The wider two-thirds of the specimen is flat and rough on one side. The other side is ground smooth and convex; this surface may have been used in rolling-type grinding operations.

Cat. No. 126
Pestle with Llama Head
Cat. No. YPM 17363
Late Horizon, Inca
Cuzco
Length: 3.4 in. (8.6 cm)
Diameter: 1.3 in. (3.2 cm)

This is a small pestle, with one end carved as a llama head. It is made from grainy black stone and is polished to a dull luster. The pestle is roughly cylindrical, with a rounded work edge at the base. The opposite end tapers into the neck and head of a camelid. Facial features are detailed, including two nostril holes, a horizontal mouth, and raised areas for the eyes. The ear flaps are carved in relief and incised, and they appear to be pointing backward.

Cat. No. 127
Pestle
Cat. No. YPM 17365
Late Horizon, Inca
Cuzco
Length: 5.4 in. (13.8 cm)
Diameter: 1.4 in. (3.6 cm)

This pestle, made from very dark gray and grainy stone, shows some evidence

of pitting. The shaft tapers gently toward the narrow end, while the thicker end has a subtle groove about 1.2 in. (3 cm) from the edge, perhaps to symbolize a phallus. Both ends show evidence of grinding, probably from its use as a pestle. The entire surface has been polished to a medium luster.

Cat. No. 128
Schist Disks
Late Horizon, Inca
Machu Picchu
Cat. No. YPM 18037
Diameter: 2.1 in. (5.4 cm)
Thickness: 0.3 in. (0.9 cm)
Cat. No. YPM 18027
Diameter: 3.9 in. (10.0 cm)
Thickness: 0.3 in. (0.8 cm)
Cat. No. YPM 18020
Diameter: 3.7 in. (9.5 cm)
Thickness: 0.4 in. (1.0 cm)
Cat. No. YPM 18067
Diameter: 1.6 in. (4.1 cm)
Thickness: 0.1 in. (0.3 cm)
Cat. No. YPM 18152
Diameter: 0.5 in. (1.2 cm)
Thickness: 0.6 in. (1.6 cm)
Cat. No. YPM 18097
Diameter: 1.6 in. (4.0 cm)
Thickness: 0.1 in. (0.3 cm)
Cat. No. YPM 18018
Diameter: 5.1 in. (13.0 cm)
Thickness: 0.6 in. (1.6 cm)
Cat. No. YPM 18153
Diameter: 0.8 in. (2.0 cm)
Thickness: 0.1 in. (0.2 cm)
Cat. No. YPM 18016
Diameter: 4.3 in. (11.0 cm)
Thickness: 0.6 in. (1.4 cm)

Thin circular disks carved from the locally available green chloritic schist were common at Machu Picchu (Bingham 1930: 200, figs. b, f, g), and 156 whole discordal schist pieces are present in the Machu Picchu collection. They were found in many parts of the site including Snake Rock, the Lower City, and the burial caves. One

group of sixteen small disks was found in a hole near Snake Rock (Bingham 1930: 204). As the disks in the exhibit here demonstrate, the sizes of these artifacts vary radically. Their diameters range from about 0.4 to 8.5 in. (1.0 cm to 21.5 cm), although most were 0.4–1.6 in. (1–4 cm) in diameter (Bridges 1984: 22).

The schist, with its naturally foliated structure, could be thinned by removing material either by grinding or by peeling off lamina-like flakes. Because the stone is soft, it could be easily cut to the desired shape using tools of a harder material. The final artifacts were produced by grinding with a rough stone, as evidenced by striations that run lengthwise along these objects. On some pieces the surfaces were finished, but on most pieces little effort was made to remove these traces of the production process. The edges of the disks were usually beveled and are thinner than the body of the disk.

Because the function or functions of this class of artifacts is unknown, Bingham considered them "problematical." Bingham (1930: 202) speculated that the disks might have been "counters," with the small ones representing single digits, medium ones serving as tens, and so forth. It is also possible that they were used for divination, or as pieces in games (Bingham 1930: 204). It seems more likely, however, that they may have been used for a more mundane purpose, such as stoppers in jars. If the latter interpretation is correct, the disks probably would have been wrapped in cloth before being placed in the vessel mouth.

Chipped Stone Tools
The Incas spread tin bronze metallurgy throughout the Andes, and metal tools became common for the first time in many regions. Nevertheless, the long-lived Andean practice of utilizing

chipped stone tools for some tasks did not disappear totally. The 1912 excavations recovered several chipped stones artifacts in the palace architecture and intervening open spaces at Machu Picchu. Some of these tools were made from materials such as chert that were available in the surrounding region, while others were produced from obsidian, an exotic raw material brought from the other side of the Andes.

Cat. No. 129
Obsidian Flakes
Cat. No. YPM 18254, 192016 A, 192016 B, 192016 C, 18253, 18241
Late Horizon, Inca
Machu Picchu, near Snake Rock area and the Sacred Plaza
Length: 0.8–1.5 in. (2.0–3.7 cm)
Width: 0.5–0.9 in. (1.2–2.4 cm)
Thickness: 0.1–0.3 in. (0.3–0.9 cm)
Publication: Bingham 1930: 199

Seven lithic artifacts recovered in 1912 were made from dark gray-black volcanic glass. All the specimens were small chipped flakes, blades, or cores (0.8–1.6 in. (2.0–4.0 cm) long). The general lack of more complex shaping and retouching indicates that these tools may have been produced for cutting and then discarded soon after their use. The presence of small chips on the edges of these artifacts provides evidence that they were actually utilized. In contrast to the cache of obsidian pebbles, these artifacts were found individually, scattered in the Snake Rock and Sacred Plaza areas (Bingham 1930: 199). Trace element analysis of the obsidian flakes indicates that most come from the Alca obsidian deposit in the Cotahuasi Valley of Arequipa, the traditional source of volcanic glass for the tools used in the Cuzco Valley. Two flakes, however, come from the more northern Quispisisa and Jampatilla obsidian sources, both located in the Department of Ayacucho (Chapter 6).

Metal Objects

The Inca drew upon three millennia of metallurgical traditions in the Andes to produce a wide range of objects from a variety of metals and alloys. Non-Inca metalworkers came from all over Tahuantinsuyu to Cuzco and other Inca centers, such as Machu Picchu (Chapter 3). One of the important activities at Pachacuti's royal estate at Machu Picchu was the production of bronze and precious metal objects that could be distributed as part of the political strategy of the royal family (*panaca*) (Chapters 3 and 7). Some types of metal items were rare or absent at the site, probably because they were not utilized there or because they were carefully returned to Cuzco when the site was abandoned.

Tweezers
Hinged tweezers, or depilators, were basic tools of personal hygiene in the prehispanic Central Andes. Indigenous peoples in South America generally have little facial or body hair, and in antiquity tweezers were used by men and

women to pluck out unwanted hair. The tradition of single-piece hinged tweezers is a long one in the Central Andes, and the Chavin civilization created similar objects over two thousand years before Machu Picchu was founded (Burger 1992: 204). Because tweezers were subjected to repeated pressure, the alloy used in their production required a mix that would provide the required toughness, to avoid cracking, without sacrificing the requisite elasticity. Judging from the metalworking by-products recovered in 1912, tweezers were among the objects being produced at Machu Picchu.

Cat. No. 130
Silver Tweezers
Cat. No. YPM 16677
Late Horizon, Inca
Machu Picchu, Cave 45
Length: 1.9 in. (4.7 cm)
Width: 1.9 in. (4.8 cm)
Publication: Bingham 1930: 187, fig. 157f; Rowe 1946: plate 78f; Rutledge 1984: 14, appendix

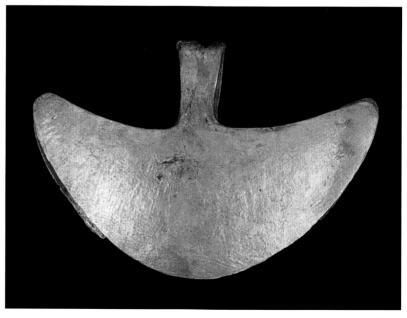

130

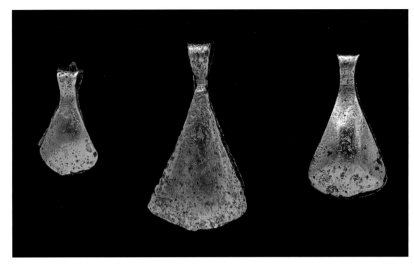

132

This crescent-shaped, large silver tweezer was found at Machu Picchu in the grave of an adult over thirty-five years of age, probably a female. During recent conservation, it was possible to join three pieces to restore the original form of this personal implement. Made of a binary silver-copper alloy, it was produced by cutting and hammering sheet metal and then burnishing the surface of the finished object. The copper in this object would have assured the toughness of the metal. The cross-member of the tweezers had been pierced so that it could be worn on a cord as a pendant or hung from a peg. The mining of silver and the production of precious metals was controlled by the Inca authorities, so it is likely that this specimen was given to the deceased individual as a symbol of royal favor.

Cat. No. 131
Silver Tweezers with Tear-drop Shape
Cat. No. YPM 17891
Late Horizon, Inca
Machu Picchu, Room 64A (Erdis 1912: 64)
Length: 1.5 in. (3.8 cm)
Width: 1.1 in. (2.8 cm)
Publication: Bingham 1930: 182, fig. 141; Rutledge 1984: appendix

Made of hammered silver of high purity, this beautiful piece corresponds to half of a silver tweezers. Like many depilators, this object was perforated so that it could be worn as a pendant, a secondary use that helps to explain the great care spent on polishing its surface. The hinge of the tweezers was a natural point of weakness, and the piece shown here is broken at this juncture. This artifact was found in a room in the Snake Rock area of Machu Picchu.

Cat. No. 132
Bronze Tweezers

While tweezers were produced from precious metal, they were more commonly made of tin bronze. Bingham (1930: 187) found half a dozen bronze tweezers at Machu Picchu. As this selection illustrates, the form and size of tweezers varied considerably, although the function and mechanical principle involved remained the same.

Cat. No. YPM 17893 (*center*)
Late Horizon, Inca
Machu Picchu, Grave 26
Length: 1.3 in. (3.3 cm)
Width: 0.7 in. (1.8 cm)
Publication: Bingham 1930: 187, fig.

157g; Eaton 1916: plate I, item 2; Rutledge 1984: appendix; Rutledge and Gordon 1987: 589, fig. 7

This artifact was recovered in the burial of a female. It has the characteristic size and curved blade of Inca tweezers from Machu Picchu. Made of a tin bronze alloy, it has an attractive golden color. The tin would have assured the elasticity desired in the tweezers, and the thickening of the metal just above where the instrument tapers would have strengthened it further. The fan-shaped blades of the tweezers display wear from repeated use. As in many examples, its central hinge has been perforated to allow it to be suspended.

Cat. No. YPM 17895 (*right*)
Late Horizon, Inca
Machu Picchu
Length: 1.0 in. (2.5 cm)
Width: 0.5 in. (1.4 cm)
Publication: Bingham 1930: 187, fig. 157a; Rutledge 1984: appendix

This small set of bronze tweezers has fan-shaped blades with rounded edges. It is well-made of thin flexible and resilient tin bronze. As in the other examples shown here, its cross-member is perforated.

Cat. No. YPM 17896 (*left*)
Late Horizon, Inca
Machu Picchu
Length: 0.7 in. (1.8 cm)
Width: 0.4 in. (1.1 cm)
Publication: Bingham 1930: 187, fig. 157b; Rutledge 1984: 52, appendix

This very small set of bronze tweezers has a curved blade with rounded edges. The metal was thickened to avoid breakage where the form is pinched. The cross-member is perforated so that the tweezers could be worn or hung; a piece of cordage remains in the hole.

133

Bracelet with Incised Decoration
Cat. No. 133
Cat. No. ypm 17873
Late Horizon, Inca
Machu Picchu, Upper City, Room 34A
Length: 6.0 in. (15.3 cm)
Max. Diameter: 2.0 in. (5.2 cm)
Width: 0.5 in. (1.3 cm)
Publication: Bingham 1930: 182, fig.
138; Erdis 1912; Rutledge 1984: 64–66,
appendix

This small hammered copper bracelet
was recovered from the excavations in
Machu Picchu's Upper City. Originally, it had a silver appearance produced by a surface enrichment technique, but only small patches of it
remain, owing to subsequent corrosion.
Three diamond designs are etched onto
the bracelet. The loop at one end of the
bracelet was formed by turning the end
back on itself; the other end was left
plain with slight rounding at the corners.

Silver Ring
Cat. No. 134
Cat. No. ypm 17874
Late Horizon, Inca
Machu Picchu
Diameter: 0.9 in. (2.2 cm)

Max. Width: 0.3 in. (0.7 cm)
Publication: Bingham 1930: 182, fig.
140; Rutledge 1984: appendix; Rutledge
and Gordon 1987: 592, fig. 10

This plain ring, made from a thick, flat
sheet of hammered silver, was joined together using solder. The squared edges
of the ring show evidence that it was
worn for some time. The ring was uncovered in Cave 53 (Erdis 1912: 37)
along with the remains of an adult male
and an adult female.

Silver Shawl Pins, or Tupus
Long pins, or *tupus*, were a basic element of female dress in the Inca Empire. The Incas did not use buttons, so
these items were essential to keep
shawls or mantles closed. Since all
women, from the most esteemed Coya
to the lowliest of retainers, wore such
garments, tupus were produced in great
quantity and are often found by archaeologists working at Inca sites. The quality of craftsmanship and the material
from which tupus were made reflected
the social status of the individuals for
which they were intended. In Inca
times, shawl pins were commonly made
of metal, although, as illustrated by the
Machu Picchu collection, they could

also be carved from organic materials
such as bone. The typical tupu has a
large head, sometimes decorated, on
top of a thin tapering shaft or pin. A circular perforation in the tupu head or
immediately below it would have allowed a string to be passed through the
hole and then wrapped around the pin
head in order to keep the garment
closed and prevent the tupu from
falling out. Used for over four millennia
prior to the expansion of the Tahuantinsuyu, tupus are still worn by women
in many highland Andean communities.

Shawl pins were among the most
common metal artifacts recovered at
Machu Picchu, and most were made of
bronze. Tupus of silver were precious
items closely associated with the generosity of the Inca state, which claimed
a monopoly on the mining of silver.
The association of silver with the female forces and the moon may have
made it particularly appropriate for the
manufacture of shawl pins. It is thus significant that a large number of silver tupus were found with the retainers
buried at Machu Picchu. Bingham mis-
took some of these for copper because
of the corrosion that covered their surfaces at the time of their excavation.
Their silver composition became obvious during the investigations of Rutledge (1984) and the conservation and
restoration by David Diestra of the
Museo Arqueológico Rafael Larco Herrera. The presence of silver tupus at
Machu Picchu probably reflects their
distribution to specially valued retainers
by the Inca elite. Their inclusion in the
burials at Machu Picchu signals the favored status of some of the *yanaconas*
(retainers) at the Inca court (Rowe
1982). The variability in the form and
size of the silver shawl pins suggests that
while some may have been locally produced, others were brought from production centers in the Cuzco area and
beyond.

135

Length: 9.2 in. (23.5 cm)
Max. Width: 2.3 in. (5.9 cm)
Publication: Rutledge 1984: 20–21, fig. 20, appendix

This silver tupu has a hemispherical pierced head and is similar to YPM 17881. The width of the cast heads of the two objects varies only slightly (Rutledge 1984: 20–21).

Cat. No. YPM 17848
Late Horizon, Inca
Machu Picchu
Length: 12.6 in. (32.1 cm)
Max. Width: 3.1 in. (8.0 cm)
Publication: Rutledge 1984: appendix

This large silver shawl pin with a spade-shaped head was cast and then hammered into the largest silver tupu recovered at Machu Picchu. Evidence of the production process has not been completely obliterated. Tear-shaped cavities exist at the junction of the head and the shaft, where the metal has not been completely smoothed; there are also elongated voids along the length of the shaft and abrasion marks and faceting that becomes more prominent nearer to the tip (Rutledge 1984).

Cat. No. 135
Cat. No. YPM 17881 (*leftmost*)
Late Horizon, Inca
Machu Picchu
Length: 9.3 in. (23.6 cm)
Max. Width: 2.6 in. (6.6 cm)
Publication: Rutledge 1984

This large silver tupu, restored from four large fragments, has a heavily forged hemispherical or semilunate head with beveled edges. The surface finishing of this piece is outstanding, but it is structurally weak due to the lack of adequate annealing during manufacture. Its central perforation and tapered shaft are typical of Inca tupus.

Cat. No. YPM 16679 A
Late Horizon, Inca
Machu Picchu, Cave 38
Length: 6.7 in. (17.0 cm)
Max. Width at Head: 1.3 in. (3.2 cm)
Publication: Eaton 1916: plate II, items 1016679b, 16679c; Rutledge 1984: 20–21, appendix

This is one of three small silver pins with flat hemispherical heads and circular perforations. It was found in Burial Cave 38 with a nearly identical tupu (YPM 16679 B).

Cat. No. YPM 17820
Late Horizon, Inca
Machu Picchu

Cat. No. YPM 17840
Late Horizon, Inca
Machu Picchu
Length: 8.6 in. (21.9 cm)
Max. Width: 1.6 in. (4.0 cm)
Publication: Rutledge 1984: appendix

This silver tupu has a spherical head form rarely recovered in the Cuzco region. Rutledge (1984) noted evidence of working on the shaft and head that allowed the two pieces to be joined.

Cat. No. YPM 17831
Late Horizon, Inca
Machu Picchu, Cave 76, approximately 218 yards (200 meters) east of the stairway

Length: 3.9 in. (10.0 cm)
Max. Diameter: 1.0 in. (2.7 cm)
Publication: Bingham 1930: 184, fig.
149a; Erdis 1912; Rutledge 1984: 52, appendix

This small silver pin has a perforated hemispherical or semilunate head typical of Machu Picchu.

Cat. No. YPM 17839
Late Horizon, Inca
Machu Picchu
Length: 11.7 in. (29.7 cm)
Max. Width: 3.2 in. (8.1 cm)
Publication: Rutledge 1984: appendix

This large silver tupu with a perforated hemispherical head is encrusted with mineralized cloth fragments. Rutledge (1984) noted abrasion marks at right angles to the axis of the shaft and on the head where it had been sharpened.

Cat. No. YPM 16679 B (*rightmost*)
Late Horizon, Inca
Machu Picchu, Cave 38
Length: 6.6 in. (16.7 cm)
Max. Width: 1.2 in. (3.1 cm)
Previous publication: Eaton 1916: plate II, items 1016679 A, 16679 C; Rutledge 1984: 20–21, appendix, fig. 20

This is one of three silver tupus from Machu Picchu with hemispherical, flat, and pierced heads. As noted, it forms a matching pair with another tupu also found in Burial Cave 38.

Cat. No. 136
Shawl Pin with Triangular Decoration
Cat. No. YPM 17843
Late Horizon, Inca
Machu Picchu
Length: 6.4 in. (16.2 cm)
Width: 2.7 in. (6.8 cm)
Publication: Rutledge 1984: appendix

The head of this shawl pin has convex sides, a rounded bottom, and a flat

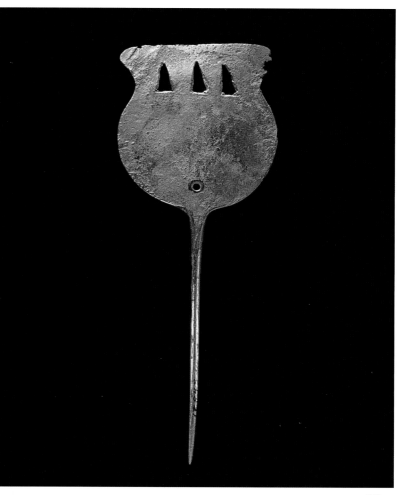

136

head. The form and proportions of the pin are unique in the collection from Machu Picchu. The three decorative triangular openings in the tupu head, perhaps created during the initial casting, are distinctive. The head of the tupu is very large in proportion to the shaft. These distinctive features are probably due to its manufacture outside of the Cuzco region. One of the few tupus with a form and decoration similar to this one is from Azapa in what is now northern Chile (D. Salazar et al. 2001: 71).

Cat. No. 137
Bronze Shawl Pin (Tupu)
Cat. No. YPM 17847

Late Horizon, Inca
Machu Picchu
Length: 9.2 in. (23.4 cm)
Max. Width: 4.3 in. (11.0 cm)
Publication: Rutledge 1984

This massive bronze tupu has a circular head that is unusually large when compared to its tapered shaft. One of the surfaces of this spherical head still shows evidence of hammering left over from the production process. The perforation of the tupu head is irregular and off center, and the metal left from punching through the tupu head to form the hole has been flattened against the surface rather than removed. The tupu also shows a crack that probably developed during manufacture. Compared with most of the tupus recovered at Machu Picchu, this was a poorly produced and finished object.

Cat. No. 138
Pair of Large Bronze Shawl Pins
Cat. No. YPM 17845
Late Horizon, Inca
Machu Picchu
Length: 18.7 in. (47.4 cm)
Max. Width at Head: 5.3 in. (13.5 cm)
Publication: Rutledge 1984: 20, 22, fig. 20
Cat. No. YPM 17846
Late Horizon, Inca
Machu Picchu
Length: 18.8 in. (47.9 cm)
Max. Width at Head: 5.7 in. (14.5 cm)
Publication: Rutledge 1984: 20, 22, fig. 20

These two massive tupus were recovered by the 1912 Yale Peruvian Scientific Expedition at Machu Picchu, but no other information on its provenance is available. The similarity in their form, size, and production suggests that they constitute a matching pair of artifacts. Both tupus have spherical heads with central perforations and a needle-like shaft. Rutledge suggested that their unusually large size could satisfy the owners' need to make an ostentatious presentation and that their lustrous appearance would make them suitable mirrors as well. Some very large tupus are shown in Guaman Poma (1980: 114). The great weight of these objects would have made their use in daily costume impractical. As an alternative, it could be suggested that they were used ritually in the dressing of inanimate objects, such as clothed stones. The dressing of sacred stones occurred during Inca times, and this practice dates back some four thousand years prior to Tahuantinsuyu.

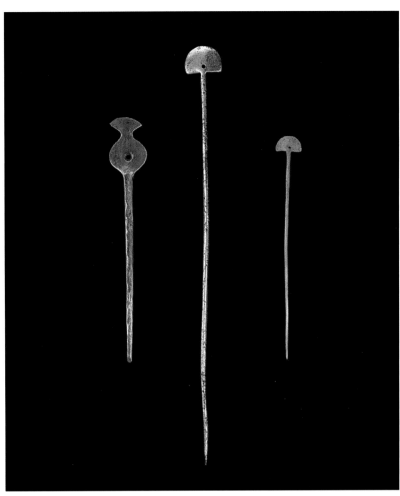

139

Cat. No. 139
Cat. No. YPM 17833 (*right*)
Bronze Shawl Pin with Semilunate Head
Late Horizon, Inca
Machu Picchu
Length: 6.1 in. (15.6 cm)
Width: 0.7 in. (1.8 cm)
Publication: Rutledge 1984: appendix

This tupu has a hemispherical head with a perforation. In his review of the distribution of Inca metal artifacts, Owen (1986: fig. 18) found that tupus with this form were widely distributed throughout Tahuantinsuyu. The examples he documented were concentrated in the central coast and highlands, the Cuzco basin, and the southern shores of Lake Titicaca, but some were found as far north as the coast of Ecuador.

Cat. No. YPM 17837 (*center*)
Large Bronze Shawl Pin with Semilunate Head
Inca, Late Horizon
Machu Picchu
Length: 11.0 in. (28.0 cm)
Width: 1.0 in. (2.4 cm)
Publication: Rutledge 1984: 20–22

This tupu is very similar to YPM 17833 but it is much larger. As with the other tupu, it has a semilunate head with a small perforation.

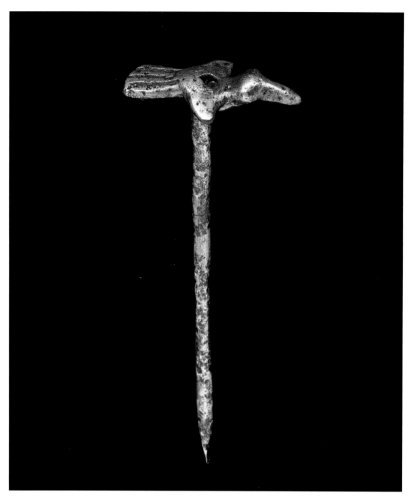

141

head so that a string could be used to prevent loss.

Lime Spoon
Cat. No. 141
Cat. No. YPM 17890
Late Horizon, Inca
Machu Picchu, Grave 26
Length: 2.1 in. (5.3 cm)
Width: 0.7 in. (1.8 cm)
Publication: Bingham 1930: 186; Eaton 1916: plate I, item 7; Rutledge 1984: appendix; Salazar 2001a

Small spoons were utilized to remove lime from specialized receptacles (*caleros*) as part of the coca chewing ritual. These tools resemble tupus, but their shafts are shorter and they end in a small, convex spoon rather than a point. The tin bronze object shown here was carefully cast to show minute details on the head of the spoon, which is shaped in the form of a bird in flight; special attention was given to the treatment of the beak and tail feathers.

Silver Headdress
Cat. No. 142
Cat. No. YPM 17872
Late Horizon, Inca
Machu Picchu
Length: 25.6 in. (65.0 cm)
Width: 1.5 in. (3.7 cm)
Publication: Rutledge 1984: 31–47, 52

This long band of silver is made from an alloy of copper and silver, with more copper than silver in the mix. Its silver appearance is due to the surface depletion of the copper. It could have been worn as a headband, and three holes have been punched in it so that it could become two different sizes. The silver sheet, heavily worked by hammering, is remarkably thin and uniform (Rutledge 1984: 52).

Headdress Adornment
Cat. No. 143

Cat. No. YPM 17844 (*left*)
Bronze Crested Shawl Pin
Late Horizon, Inca
Machu Picchu
Length 6.8 in. (17.2 cm)
Width: 1.0 in. (2.6 cm)
Publication: Rutledge 1984: 43–44, appendix

The head of this bronze tupu has the shape of a disc with a crest. The perforation of the tupu was placed in the center of the disc for reasons of design. The rounding of the shaft was incomplete and this piece appears to be a work in process, representing one of the final stages of shawl pin production (Rutledge 1984: 43–44).

Cat. No. 140
Bronze Shawl Pin with Aryballos-Shaped Head
Cat. No. YPM 17842
Late Horizon, Inca
Machu Picchu
Length: 6.0 in. (15.0 cm)
Width: 0.8 in. (2.0 cm)
Publication: Rutledge 1984: appendix
Related objects: Joyce 1912: 130, fig. 11C

This bronze tupu has a distinctive head in the form of an Inca storage vessel (*aryballos*); the sides of the miniature vessel are shown with vertical strips of metal. The head of the tupu was probably cast onto the shaft in a two-step process. A small loop so attached to the

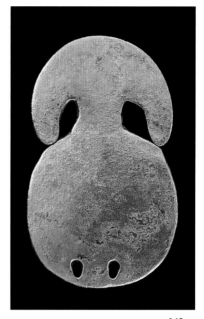

142

143

Cat. No. YPM 17878
Late Horizon, Inca
Machu Picchu
Length: 2.7 in. (6.9 cm)
Max. Width: 1.7 in. (4.4 cm)
Publication: Rutledge 1984: appendix

This silver headdress ornament was crafted by cutting and polishing hammered silver sheet metal. The composite shape of the ornament consists of a lunar form mounted on a sphere. Two perforations were made near the bottom so that it could be attached to a cloth backing. Analogous, but somewhat different, metal objects are shown in Guaman Poma (1980: 313, 315, 336) as headdress ornaments and pendants.

Silver Disks
Hammered precious-metal disks or bangles were widely produced in the Central Andes prior to Inca expansion. They were especially popular among the Chimu metalworkers of Peru's north coast, where hammered plaques of gold and silver were sewn onto shoes, tunics, mantles, neckpieces, crowns,

and other items of dress (e.g., Rowe 1984: 160, 161). This tradition continued into Inca times. The 1912 Yale Peruvian Expedition encountered several silver disks during their work at Machu Picchu.

Cat. No. 144
Plain Silver Disks
Cat. No. YPM 17886 (*right*)
Late Horizon, Inca
Machu Picchu, Snake Rock area
Max. Diameter: 0.8 in. (2.1 cm)
Publication: Bingham 1930: 187, fig. 158; Rutledge 1984: appendix
Cat. No. YPM 17850 (*center*)
Late Horizon, Inca
Machu Picchu, Section 41A
Diameter: 3.6 in. (9.1 cm)
Publication: Bingham 1930: 187; Erdis 1912; Rutledge 1984: 52, appendix
Cat. No. YPM 17888 (*left*)
Late Horizon, Inca
Machu Picchu, Snake Rock area
Max. Diameter: 0.9 in. (2.2 cm)
Publication: Bingham 1930: 187, fig. 158; Rutledge 1984: appendix

Five small silver disks were found together in the Snake Rock zone of Machu Picchu. The small disks were hammered, punched, and then hammered again. They probably were created to be attached to a headband or other type of textile. In contrast to the large disk, the small disks appear to be made from silver of high purity and were nicely polished.

Found along with the small disks was a large disk of silver foil that had been perforated so that it could be sewn to a textile or some other object. It was made of a low-grade copper-silver alloy, but the surface was enriched to produce the strong silver coloration. Prior to being discarded, it was folded and unfolded, perhaps in preparation for reworking at Machu Picchu into another silver object. At sites on the Peruvian coast, folded silver sheet metal from previously used artifacts sometimes appears in the kits or burials of metalworkers, so it is conceivable that all of the silver disks were going to be melted down and transformed into new objects.

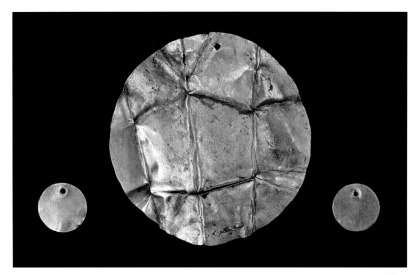

144

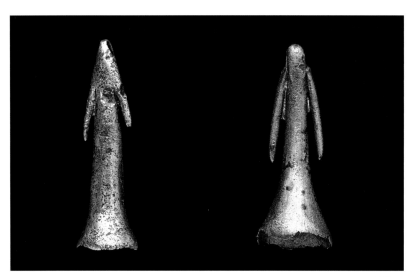

145

Bronze Bells
Cat. No. 145
Cat. No. YPM 18427 (*right*)
Late Horizon, Inca
Machu Picchu, Cave 57
Height: 1.4 in. (3.5 cm)
Width: 0.5 in. (1.3 cm)
Cat. No. YPM 18428 (*left*)
Late Horizon, Inca
Machu Picchu
Height: 1.3 in. (3.5 cm)
Width: 0.4 in. (1.1 cm)
Publication: Bingham 1930: 189, fig.
159d; Rutledge 1984: appendix

This pair of matching bronze objects
has a distinctive shape formally reminiscent of the cantu flower, a popular image in Inca art and poetry. Each object
has concave walls that flare at the open
base and two appendages that emerge
from the top. At the tip is a hole to permit hanging from a cord. Although
Eaton and Bingham suggested that
these were earrings or ear pendants,
scholars at the Museo Inka in Cuzco
have more plausibly interpreted similar
pieces as bells that were strung and
worn around the ankles during dances

(Guaman Poma 1980: 146, 297). Although these artifacts have no means of
attaching a clapper, they would have
made a ringing sound when they con-
tacted one another during dancing.

Silver Plumb Bob or Plummet
Cat. No. 146
Cat. No. YPM 18426
Late Horizon, Inca
Machu Picchu
Length: 1.3 in. (3.3 cm)
Max. Width: 1.3 in. (3.3 cm)
Publication: Bingham 1930: 188, fig.
153; Rutledge 1984: appendix

This is one of the most remarkable objects recovered by the 1912 Yale Peruvian Expedition. Identified as a bola
weight by Bingham (1930: 184), this
spherical artifact was cast in solid silver.
A casting core was employed to create a
recess within the ball that was crossed
by a pin. The object was finished by
hammering the outer surface, and the
blows left by this process are still visible.
The form of this distinctive object allowed it to be suspended by a string. It
differs so profoundly in form and production from the stone bolas that some
other interpretation would seem to be
called for. It is hypothesized that this
finely made object served as a plumb
bob rather than a bola weight. The use
of a precious metal for this object suggests that if it was employed as a plumb
bob, its use would have been linked to
ritual activities such as astronomical observations or construction of ceremonial architecture. Archaeoastronomers
have posited the use of a plumb bob in
the solstice observances at the Torreón,
and this object could have played such
a role (Dearborn and White 1983).

Bronze Mirrors
The use of mirrors for personal and ceremonial purposes has a long history in
the Central Andes. During most of Peruvian prehistory, mirror surfaces were

fashioned out of naturally reflective materials such as anthracite coal or pyrite (Muelle 1940). In Inca times, however, artisans produced tin bronze mirrors with a disk shape, a parabolic curvature, and a hang tab by which they could be suspended or held. These mirrors were made by specialized metallurgists who, at least in some cases, produced a silver surfacing on these pieces. In the drawings of Guaman Poma, adult males are frequently shown wearing items that resemble these parabolic mirrors around their necks during ceremonies and in battles (Salazar 2001a: 122). The first Inca queen, Mama Uaco, is depicted as viewing her image reflected in one of these mirrors while her attendants arrange her hair (Guaman Poma 1980: 98, 128, 134, 136, 140, 226).

At Machu Picchu, four mirrors were recovered. All were circular in form and parabolic in curvature. Owing to corrosion, little of the silver surfacing on these mirrors has survived. Most were found near Snake Rock in the southwestern sector of the site. Parabolic bronze mirrors with perforated tabs have been found at other Inca sites in the Cuzco drainage and around Lake Titicaca (Owen 1986: fig. 51).

147

Cat. No. 147
Cat. No. YPM 17877 (*upper left*)
Late Horizon, Inca
Machu Picchu, Station 9A near Snake Rock
Width: 2.7 in. (6.9 cm)
Length: 2.9 in. (7.3 cm)
Publication: Bingham 1930: 182, fig. 137a; Erdis 1912; Rutledge 1984: 64, appendix; Salazar 2001a

Like the other mirrors from Machu Picchu, this round parabolic bronze mirror has a perforated rectangular stem or handle. However, the specimen is unusual in having incised chevron designs engraved on one side of the stem or handle and upper edge.

Cat. No. YPM 18454 (*upper right*)
Late Horizon, Inca
Machu Picchu, Erdis's Station 9A (a small cave near Snake Rock)
Width: 1.4 in. (3.6 cm)
Length: 1.8 in. (4.5 cm)
Publication: Bingham 1930: 182, fig. 137b; Eaton 1916; Rutledge 1984: appendix

This circular mirror has the same form as the larger mirrors, but it is only a fraction of the size. Its parabolic shape and careful production suggest that it was designed to serve as a mirror as well as a pendant.

Cat. No. YPM 18480 (*lower left*)

Late Horizon, Inca
Machu Picchu, Grave 26
Height: 3.8 in. (9.7 cm)
Width: 3.1 in. (7.9 cm)
Publication: Bingham 1930: 182, fig. 137c; Eaton 1916, plate I, item 4; Mathewson 1915; Rowe 1946: plate 79d; Rutledge 1984: 36–40, appendix; Salazar 2001a: 121

This beautiful cast bronze mirror, made from an alloy of copper (94.35 percent) and tin (5.34 percent), was found in the grave of a 45- to 55-year-old woman at Machu Picchu. The mirror's "hang tab" is decorated with delicately delineated chevrons, and the entire artifact originally had a silver-plated surface.

Similar mirrors were recovered during the 1912 Machu Picchu investigations, but none were as large or elaborate as this one. It was polished to a brilliant surface and provided an even more reflective silver surface (Mathewson 1915; Rutledge 1984: 38–40).

Cat. No. YPM 17849 (*lower right*)
Late Horizon, Inca
Machu Picchu, Snake Rock area
Length: 4.2 in. (10.8 cm)
Max. Width at Head: 3.7 in. (9.5 cm)
Weight: 4.3 oz. (123.0 g)
Publication: Bingham 1930: 182, fig. 137d; Rutledge 1984: appendix

This parabolic bronze mirror has a damaged handle. Examination of the corrosion on it reveals impressions of leaves and cloth in the encrustation. This object may originally have been silver-plated (Rutledge 1984: appendix).

Tool Ornament
Cat. No. 148
Cat. No. YPM 17912
Late Horizon, Inca
Machu Picchu, near southeast side of Sacred Plaza
Length: 3.5 in. (9.0 cm)
Max. Width: 2.0 in. (5.0 cm)
Publication: Bingham 1930: 182, fig. 142; Rutledge 1984: 57–58

Bingham thought this bent cone–shaped object was an armlet, but a more plausible interpretation is that this hammered sheet metal object served as an ornamental top for a staff or ceremonial tool. Made of copper and silver alloy, its silver appearance is due to surface depletion. Much of the original silver color has been obliterated, but traces of it remain. The edges of this object were turned over and hammered down, and tabs were used to join the sheet together (Rutledge 1984: 57). In Inca times, it was customary to add precious metal ornaments to wooden tools

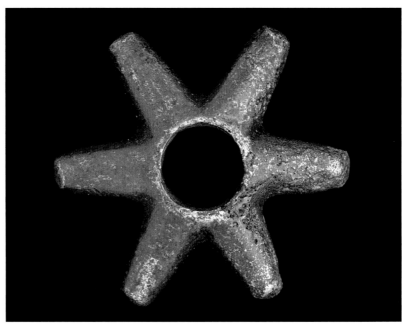

149

used on ritual occasions in order to distinguish them from simple utilitarian tools. A good example of this practice is the existence of gilded canal cleaning instruments from the south coast of Peru (Menzel 1977: fig. 8b).

Bronze Mace Head
Cat. No. 149
Cat. No. YPM 18425
Late Horizon, Inca
Machu Picchu
Width: 3.5 in. (8.8 cm)
Thickness: 1.0 in. (2.4 cm)
Bore Diameter: 0.9 in. (2.3 cm)
Publication: Rutledge 1984

The 1912 expedition recovered a single six-pronged mace head at Machu Picchu. Made of tin bronze, this object shows evidence of uneven cooling at the time it was cast. It has striations from polishing and wear from being hit against a hard object. As already noted, a mace head such as this one would have been hafted on a wooden shaft. The role of maces as accessories in royal dress has been noted, but the un-

remarkable quality of this object and the evidence of wear suggest that this mace head probably functioned as a weapon. Recent excavations at Machu Picchu have revealed evidence that mace heads like this one were being cast in the southwest sector of Machu Picchu (Astete 2001: 106). Bronze star-shaped mace heads were widely distributed through Tahuantinsuyu and have been documented in many areas, including the south coast of Peru and the shores of Lake Titicaca (Owen 1986: fig. 12).

T-Shaped Bronze Ax Heads
Like many classes of Inca utilitarian objects, T-shaped axes were produced for thousands of years before the emergence of the Inca state. However, in the case of axes, ground stone rather than bronze was the technology utilized for most of Andean prehistory. At Machu Picchu and other sites in the Urubamba drainage, T-shaped axes were commonly made of the tin bronze alloy associated with Tahuantinsuyu. Although bronze axes were relatively

common at Machu Picchu and other sites in Peru's southern highlands and Bolivia (Mayer 1994), they have not been well documented for the more northern highlands or the coast. As a consequence, they may not have been symbolically associated with the Inca state as was the case for tumi knives or tupus (Owen 1986: 32). It is generally assumed that the flat edge of the T-shaped ax head was hafted on a wooden shaft, enabling the tapered blade to be used as a cutting tool for the felling of trees and for other activities. Because of the mechanical properties of bronze, ax heads made of this material would have had considerable practical advantages over those made of stone. In the tropical forests of the eastern lowlands in the nineteenth- and twentieth-century, ethnographers documented the use of similar tools for the clearing of trees and brush in preparation for cultivation.

Both bronze and stone T-shaped ax heads were recovered in 1912 by the fieldworkers at Machu Picchu. Almost all of the bronze ax heads in the Bingham Collection show wear on the crossbar as well as the edge, suggesting that axes were sometimes used for hammering as well as cutting. This could mean that they were sometimes used without hafting or that they were hafted in such a way as to provide access to the flat, platform-like top of the crossbar. Like the knives, most of the bronze axes found at Machu Picchu came from within the palace complex rather than from the burial caves.

Cat. No. 150
Bronze T-Shaped Ax Heads and Chisels
Cat. No. YPM 17902
Late Horizon, Inca
Machu Picchu
Length: 5.1 in. (13.0 cm)
Max. Width: 4.3 in. (10.9 cm)
Publication: Gordon 1985: 312, 316, 319–23, 325; figs. 3, 5, 8, fig. 5; Rutledge 1984: appendix

This bronze T-shaped ax with crescent-shaped edge, made from an alloy of copper (94.3 percent) and tin (5 percent), was very heavily used judging from the wear on both the blade edge and the upper surface (Gordon 1985; Rutledge 1984). The working edge of this artifact contains striations and indentations that suggest the artifact was used on material harder than bronze, possibly on stone. The upper flat surface had been struck with such force that the crossbar is now concave (Rutledge 1984)

Cat. No. YPM 17967
Late Horizon, Inca
Machu Picchu, north wall of Room 24A
Length: 4.0 in. (10.3 cm)
Max. Width: 3.9 in. (10.0 cm)
Publication: Erdis 1912; Gordon 1985: 312, 316, 318–19, 325, fig. 4, p. 312, fig. 5 (no. 4), p. 31; Mathewson 1915; Rutledge 1984: 20–21, fig. 20, appendix

This classic Inca bronze ax, made of an alloy of copper (95.6 percent) and tin (4 percent), was discovered by Erdis during the 1912 excavations of Room 24A at Machu Picchu. The broken edge of the blade and the traces of hammer blows on the crossbar provide evidence of its use at the site. Gordon (1985) suggests that the crossbar atop the artifact may have been used to provide protection for the user's hand if the object were to be used in conjunction with a hammer.

Cat. No. YPM 17898
Late Horizon, Inca
Espiritu Pampa
Length: 4.2 in. (10.7 cm)
Max. Width: 5.1 in. (13.0 cm)
Publication: Foote and Buell 1912; Gordon 1985: 312, 316–18, 320, 324; figs. 1, 5, 6; Gordon 1986: 234–36, 239; Rutledge 1984: appendix

This T-shaped ax head has a broad, sharp edge and an asymmetric crossbar. Metallurgical analysis has demonstrated that it was made of an alloy of copper (87.6 percent) and tin (12 percent). During casting, the ax was subjected to prolonged annealing. The composition and manufacture of this tool would have allowed the tool to maintain its edge after repeated blows to organic material, and it would have been suitable as a woodworking tool (Gordon 1984). Analysis of wear indicates that the crossbar of this artifact has been hammered either on or with, suggesting a secondary use for this tool.

Cat. No. YPM 17900
Late Horizon, Inca
Rosalina
Length: 4.6 in. (11.6 cm)
Max. Width: 4.7 in. (12.0 cm)
Publication: Foote and Buell 1912: object 2; Gordon 1985: object 2; Gordon 1986: object E; Rutledge 1984: appendix

This T-shaped ax head, made of an alloy of copper (93.7 percent) and tin (5.6 percent), shows heavy wear both on its edge and on the crossbar. The wear is particularly heavy on the tapered blade, and the edge has been flattened and split. Gordon (1984) interpreted this tool as having been used for stonework. According to his study, the working edge of this artifact contains striations and indentations that suggest the artifact was used on material harder than bronze, possibly on large free stone structures where insertion into cracks and crevices was not required. Microstructural analysis has indicated that the working edge of the artifact was blunt at the time of its use. This artifact also contains small breaks and incomplete fractures or small cracks (Gordon 1985). The upper surface of the crossbar shows evidence of the tool having been used as a hammer. It was probably used for multiple purposes.

151

Cat. No. 151
Bronze T-Shaped Ax Heads and Chisels
Cat. No. YPM 17905 (*top left*)
Late Horizon, Inca
Machu Picchu
Length: 3.1 in. (8.0 cm)
Max. Width: 3.7 in. (9.5 cm)
Publication: Rutledge 1984: 41, appendix
Related objects: Mayer 1994: 3; plates 11, 45

This T-shaped bronze ax with a crescent-shaped edge was cast and then reworked by heavy forging; the joining scar where the two halves of the mold met is visible. As in several of the so-called ax heads, this piece could either be hafted or used by itself as a hand-held tool when grasped by the upper cross-member (Rutledge 1984: 41).

Cat. No. YPM 17904 (*top right*)
Late Horizon, Inca
Machu Picchu
Length: 3.5 in. (9.0 cm)
Width: 5.8 in. (14.8 cm)
Publication: Rutledge 1984: 41, appendix
Related objects: Mayer 1994: 39; plates 11, 45

This T-shaped bronze ax head has a crescent- or anchor-shaped edge, which is not common at Machu Picchu but is common on ax heads from sites in Bolivia (Mayer 1994). This tool was cast and then reworked by heavy forging; despite this, the joining scar where the two halves of the mold met was visible at the time of analysis (Rutledge 1984: 41). The edge of this artifact was broken and bent as a result of use on a very hard

material, possibly rock. There is also evidence of wear on the crossbar.

Cat. No. YPM 17907 (*bottom left*)
Late Horizon, Inca
Machu Picchu, Eastern Terrace
Length: 2.6 in. (6.5 cm)
Max. Width: 1.6 in. (4.0 cm)
Publication: Gordon 1985: 312, 316, 318–19, 321; fig. 8; Gordon 1986: 234, 236; Rutledge 1984: 14, appendix

This bronze chisel, made of a copper (93.1 percent) and tin (6 percent) alloy, is smaller than the bronze axes and lacks the distinctive crossbar. The absence of a crossbar would allow this artifact to be inserted into a wooden shaft or handle. There is considerable evidence that this tool was heavily used. Incomplete fractures and small cracks have been noted throughout the artifact, along with deformations from pounding the striking platform (Gordon 1985; Rutledge 1984). The cutting edge is dull, flattened by wear and covered with abrasion marks.

Cat. No. YPM 17908 (*bottom center*)
Late Horizon, Inca
Machu Picchu
Length: 4.7 in. (12.0 cm)
Max. Width: 2.4 in. (6.1 cm)
Publication: Gordon 1985: 312, 316, 318, fig. 5, no. 12; Rutledge 1984: appendix

This bronze chisel is well worn and is rounded on both sides across the top. The deep grooves across the artifact and nicks on the cutting surface suggest that it was heavily utilized (Rutledge 1984).

Cat. No. YPM 17899 (*bottom right*)
Late Horizon, Inca
Machu Picchu
Height: 3.7 in. (9.4 cm)
Length of Blade: 3.5 in. (9.0 cm)
Max. Width: 3.8 in. (9.8 cm)
Publication: Gordon 1985: 312, 316, 321–32, 324, fig. 7; fig. 5: "7"; Rutledge 1984: appendix

This T-shaped ax head from Machu Picchu is unusual in having very high copper content (98.7 percent) and very low tin content (0.7 percent). Because of this composition, its utilitarian functions would have been limited. Despite this, the flat upper portion shows evidence of heavy pounding and the sharpened blade edge displays numerous nicks. A channel exists on both sides of the top of the artifact, possibly to facilitate hafting (Rutledge 1984).

Cat. No. 152
Large Bronze T-Shaped Ax
Cat. No. YPM 17906
Late Horizon, Inca
Machu Picchu
Length: 5.9 in. (15.0 cm)

Width: 5.5 in. (14.0 cm)

This bronze ax is unusually large and heavy, almost twice the size of most axes from Machu Picchu. It was, however, utilized as a tool. It was polished to sharpen its edge, and it shows wear from cutting thin objects. As with most of the axes, the crossbar also shows evidence of numerous heavy blows.

Silver Plate Handle
Cat. No. 153
Cat. No. YPM 17897
Late Horizon, Inca
Machu Picchu
Length: 1.8 in. (4.7 cm)
Max. Width at Head: 0.6 in. (1.5 cm)
Publication: Bingham 1930: 189, fig. 189; Rutledge 1984: 18, 35–36, 56–57, appendix

According to the Spanish chroniclers, the Inca royalty used serving vessels made of gold and silver. Although most of these were melted down by the Spanish, enough examples have been recovered from archaeological sites to lend credibility to these historical accounts. One would imagine that such vessels would have been used at a country palace such as Machu Picchu but that

they were returned to Cuzco when the site was abandoned. The silver handle shown here, recovered by Bingham near Machu Picchu's City Gate, constitutes the only empirical evidence of such vessels at the site.

The handle was made from several pieces of hammered silver sheet soldered together and shaped. The silver-plate handle is hollow and has an interior tube that supports the outer sheet. The vessel fragment resembles the bird-head handles of ceramic plates such as YPM 16950 and YPM 16449 in size and form, and it seems reasonable to postulate that this is a silver version of these pottery vessels. The beak of the bird is missing, and the handle is broken off at its juncture with the plate. The round eyes were made by pounding a boss against the interior of the sheet, a technique known as repoussé (Rutledge 1984: appendix). This silver plate fragment may have been discarded when it was no longer serviceable or perhaps artisans intended to rework it in future craft activity at the site.

Knives
Knives were one of the most common and widely disseminated metal tools produced in Inca times. Typically made

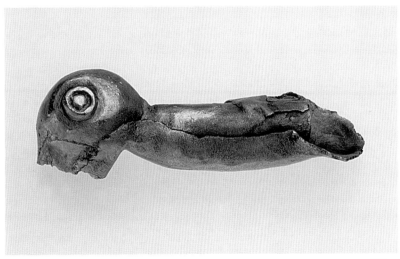

153

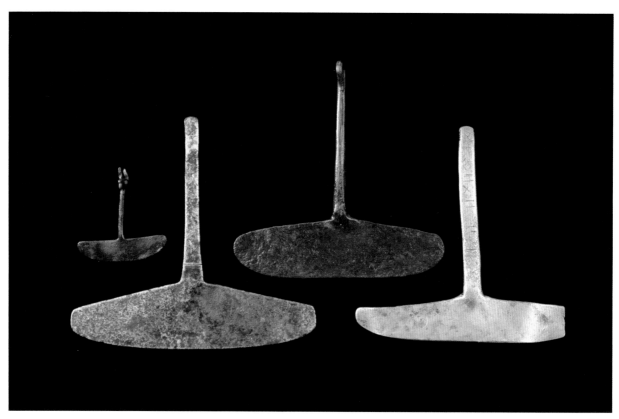

154

of copper or tin bronze, these objects, known as *tumis*, usually have long curved blades at right angles to the handles. The handles are narrow, and some have decorated heads attached their end. It is common for Inca knives to have a loop or perforation that permits them to be hung around the neck as a pendant. Comparative studies reveal that the variants of Inca knives were distributed throughout Tahuantinsuyu from Chile to Ecuador (Mayer 1994: 44–45, plates 48, 49; Owen 1984: 37). This class of objects appears to be linked to the state, and the government probably played a role in their production and distribution. At Machu Picchu twenty-three knives were unearthed in the 1912 excavations, constituting roughly 10 percent of the metal artifacts recovered. All but a few of these came from the palace complex. The four found in burial caves

were associated with males (Bingham 1930: 188).

Cat. No. 154
Cat. No. YPM 17868 (*left*)
Bronze Knife with Llama-Head Finial
Late Horizon, Inca
Machu Picchu, Cave 54
Length: 1.9 in. (4.8 cm)
Max. Width: 1.8 in. (4.6 cm)
Publication: Bingham 1930: 185, fig. 156a; Eaton 1916; Rutledge 1984: appendix

The handle of this small bronze knife, or *tumi*, is decorated with a finial modeled as a llama's head on top of a short, round shaft. A loop on the back of the llama's head would allow the knife to be suspended, perhaps so it could be worn as a pendant. The tool was made of an alloy of copper (96.8 percent) and tin (3 percent). Unlike YPM 17862, this knife

was cast in one piece. The knife is well sharpened, and abrasion marks from usage can be observed near the edge of the blade.

Cat. No. YPM 17862 (*second from left*)
Undecorated Bronze Knife
Late Horizon, Inca
Machu Picchu
Length: 4.7 in. (11.8 cm)
Max. Width: 5.15 in. (12.9 cm)
Publication: Mathewson 1915; Rutledge 1984: appendix

This plain T-shaped knife of tin bronze (copper 94.5 percent, tin 5.1 percent) has a rectangular shaft and thin intact blade. It does not have a loop for suspension and is not decorated.

Cat. No. YPM 17855 (*third from left*)
Bronze Transverse Knife with Loop Handle

Late Horizon, Inca
Machu Picchu
Length: 4.3 in. (11.0 cm)
Max. Width: 4.3 in. (11.0 cm)
Publication: Rutledge 1984: appendix

This heavy, undecorated bronze knife was forged on both sides. The shaft terminates in a hook made from a tapered point. The sharp blade shows evidences of marks parallel to the edge as a result of use.

Cat. No. YPM 17864 (*right*)
Decorated Bronze Knife
Late Horizon, Inca
Machu Picchu
Length: 4.3 in. (11.0 cm)
Max. Width: 4.2 in. (10.9 cm)
Publication: Mathewson 1915; Rutledge 1984: 64–65, appendix

This T-shaped bronze knife, made from gold-colored tin bronze (92.5 percent copper, 7 percent tin) has a handle decorated on both sides with common Inca geometric motifs. Rutledge noted abrasion marks across the blade as well as deep gouges that suggest use as a chisel as much as a knife. One extreme of the blade had broken off in antiquity, and stresses from use resulted in bending on both the vertical and horizontal planes. This is one of the few knives decorated on the rectangular handle or shaft. Both sides of the handle are decorated with a column of alternating rhomboids, X's, and horizontal lines etched into the metal.

Cat. No. 155
Duplex Cast Bronze Knife with Llama Finial
Cat. No. YPM 17962
Late Horizon, Inca
Machu Picchu, Cave 54
Length: 3.0 in. (7.6 cm)
Max. Width: 0.8 in. (2.0 cm)
Publication: Bingham 1930: 188, fig. 156b; Erdis 1912: 41; Gordon and Rutledge 1984: 585–86, figs. 1, 2; Mathewson 1915; Rutledge 1984: 53, 58–61, appendix

This small *tumi* with a handle decorated in the shape of a llama's head was recovered in 1912 from Cave 54 at Machu Picchu. The crescent form of the blade is typical of Inca ritual knives from Cuzco and other portions of the empire. Decorated tumis such as this one may have been used for ceremonial purposes, although their utilization on more mundane occasions should not be ruled out.

This unique specimen has special significance because of the unusual process by which it was produced. It was cast in two pieces, with the upper modeled handle being cast onto the lower stem and blade. The two sections differ in their metallic composition. The lower portion is a mixture of tin (3 percent) and copper, typical of many Cuzco Inca metal artifacts, and the upper section is a combination of copper with a higher amount of tin (9 percent) and, most surprisingly, bismuth (18 percent). A detailed study of this object by Yale geologist Robert Gordon (Gordon and Rutledge 1984) has concluded that the bismuth had been intentionally added to the alloy, perhaps in order to give the handle its unusual golden color and to facilitate the duplex casting process. This is the only documented instance of Inca experimentation with bismuth in its characteristic tin bronze alloys.

Cat. No. 156
Straight Knife with Modeled Fisherman
Cat. No. YPM 17973
Late Horizon, Inca
Machu Picchu, Room 24A near Snake Rock
Length: 5.1 in. (13.1 cm)
Max. Width: 1.8 in. (4.6 cm)
Thickness: 0.2 cm
Publication: Bingham 1930: 188, 192,

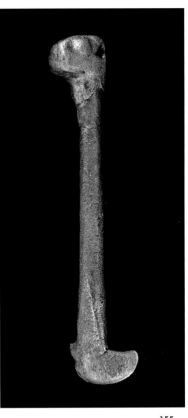

155

fig. 191, item 169; Erdis 1912: 31; Mathewson 1915: 583, 599; Rutledge 1984: 27, 29, appendix
Related objects: Jones 1964: fig. 54

This bronze knife, made from an alloy of copper (88 percent) and tin (9.4 percent), is unlike any other knife at Machu Picchu, having a straight rather than a transverse blade. During the Late Horizon, this form of knife was popular on the north coast of Peru (e.g., Jones 1964: fig. 54) but was very uncommon in the Cuzco area. The upper edge of the knife is decorated with a depiction of a fisherman and his fish. Bingham (1930: 191) considered it the finest example of casting found at Machu Picchu.

The details are remarkable — even the twists in the fishing line are shown. For this artifact, the metallurgist proba-

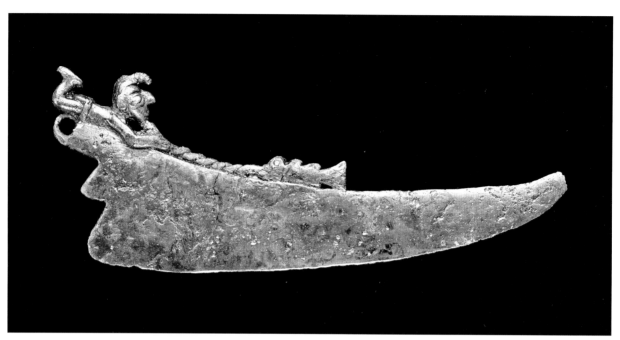

156

bly chose an alloy with high tin content for its expansion properties when cooling. This composition allowed the molten alloy to remain in a liquid state and consequently to flow for a longer time before solidifying, thereby filling the fine recesses of the mold. Bingham (1930: 192) described the scene depicted on the top of the knife as follows: "The boy has the characteristic beaked nose of the Incas; his cap has the usual earflaps; the expression of his face is one of grim determination and, judging by the eye of the fish, he looks as though he were having considerable difficulty in hauling in his prey. The right hand grasps the rope firmly with extended fingers slightly in front of the left hand, and the end of the rope touches the boy's chin. His feet are up in the air, and the general impression is given that he is lying on the bank of a stream, or possibly on the sea beach." A small loop beneath the fisherman would have allowed the knife to be suspended from a string and worn as a pendant.

Cat. No. 157
Crescent-Shaped Bronze Knife-Pendant

with Curvilinear Adornment
Cat. No. YPM 17876
Late Horizon, Provincial Inca
Machu Picchu
Length: 3.8 in. (9.7 cm)
Width: 2.2 in. (5.6 cm)
Publication: Rutledge 1984: 18, 28–30, 39, appendix

Many objects found at Machu Picchu differed from classic Inca creations in their style and production. This is the case for this crescent-shaped knife of tin bronze with wave-like projections from its upper edge. A loop at the top-center of the object was created for its suspension as a pendant. The unusual golden

157

194

158

musician is dressed in a loincloth with plied fringe, and a similar textile is hanging from the shoulders. A semi-hemispherical hat with a decorated border and a set of ear plugs completes the attire of this well-dressed man. The top of the cylindrical handle has a small loop so that the knife could be hung as a pendant.

Cat. No. 159
Knife with Pinwheel Motif Handle
Cat. No. YPM 7100
Late Horizon, Provincial Inca
Peru
Height: 5.7 in. (14.5 cm)
Max. Width: 6.2 in. (16.0 cm)

This large and unusual bronze knife with a semilunate blade was cast in a single piece and then hammered to give the piece its final form. Rather than having a solid shaft as its handle, it has an open geometric handle decorated with a pinwheel motif. The piece is an elegant example of Inca metallurgy, but it was also employed as a tool, and wear and damage are evident on its blade.

Cat. No. 160
Knife with Modeled Bird Finial
Cat. No. YPM 7101
Late Horizon, Inca
Peru
Height: 7.2 in. (18.5 cm)
Max. Diameter: 6.4 in. (16.3 cm)

This tin bronze *tumi* has a curved transverse blade and a cylindrical shaft that ends in a finely modeled finial. The sculpted image represents a crested bird; it holds a snake, with a missing piece of midsection, in its beak and claws. This finely cast piece must have been made in a complex mold using the lost-wax method. Despite the quality of this knife, it was heavily used and shows wear on its edge.

color of this cast bronze object is due to the higher proportion of tin (28 percent) incorporated into the alloy. The style of this object is also distinctive because of the crescent shape of the blade and the distinctive filigree-like elements that decorate it. The high tin bronze mix would have resulted in a longer liquid state, thereby giving the metallurgist more time to work the molten bronze into the recesses of the elaborate mold. Knives such as this one were not typical of Cuzco, and this distinctive piece was probably brought from another part of Tahuantinsuyu. Comparisons with Inca assemblages in other regions suggest that its source may have been the Cañari ethnic group from the eastern Andean slopes of Ecuador.

Cat. No. 158
Knife with Musician Finial
Cat. No. YPM 5205
Late Horizon, Inca
Cuzco
Height: 5.7 in. (14.5 cm)
Max. Width: 4.5 in. (11.5 cm)

This knife was acquired by the Yale Peabody Museum's first director, O. C. Marsh. It was made by the lost-wax method and was cast as a single piece. Its thick transverse blade has marks of heavy wear, and the sides are broken. The cast finial on the top of the knife handle depicts a flat, rectangular platform or raft on which an individual in a prone position is shown lying on a pillow and playing a kind of flute. The

159

160

Metal Effigies
Cat. No. 161
Gold Maize Effigy
L.1979.109.2
Mint Museum of Art, Charlotte, North
Carolina
Late Horizon, Inca
Peru
Length: 8.9 in. (22.5 cm)
Width: 2.8 in. (7.0 cm)
Related objects: Curatola 2001: 339;
Disselhoff 1967: 27

The central role of maize in Inca ritual
and subsistence was described by the
Spanish chroniclers (Murra 1960), and
it has been substantiated by archaeological research (e.g., Burger, Lee-Thorp,
and Van der Merwe 2003; Hastorf 1990;
Hastorf and Johannessen 1993). In addition to maize effigies (illas) that were
sculpted from stone or shaped from
clay, the Inca produced representations
of corn in gold. Some idea of the role of
these golden effigies can be gleaned
from historical accounts. In their accounts of the Coricancha in Cuzco, the
most sacred temple of the Inca, the
Spanish chroniclers recounted that

maize was grown in the ceremonial
courtyard, cultivated by the Sapac Inca
himself. The Incas also erected life-size
maize plants in the Coricancha courtyard at the time of planting, harvesting,
and during the major puberty ceremony (Rowe 1944: 39). Samuel Lothrop
(1938: 5) notes that one of the objects
collected as ransom for Atahualpa — "A
stalk of maize, of gold, with three leaves
and two ears" — was sent to Spain in
1534 rather than being melted down
into ingots.

The maize effigy shown here is a full-
scale representation of an ear of maize
with an indication of leaves at its base. It
is made of hammered gold sheet metal,
and great care has been taken to realistically represent the rows of maize kernels. It is possible that an actual ear of
maize was used as the model for the
hollow effigy.

Cat. No. 162
*Gold Figurine of a Seated Figure with
Tweezers*

161

Cat. No. 86.224.33
Brooklyn Museum of Art
Late Horizon, Provincial Inca
Lambayeque Valley (?), north coast of
Peru
Height: 1.8 in. (4.7 cm)
Publication: Jones 1964: 50, fig. 52

Small figurines of gold and silver were produced during the Late Horizon by joining and shaping hammered sheet metal. This tradition has deep roots on Peru's north coast that date back to over 1,500 years to the Early Horizon (Burger 1992: 201). The hollow figurine from the Brooklyn Museum of Art is made of gold sheet. It represents a seated male who wears a round helmet or headdress and circular ear spools. The figure appears to be removing facial hair with tweezers. The figure's arms are bent, suggesting movement, but his expressionless face is rendered in a stylized manner. His feet lack even the schematic treatment that characterizes the hands and face.

Precious-Metal Drinking Vessels, or Aquillas

The gold and silver drinking vessels the Inca artisans produced were emblematic of Inca wealth and power (Cummins 2002). They were also associated with the generosity of the state, since they were acquired as a result of royal favor rather than by purchase or exchange in a market setting. These drinking vessels were made in pairs for ritual drinking, which always occurred between two parties. The distribution of the *aquillas* and the material from which they were made was determined by social rank. Several sixteenth-century Spanish chronicles report that aquillas were among the gifts offered to unconquered groups prior to a violent confrontation; acceptance of the vessels and other signs of royal generosity symbolized capitulation and incorporation into Tahuantinsuyu. While wooden

162

and ceramic drinking vessels were used by the general population of the Inca empire, the Inca court and their provincial administrators were provided with aquillas for consuming corn beer. As illustrated by the drawings of Guaman Poma (1980: 126, 224), their role as symbols of high status was particularly conspicuous during state and religious rituals.

Cat. No. 163
Gold Beaker in the Form of a Man's Head
Brooklyn Museum of Art
Cat. No. 43.87.7
Late Horizon, Provincial Inca
Coastal Peru
Height: 3.3 in. (8.3 cm)
Diameter: 1.8 in. (4.5 cm)
Silver Beaker in the Form of a Man's Head
Brooklyn Museum of Art
Cat. No. 36.358
Late Horizon, Provincial Inca
Coastal Peru
Height: 3.1 in. (8.0 cm)
Diameter: 2.2 in. (5.6 cm)

The creation of ritual drinking vessels in the form of human heads predates the Inca by some five centuries, and

164

such vessels were widely used on the Peruvian coast during the two centuries immediately preceding Inca expansion. Beakers representing faces with prominent beak-like noses were particularly common during Inca times along the southern and central coast of what is now Peru (King 2000: 53; Menzel 1977). The almond-shaped eyes and simple upturned mouth on the two vessels illustrated here suggest that they were produced on the central or southern Peruvian coast. Effigy beakers were made by beating flexible gold or silver sheet metal over a solid wooden form (Bouchard 1987: fig. 378).

Cat. No. 164
Gold Beaker in the Form of a Man's Head
Private Collection
Late Horizon, Inca
Coastal Peru
Height: 5.9 in. (15.0 cm)
Diameter: 3.1 in. (8.0 cm)

This gold beaker, probably from the southern or central coast of Peru, resembles the Brooklyn Museum of Art gold beaker in many respects, although the treatment of the mouth, cheeks, and nose is slightly less stylized. This

165

specimen has a raised horizontal band above the forehead, corresponding to a textile sling used as a headdress. Of special interest are the two ears of maize (corn) shown on the back of the cup, images consistent with the idea that *aquillas* such as this one were used to consume corn beer. Other gold and silver aquillas are also decorated on their backs with maize motifs (Jones 1964: figs. 64, 65).

Male and Female Figurines of Precious Metal

Inca metalworkers produced small effigies of male and female individuals for use in special offerings. Made of gold or silver, these hollow or solid figurines represent individuals without distinctive personal characteristics. The sex of the effigies was made explicit through the representation of primary and secondary sexual characteristics, and it was not uncommon for the effigies to appear in male/female pairs. The modeled metal effigy itself was always shown without clothing, except in some cases where ear spools appear on males. On the other hand, special care was taken to represent the hairstyle of the figures. The hair of male figurines was short and adorned with cords wrapping horizontally around their heads. The female figurines usually are shown with long hair arranged in braids. Another gender-based difference is that male effigies sometimes were shown with a bulging cheek, signifying the chewing of coca; this detail is missing on the female figurines (Rowe and Rowe 1996: 302–4).

The naked appearance of these effigies is misleading. Figurines encountered in optimal environmental conditions, such as on snow-capped mountain peaks or in the coastal deserts, were elaborately dressed. These effigies wore miniature versions of male or female elite garments, including tunics or mantles, coca bags, and feather headdresses. In those cases where figurines were found without any clothing, such as in the central plaza of Cuzco, this usually can be explained by the destructive impact of the elements during the five centuries since burial.

Small gold and silver figurines are distinctive Inca artifacts, and they appear to have been an Inca innovation. Precious-metal effigies produced by the Incas have been encountered throughout Tahuantinsuyu; similar offerings were sometimes made of effigies carved from spondylus shell, a material available only off the warmer waters north of the modern Peru/Ecuador border. In recent years archaeologists and mountain climbers have encountered elabo-

rately dressed gold and silver figurines on the summits of mountains in southern Peru, northwest Argentina, and northern Chile (Reinhard and Ceruti 2000; Schobinger 2001). They have also been found on the Isla de la Plata, an island off the coast of southern Ecuador (McEwan and Van de Guchte 1992), and in the coastal temples on the north coast and central coast (Heyerdahl et al. 1995). Examples discovered on mountaintops are often associated with evidence for the Capacocha ritual, an important ceremonial act that involved the sacrifice of unblemished children. The remaining contexts suggest that the figurines were offered to the gods on other occasions as well. No gold or silver figurines were unearthed by Bingham at Machu Picchu, nor have they been discovered there during the subsequent decades of archaeological investigations.

Cat. No. 165
Male Silver Figurine
Dumbarton Oaks B-474
Inca, Late Horizon
Height: 8.9 in. (22.7 cm)
Width: 2.0 in. (5.2 cm)
Publication: Alcina 1979: fig. 714; Benson 1963: no. 419; Bliss 1957: no. 338; Boone 1996: plate 89

This large, hollow figurine representing an Inca male is unusually well made. The carefully modeled face with its almond-shaped eyes, straight closed mouth, and broad nose resembles other male figurines, as does the placement of the hands on the chest and the simplified feet. The bulge in the figure's left cheek indicates that he is chewing a wad of coca leaf, and the perforated and distended earlobes identify the individual as a member of the Inca elite; ear ornaments of perishable materials probably once adorned this figurine. The indented space on the upper head of the figure was designed to accommodate a

166

167

168

braided headdress of horizontal cords. Known as *llawt'u* in Quechua, these headdresses are sometimes represented on male figurines, and actual examples of such a headdress were found by Max Uhle in his excavations at Pachacamac (Rowe and Rowe 1996: 306). The headdresses could be black or multicolored; one example featured a pattern of concentric diamonds in red, blue, and yellow (Uhle 1903: 40). According to Heather Lechtman, most of this figurine was made from a single thick silver sheet that was hammered into shape and soldered at the back seam. The crown, ears, feet, and penis were made from separate pieces of silver connected to the body using solder or pressure welding (Lechtman 1996: 308–9).

Cat. No. 166
Male Gold Figurine
The Metropolitan Museum of Art
Gift and Bequest of Alice K. Bache,
1974, 1977 (1974.271.7)
Late Horizon, Inca
Height: 2.5 in. (6.3 cm)

This small hammered hollow gold figurine represents a standing nude male figure with his hands pressed against his

chest. The elongated perforated ears were carefully modeled and designed for ear ornaments. This figurine represents the braided cord headdress (*llawt'u*) rather than simply leaving a space for it. The representation of the cylindrical torso and limbs is schematic and crude compared to the detailed treatment of the head.

Cat. No. 167
Male Gold Figurine
YAG 2002.15.3
Yale University Art Gallery
Late Horizon, Inca
Height 2.2 in. (5.7 cm)

This small male effigy crafted from hammered gold sheet metal differs from the others shown here only in small details. For example, the penis is more prominent. The braided cord headdress has seven turns of the cord, rather than six, and it lacks the broader bands at the top of the headdress. At the same time, it resembles the other male figurines in the elaboration and large size of the perforated ears, the careful modeling of the face, and the schematic treatment of the torso and lower limbs. On this piece, the feet are

represented by flat rectangular pieces of thick sheet metal, with toes indicated only by straight incisions.

Cat. No. 168
Female Gold Figurine
The Metropolitan Museum of Art
Gift of Louise Reinhardt Smith, 1995
(1995.481.5)
Late Horizon, Inca
Height: 5.9 in. (15.0 cm)

This medium-sized female figurine is standing with hands pressed beneath the modeled breasts against her chest or ribs. The treatment of the arms and hands is simplified, and the lower limbs were modeled with even less care. The

169

170

knees and toes are not depicted. In contrast, the face was shown with care and the long braided hair was carefully detailed. This figurine, like most Inca female figurines, does not represent the ears, presumably because females did not wear ear ornaments, and the symbolic piercing of the ears to represent the achievement of adulthood was limited to male adolescents.

Cat. No. 169
Female Gold Figurine
The Metropolitan Museum of Art
The Michael C. Rockefeller Memorial Collection
Bequest of Nelson A. Rockefeller, 1979 (1979.206.1058)
Late Horizon, Inca
Height: 2.4 in. (6.1 cm)

This small, hollow gold female figurine strongly resembles the medium-sized gold figurine from The Metropolitan Museum of Art (1995.48.5). This piece, however, was less carefully modeled, and the breasts are only suggested rather than represented. The long hair is detailed, but the lower limbs received

only cursory treatment. The position of the arms and heads varies little among the figurines, regardless of sex.

Cat. No. 170
Silver Llama Figurine
The Metropolitan Museum of Art
Gift and Bequest of Alice K. Bache, 1974, 1977 (1974.271.36)
Late Horizon, Inca
Height: 2.0 in. (5.2 cm)
Related objects: Morris and von Hagen 1993: 226

Precious-metal figurines of llamas were produced with the same techniques used to make male and female figurines. This hollow effigy shows the llama recently shorn, with upright ears and a short projecting tail. As in the human figurines, the face was treated with some care but the body and lower limbs were given only slight attention. The genitals are depicted to indicate that the figurine is male. A silver llama figurine like the one shown here was recovered from the summit of the Llullaillaco Volcano in Argentina, in association with human remains, classic Inca ceramics,

precious-metal human effigies, and llama effigies carved from spondylus shell (Reinhard and Ceruti 2000: fig. 30). Presumably, silver llama effigies also were used in rituals related to the fertility of the camelid herds.

Bone Objects

Throughout Andean prehistory, objects were carved out of bones as tools, ornaments, and other items. With the increasing frequency of metal objects, bone appears to have declined in importance as a raw material, but bone objects continued to be produced, particularly as weaving tools. Bone artifacts were relatively rare at Machu Picchu, but there is evidence that some of them were produced at the site by the retainers.

Bone Shawl Pin
Cat. No. 171
Cat. No. YPM 17466
Late Horizon, Inca
Machu Picchu, Cave 85
Length: 3.4 in. (8.6 cm)
Width: 0.8 in. (2.0 cm)
Publication: Bingham 1930: 220, fig. 213; Eaton 1916: plate IV, no. 7; Miller 2003: 48

This polished bone shawl pin, or *tupu*, is unique among the materials Bingham recovered. Found in the burial of a gracile individual of indeterminate sex, it features an elaborately carved head and a straight shaft that tapers to a point. Most of the shawl pins encountered at Machu Picchu are made of metal, and this bone tupu displays exceptionally delicate workmanship. It is carved with the same image on both sides and depicts two perched birds in profile kissing or "billing." The wings are represented by diagonal incisions, and the tail features of each bird are shown along the edges of the tupu. The

171

rectangular form upon which the birds perch is decorated with two rows of circle-dot designs. Like metal tupus, this bone shawl pin is perforated immediately below the artifact head; this would have allowed a cord to be attached that could be use to secure the shawl and prevent the tupu from slipping out. Given the rarity of this artifact, it may have been brought from outside the Cuzco area. Similar artifacts are common at some Inca sites in Ecuador, most notably the Pucará de Rumicucho, a fortress-like site near Quito. Bingham (1930: 220) mentions

that a similar artifact was found on the coast of Chile.

Bone Pins and Weaving Tools
Cat. No. 172
Bone Pick
Cat. No. YPM 19620
Late Horizon, Inca
Machu Picchu
Length: 3.1 in. (7.8 cm)
Width: 0.3 in. (0.9 cm)
Publication: Miller 2003: 53

This bone shaft fragment was polished to a point so that it could be used as a tool. Judging from its form and wear patterns, it appears to have been used in textile production to separate or pack threads during the weaving process.

Cat. No. YPM 19623
Bone Shawl Pin
Late Horizon, Inca
Machu Picchu
Length: 4.3 in. (10.9 cm)
Width: 0.5 in. (1.2 cm)
Publication: Bingham 1930: 220, fig. 212; Miller 2003: 53

This bone shawl pin has a small oval head and a perforation at the top of its shaft to facilitate fastening and prevent the ornament's loss. It lacks the evidence of wear commonly found near the tips of bone weaving tools and appears to have been a poor woman's equivalent of a bronze or silver tupu.

Cat. No. YPM 19621
Bone Weaving Tool and Shawl Pin
Late Horizon, Inca
Machu Picchu
Length: 4.3 in. (10.9 cm)
Width: 0.5 in. (1.2 cm)
Publication: Miller 2003: 53

Beautifully carved and polished, this tool has a finely drilled hole in the upper part of the shaft. It was produced by sawing off the end of the bone and by

splitting the shaft to permit a tapered point. The tool was completed by carefully polishing the entire object. The truncated end of the bone constitutes the ornamental head of the tool. Considering its strength, form, and polish, its main function was probably as a weaver's tool, but judging from the perforation, it probably had a dual use as a shawl pin.

Cat. No. YPM 19624
Weaving Tool and Shawl Pin
Late Horizon, Inca
Machu Picchu
Length: 3.9 in. (9.8 cm)
Width: 0.4 in. (1.0 cm)
Publication: Miller 2003: 53

This bone pick was made by carving a fragment of shaft to a tapered point. It was perforated so that it could double as a shawl pin. The head of the pin was simply rounded rather than being carved into a distinctive shape. The tip of the tool was damaged in antiquity and is now missing.

Bone Flute, or Quena
Cat. No. 173
Cat. No. YPM 17525
Late Horizon, Inca
Machu Picchu
Length: 7.3 in. (18.6 cm)
Max. Diameter: 1.2 in. (3.0 cm)
Publication: Miller 2003: 49
Related objects: Olsen 2002: 40, fig. 3.2

This musical instrument features four equally spaced finger holes on the upper surface and a thumb hole on the bottom surface. Its distal end is cut lengthwise and notched to form a mouthpiece. While this object resembles modern highland *quenas*, it is different because it has two fewer finger holes and is made of bone rather than cane. This polished bone flute was made by carving the leg bone of a llama or an alpaca (Miller 2003).

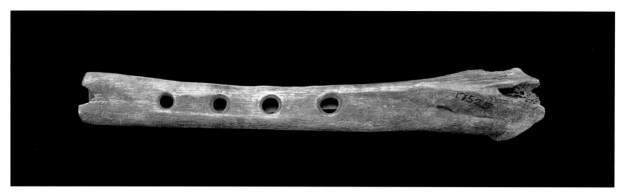

173

Incised Bone Tube
Cat. No. 174
Cat. No. YPM 17527
Late Horizon, Inca
Machu Picchu
Length: 3.6 in. (9.2 cm)
Diameter: 0.7 in. (1.7 cm)
Publication: Miller 2003: 48

Unique among the bone artifacts recovered at Machu Picchu, this polished bone tube was found in the ruins of the palace complex. It has a concentric diamond bisected at its midsection by two parallel lines. This motif is situated on a field textured by incised dots, and a pair of lines encircles each of the extremes of the object. It may be significant that the bone has been completely hollowed out and that both ends of the tube are chamfered and polished. While most of the artifact shows little evidence of wear, the broader end shows numerous small scratches. The purpose of this artifact is unknown, and a wide range of possibilities exists, such as a tool for the inhalation of snuff or, alternatively, as a spool around which thread could be wrapped. Decorated snuff tubes have been documented from an Inca mountaintop sacrifice at Cerro Esmeralda in northern Chile (Cornejo 2001: 109). Another possibility is that it was a needle case for these delicate tools of wood and cactus spine.

Bone Spindle Whorls
At Machu Picchu, weaving was an important activity, and the spinning of thread from camelid wool was a crucial component of this productive process. Toward this end, spindle whorls were produced from animal bone, as well as from pottery and stone. Spindle whorls made from bone were comparatively rare at Machu Picchu, but judging from the incomplete examples recovered during the 1912 excavations, they were locally manufactured from the bones of slaughtered llamas and/or alpacas. Because these bone whorls were comparatively light, it is likely that they were intended for the spinning of fine thread. At least five spindle whorls and spindle whorl blanks were recovered, most coming from Cave 56 of the southernmost cemetery of Machu Picchu.

Cat. No. 175
Spindle Whorl
Cat. No. YPM 196401 A
Late Horizon, Inca
Machu Picchu, Cave 56
Diameter: 1.6 in. (4.1 cm)
Publication: Miller 2003: 50

This spindle whorl was made by drilling the head cap of a camelid humerus. It was the only completed example encountered.

Cat. No. YPM 196401C
Late Horizon, Inca

Machu Picchu, Cave 56
Diameter: 0.9 in. (2.3 cm)
Publication: Eaton 1916: plate IV, fig. 4; Miller 2003: 50

This incomplete spindle whorl was in the process of being fabricated from the severed head of a camelid femur. It had been drilled but the shaping had not yet begun.

Cat. No. YPM 196401B
Late Horizon, Inca
Machu Picchu, Cave 56
Diameter: 1.3 in. (3.3 cm)
Publication: Eaton 1916: plate IV, fig. 5; Miller 2003: 50

This artifact illustrates the first stage of spindle whorl production. The head of a camelid femur has been severed to serve as a blank for subsequent carving. Drilling had begun from the underside but had not yet been completed.

Bone Weaving Tools, or Wichuñas
Bone weaving tools, known as *wichuñas* or *rukis* among contemporary Quechua-speaking highland peoples, were among the most common bone artifacts recovered during the 1912 excavations at Machu Picchu (Bingham 1930; Eaton 1916). Observation of modern weavers leads us to believe that these pointed tools were used to pack the threads together and to separate the

warp from the weft when producing designs. A recent study by Miller (2003) identified numerous bones in the Bingham Collection that had been worked to create blanks for the production of wichuñas. This implies that these weaver's tools were locally manufactured at Machu Picchu from alpaca or llama bones.

Cat. No. 176
Cat. No. YPM 58338 (top)
Late Horizon, Inca
Machu Picchu, Cave 52
Length: 6.0 in. (15.2 cm)
Max. Diameter: 1.5 in. (3.8 cm)
Publication: Eaton 1916: plate IV, fig. 10; Miller 2003: 53

This *wichuña* was made from a llama tibia. The tip of the tool is highly polished from wear, and cut marks are visible on the shaft. The articulating end of the bone was left unmodified as a handle.

Cat. No. YPM 58340 (middle)
Late Horizon, Inca
Machu Picchu, Cave 27
Length: 6.9 in. (17.6 cm)
Max. Diameter: 0.9 in. (2.2 cm)
Publication: Eaton 1916: plate IV, fig. 11

Made from a deer or small camelid tibia, the tip of this weaving tool is highly polished as the result of wear.

Cat. No. YPM 18625 (bottom)
Late Horizon, Inca
Machu Picchu, Cave 9
Length: 10.0 in. (25.5 cm)
Max. Diameter: 1.5 in. (3.8 cm)
Publication: Bingham 1930: 212, fig. 185; Eaton 1916: plate IV, fig. 9; Miller 2003: 53

This weaver's point, or *wichuña*, was carved from a llama tibia. It shows extensive polish and wear near its tip, as well as cut marks along its shaft.

Bone Trowel
Cat. No. 177
Cat. No. MP 71.1
Late Horizon, Inca
Machu Picchu, Cave 71
Length: 5.8 in. (14.8 cm)
Width: 3.7 in. (9.5 cm)
Publication: Miller 2003: 57

During his reanalysis of the faunal collection, George Miller (2003) identified eleven camelid pelvis fragments that had been modified and used as tools. This trowel, as in the other cases, has a broad end (the iliac blade) that displays scratches and abrasion, while the narrow end (the iliac neck) shows evidence of hand-polishing. This suggests that these tools were repeatedly used for a yet undetermined purpose, such as the preparation of skins or some other material. With one exception, all of the examples of "pelvic trowels" encountered had been included in the burials of retainers interred in the southern cemetery of Machu Picchu. This trowel was found with the body of a young adult male between the ages of 19 and 24.

Wood Objects

Few wooden objects survived the climate of Machu Picchu, with its heavy precipitation and sharp fluctuations in temperature. In addition to the fragment of a small wooden dish, Bingham (1930: 215) recovered three wooden tools used in sewing and crocheting. The expedition also encountered a sewing needle made from a cactus.

Wooden Textile Implements
Cat. No. 178
Cat. No. YPM 19625
Wooden Needle
Late Horizon, Inca
Machu Picchu
Length: 4.6 in. (11.6 cm)
Width: 0.1 in. (0.3 cm)

This long wooden needle has a broad, tapered head that has been perforated to allow fine thread to be passed through it. The shaft is wafer-shaped near the head but rounded in the lower section, which tapers to a sharp point.

Cat. No. YPM 19618
Wooden Crochet Hook
Late Horizon, Inca
Machu Picchu
Length: 5.5 in. (13.9 cm)
Width: 0.2 in. (0.6 cm)

176

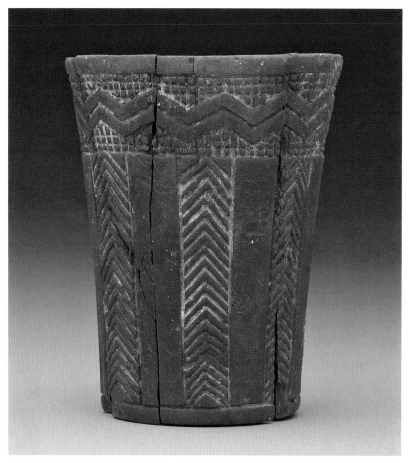

179

This remarkable object is one of the few crochet tools to be documented for prehispanic Peru. The handle of the crochet hook is flattened and incised on one side with a vertical column of chevrons; the other side was left plain. The edges of the handle were carved to form a tooth-like decoration. The shaft tapers but ends in a small hook rather than a simple point. In Peru, textiles that seem to be made by crocheting go back at least as far as the Paracas culture, which flourished during the first millennium BC, but crochet hooks have not been found. As a consequence, some skepticism has existed concerning this interpretation of the cloth. The Machu Picchu wooden crochet hook implies that this technique was being employed at the royal estate during Inca times.

Cat. No. YPM 19617
Wooden Needle
Late Horizon, Inca
Machu Picchu
Length: 5.0 in. (12.7 cm)
Width: 0.1 in. (0.2 cm)

This wooden needle is very similar in form to YPM 19625 but slightly longer.

Wooden Ritual Drinking Vessel, or Qero
Cat. No. 179
Cat. No. YAG 1940.601
Yale University Art Gallery
Late Horizon, Inca
Height: 4.0 in. (10.0 cm)
Diameter: 3.2 in. (7.8 cm)
Related objects: Flores Ochoa et al. 1998: 17

Qero, as defined in the 1608 Colonial Quechua dictionary compiled by Gonzáles Holguín (1608), signifies a wooden drinking vessel. These beaker-like vessels, produced in matching pairs, were used for the consumption of corn beer in public settings. During Inca times, they were typically decorated with geometric motifs carved into their dark outer surfaces (Rowe 1961). Pigments were sometimes added to the incisions to highlight the designs, many of which resemble the motifs on ceramics and textiles. Wooden qeros were similar in form and function to the more prestigious silver and gold drinking vessels (*aquillas*).

The classic Inca qero shown here has the characteristic Inca form with slightly concave sides, a flat base, and rounded rim. Decoration consists of a broad horizontal band immediately beneath the vessel rim. This band is decorated with a dual horizontal zigzag line against a crosshatched background. The rest of the vessel exterior is adorned with a series of vertical bands filled with chevrons. A basal incision demarcates the end of the vessel's decoration. White pigment has been applied to make the decoration more visible. As on many qeros, time has taken its toll on this vessel, producing a series of vertical fissures. A similar qero was encountered with a human offering at 19,194 feet (5,850 meters) above sea level on the summit of Mt. Ampato in Arequipa, and an almost identical piece exists in the collection of the Museo Inka in Cuzco (Flores Ochoa et al. 1998: 53, 17).

Textiles

Quipu
Cat. No. 180
Cat. No. YPM 19236
Late Horizon, Inca
Coastal Peru

Length (main cord): 67.6 in. (171.8 cm)
Max. Width (pendant cords): 14.1 in. (36.0 cm)
Max. Thickness (tassel): 0.8 in. (2.0 cm)

Knotted string records, known as *quipus*, were the principal recordkeeping device used by the Incas to record the accounts, tribute lists, and other economic matters in Tahuantinsuyu. These devices were kept by Inca officials, known as *quipucamayocs*, who were trained by the state in their use. Most quipus were dedicated to recording numerical information using the knots that signified numbers in a base-ten place notation. Most knotted cords served as mnemonic devices to aid the memory of officials at the local, provincial, and imperial levels of government. The relationship of the recorded numbers to one another was represented by their positions on pendant cords along a main cord or as secondary or tertiary cords along a pendant cord (Ascher and Ascher 1981). Analysis of numerical quipus yields a hierarchical arrangement of sets and subsets of numbers; in this regard, they resemble computer spreadsheet with notation accomplished through knots rather than Arabic numerical notation. Cultural conventions existed concerning the hierarchical organization of the quipus (Murra 1990), but color and color patterning were also manipulated to help signal object significance. Recent research, as

well as some statements in the Colonial historical documents, suggest that some quipus may have also been used to record nonnumerical information such as historical accounts and poetry (Urton 1995). The way in which such nonnumerical quipus may have functioned is still under investigation (Quilter and Urton 2002). Knotted string records continued to be utilized during Colonial times, and in some isolated villages within the Peruvian highlands simple knotted string records were used until recently (Mackey 1990).

The large quipu shown here is in the collection of the Yale Peabody Museum and was acquired by Hiram Bingham. It has been documented by Daniel Koloski (1996), and the following description is based on his observations. The quipu's main cord is over five feet long, and its one intact end terminates in a large yellow on red tassel. Made of camelid (probably alpaca) wool and cotton fiber, the quipu is also decorated with small alternating yellow and red tassels that were looped around the main cord. Hanging from the main cord are 582 pendant cords, all of which are S-spun and Z-plied and filled with S-tied knots. The pendant cords are grouped into 29 clusters. These clusters can be subdivided into three sections based on the number of cords in each. The pendant cords exhibit a general coloration pattern consisting of a dark

brown cord followed by a light brown cord and then a white cord. Another pattern emerges: many cluster sections end in a series of colored cords consisting of a bicolored cord, of maroon and green. Based on his detailed examination of the Yale quipu, Koloski (1996) concluded that the features present in the specimen cannot be explained solely as a numerical record and that its structure supports Urton's arguments that knotted records also encoded other classes of information.

Inca Tunics

The most important garment worn by Inca men was a woven sleeveless tunic, or *uncu*. These garments, longer than they are wide, were worn loose to about knee length. The finer tunics were produced using a tapestry technique, with a neck slit woven into the garment using discontinuous warps. Since fabric was not cut or otherwise tailored, the uncus were woven to the desired size. The cloth for the tunics was woven in a single piece and then folded over and sewn at the seams leaving openings for the arms. The finest Inca tunics were produced by female and male specialists in government facilities and then distributed as gifts to express royal favor and symbolize elite status (Murra 1962; Salazar and Roussakis 2000). Many of the Inca tunics that have survived bear a limited range of motifs, and there is considerable evidence for standardiza-

180

181

Tupa, and Tupa Amaru all wear tunics of this kind (e.g., Guaman Poma 1980: 86). That the Dumbarton Oaks uncu has no known surviving equivalent lends credibility to the idea that it may be a garment that was created for the emperor. Because this tunic makes use of a cotton warp, it is likely that it was produced along Peru's coast. The neck and ends of the garment are covered with embroidered bindings that are visible as colorful bands. Analysis of the Dumbarton Oaks tunic indicates that it was actually worn in antiquity, and its repeated use led to structural damage at both ends of the neck slits. This problem was repaired in antiquity using a thin, clear filament believed to be human hair (Rowe and Rowe 1996: 457).

The elaborate decoration of this tunic employs some 23 basic patterns transmuted into the 156 distinctive tocapu units on each side of the garment. While many of the design elements are familiar from other Inca textiles, the only representation of a recognizable object is a miniature black, white, and red checkerboard tunic. Scholars have struggled in vain to understand the significance and patterning of the tocapu units. It has been suggested that individual tocapu units might correspond to specific places or lineages. Attempts to interpret the complex sequence of tocapu designs as a form of writing (Barthel 1971) has been met with skepticism by most specialists. While the actual meaning of the symbols on this tunic remains uncertain, there can be little doubt that this distinctive style of tunic decoration served as an effective visual designation of the unique status of the Inca ruler. The enormous skill and considerable time required to produce such an uncu provided ample testimony to the power of the Sapac Inca.

Cat. No. 182
Tunic Decorated with Key-Checkerboard Motif

tion, reflecting the hierarchical sociopolitical structure of Tahuantinsuyu (Rowe 1979). Most Inca tunics were made exclusively of camelid wool or a combination of camelid wool and cotton. Camelid wool lent itself to the bright colors that characterize many of these garments because it can be dyed more effectively than cotton.

Cat. No. 181
Tunic with Tocapu Decoration
Dumbarton Oaks Collection B-518
Late Horizon, Inca
Coastal Peru
Height: 35.8 in. (91.0 cm)
Width: 30.0 in. (76.0 cm)
Publication: Horkheimer and Kauff-

mann Doig 1965: 141; Morris 1992: 594; Rowe 1979: 257–59; Rowe and Rowe 1996: 457–65

This tunic from the Dumbarton Oaks Collection is the only known surviving example of an Inca textile of royal quality (Rowe and Rowe 1996: 457). Finely woven in camelid wool and cotton using a tapestry technique, this garment is completely covered with geometric designs within small rectangular units; these designs, called *tocapu*, were a royal prerogative. Only the Inca rulers or Sapac Inca wore tunics completely covered with tocapu designs. In Guaman Poma's illustrations, Viracocha Inca, Tupa Inca, Huayna Capac, Sayri

Private Collection
Late Horizon, Inca
Coastal Peru
Height: 33.0 in. (84.0 cm)
Width: 28.1 in. (71.5 cm)
Related objects: Cummins 2002: fig.
4.3; Jones 1964: 43; Morris 1992: 593;
Rowe 1979

In most respects, this key-checkerboard tunic exemplifies one of the most common kinds of high-status garments produced by the specialized weavers of the Inca state. The upper two-thirds of the tunic was decorated by alternating and contrasting light and dark squares filled with what archaeologists refer to as the "Inca key motif." The color contrast between the repeating decorative units is reinforced by the shifting orientation in the key motif itself. The lower third of the tunic is decorated with broad red horizontal bands as well as with an embroidered zigzag design and embroidered binding. Garments such as this one have been found at Los Majuelos in the Nasca drainage and at other sites along Peru's south coast. The key motif was widely used by Inca artists, and variants of it appear on Inca ceramics and on the wooden and precious-metal drinking vessels known as *aquillas* (Cummins 2002: fig. 4.7a; Jones 1964: 13–14).

The color, fineness, and sheen of the fiber utilized in this tunic suggest that vicuña wool rather than alpaca wool was utilized. The vicuña, the wild relative of the alpaca, flourishes at very high elevations, usually 14,000 feet above sea level or more, and its wool was especially prized. Special royal hunts were organized to capture and shear these animals, and the use of their fiber was reserved for the Inca emperor and his court (Garcilaso 1958). Textiles such as this one had enormous symbolic value, communicating a kind of wealth more highly valued by the Incas than gold or silver (Salazar and Roussakis 2000).

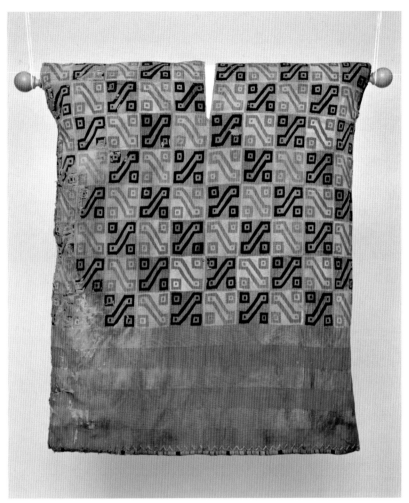

182

Coca Bag with Llamas
Cat. No. 183
Cat. No. YPM 17897
Late Horizon, Inca
South Coast of Peru
Length: 19.7 in. (50.0 cm)
Width: 7.9 in. (20.0 cm)
Related objects: Stone-Miller 1992:
plate 66

The woven bag was an essential element in the wardrobe of Inca men. Guaman Poma de Ayala's portrait of the Inca emperor Manco Capac shows such a bag hanging from his wrist. Leaves of the coca plant (*Erythroxylon* spp.) were kept in these bags. They chewed the leaves with lime for a

mildly stimulating effect, to reduce the stress of living and working in the Andes. According to some early historical accounts, the Inca rulers controlled the production and consumption of coca, distributing it as a gift to members of the elite and other favored subjects. Coca, considered a sacred crop, was used in many Inca ceremonies as an offering to the deities.

This example of a coca bag is woven of camelid wool, probably alpaca, and cotton, using many different construction techniques, including interlocked tapestry, looping, knotting, netting, and plied fringe. Woven rows of llamas, the Andean pack animal central to the functioning of the Inca economy and

184

army, are the bag's main decoration.

The lateral edges of the bag depict a line of stylized yellow birds in flight against a red background, while the lower edge of the bag is adorned with a line of red birds against a yellow ground. The two sides of the bag are decorated with a vertical line of small white crosses. While the style of the profile birds is characteristic of Peru's south coast in valleys such as Ica, the colors of the bag (two shades of dark red and a golden yellow) and the design of the llamas in profile are typical of Inca imperial style. These stylistic features and the excellent preservation of the bag suggest that it came from Peru's southern coastal desert. Abundant dark red and

golden cords (Z-plied) hang from the bottom of the bag as an elaborate ornamental fringe. The upper section of the bag, including its shoulder strap, is missing from this specimen (see Stone-Miller 1992: 178, plate 66, for a complete example).

Textile Miniatures
Cat. No. 184
Brooklyn Museum of Art
Late Horizon, Inca
Central Andes
Miniature Mantle
Cat. No. 41.1275.107
Length: 10.6 in. (26.9 cm)
Width: 9.4 in. (23.9 cm)
Miniature Mantle

Cat. No. 41.1275.110
Length: 5.6 in. (14.2 cm)
Width: 4.7 in. (12.0 cm)
Miniature Headdress
Cat. No. 41.1275.108 A
Length: 10.2 in. (26.0 cm)
Width: 5.0 in. (12.7 cm)
Miniature Headdress
Cat. No. 41.1275.108 B
Length: 4.5 in. (11.4 cm)
Width: 3.2 in. (7.9 cm)

High-quality miniature textiles were produced to adorn the gold and silver figurines that were incorporated in offerings during the Capacocha and other important religious ceremonies. The textiles shown here from the Brooklyn

Museum of Art appear to have come from a single offering context, given the similarity between the two mantles and the two headdresses. Despite the apparent presence of matching pairs, the textiles contrast with each other in terms of size and color patterning. For example, one mantle is dominated by a central green band, while the larger mantle features a central black band. Yet both mantles have the same banding and similar embroidery encircling the garment's edge. Both headdresses feature a feathered crown with a long cream-colored neck flap that ends in brown tassels, and each has a red embroidered zigzag pattern above the tassels. Nonetheless, the smaller headdress is dominated by red-yellow feathers, while the larger headdress is dominated by white feathers in the crown section. Similar red and white feather headdresses adorned the pair of gold and silver female figurines left as part of a human offering on the summit of Volcán Llullaillaco in northwestern Argentina (Reinhard and Ceruti 2000: 184–85; plates 37, 38). The form and decoration on the miniatures resemble typical Inca textiles; for example, the mantles are adorned with a variant of the Inca key motif, one of the most common designs on Inca tunics.

Colonial Andean Objects

Although Tahuantinsuyu was destroyed and Machu Picchu was abandoned around AD 1532, many aspects of Inca culture and society survived and even flourished. The survival and transformation of Inca culture was expressed through the material objects produced during the two centuries following the Spanish Conquest. These include familiar forms as well as some newly introduced modes of expression, such as oil paintings on canvas.

Colonial Pottery

Cat. No. 185
Aryballos
Cat. No. YPM 17468
Colonial, 16th century
Chile
Height: 15.0 in. (38.0 cm)
Rim Diameter: 6.1 in. (15.4 cm)
Max. Diameter: 11.2 in. (28.5 cm)

This polished bichrome aryballos is heavily painted in red over a thin, cream-colored slip. The neck and conical base are red, while the chamber and strap handles are covered with detailed geometric and figurative representations. The aryballos form was inspired by the Inca ceramic tradition, but it departs from standard Cuzco conventions by the low placement of the lateral strap hands, the unusual shape of the neck, which is more constricted and less flaring than the norm, and the flattened bottom of the conical base. Now broken, the pierced "ear" nubbins of the aryballos are unusually large. The vessel's decoration shows strong Inca influence, most notably the rows of repeating triangles, the horizontal bands of cross-hatching, and the use of the "hourglass" motif. Yet the manner of organizing these designs is distinctively provincial. For example, rather than simply repeating, as they do in classic Inca pottery, the hourglass designs alternate between a vertical and a horizontal position. The upper register of the chamber is decorated with a procession or caravan of llamas, judging from their long necks, short hair, and upright tails. The strap handles are painted with alternating red circles and triangles separated by a zigzag line. The back of the aryballos is decorated with two lower bands of red triangles and a series of rectangular and triangular zones filled with cross-hatching. The style of the painting, unlike anything seen in the Inca heartland, suggests that the piece was produced in the southern Andes,

perhaps northern Chile.

The interpretation of this piece as Colonial is based primarily on the vessel's replacement of the central feline lug with a detailed model thatched building in whose doorway sits a stylized human male. This representation is reminiscent of the placement of churches with priests as ornaments on the post-Conquest ceramic vessels from the central and southern highlands of Peru. In addition, several of the decorated registers are framed within a curved or arched form, a shape reminiscent of Christian church doorways or windows.

Cat. No. 186
Zoomorphic Effigy Bottle
Cat. No. YPM 18549
Colonial, late 16th century
Ollantaytambo, Cuzco
Height: 7.3 in. (18.5 cm)
Rim Diameter: 1.8 in. (4.5 cm)
Max. Diameter: 8.9 in. (22.5 cm)

This large brown bottle, shaped like a four-legged creature reminiscent of a dragon, was produced sometime after the Spanish Conquest. The head of the creature is shown with large upright ears, prominent oval eyes, a long snout, and thick lips; an anomalous protuberance occurs above the nose. The creature has a prominent barrel-shaped chest, but the rest of its body is thin and elongated. Small nubbins represent the front legs, while the back legs are shown flexed against the body in low relief, each ending in what appears to be a split or cloven hoof. The pose suggests that the creature is in a prone position raised slightly on its front legs. The creature also has a large, long tail that curls upward and rests against the back of the its head. This tail doubles as the tubular stirrup for this stirrup-spouted vessel. The pattern of the creature's coat is indicated by surface texturing. The area of the chest is marked by linear in-

186

cisions, while the back of the head is covered with irregular punctations. The rest of the body is smooth and well-polished.

The features linking this piece to the prehispanic traditions of Peru's north coast are its production using a two-piece mold, the focus on figurative three-dimensional representation, and the presence of a truncated, stirrup-spouted handle. However, no creature comparable to this zoomorphic one appears on prehispanic pottery from the Central Andes, and while Colonial ceramics are poorly known, there are parallels between this figure and the representation of dragons that figure prominently on Colonial *qeros* (Flores Ochoa et al. 1998: 306–7). The elongated body, treatment of the legs and feet, and long curled tail provide support for the interpretation of this figure as a dragon, although elements of feline and other animal representations may also have been melded to produce this supernatural image.

Cat. No. 187
Effigy Head Cup
Cat. No. YPM 18517
Colonial Period, 17th century
Ollantaytambo, Cuzco
Height: 4.8 in. (12.1 cm)
Rim Diameter: 1.6 in. (4.0 cm)
Max. Diameter: 3.1 in. (8.0 cm)
Related object: Schindler 2000: 297

This cup is modeled with a stylized portrait of an African individual. His red-slipped face is round, with open eyes and a mouth covered with a very thin layer of white paint. The hair, also painted a pale cream color, is fashioned in rows of three-dimensional volutes. A white band separates the face from the conical pedestal base. A low vertical neck rises from the top of the head cup. The use of a two-piece mold and the modeling technique, along with the short vertical neck and conical base, link this cup to the ceramic tradition of Peru's north coast, but this piece was acquired by Bingham in Ollantaytambo.

The Spanish brought African slaves and free people of African descent to

the Central Andes. Francisco Pizarro, for example, was granted fifty African slaves in 1534 (Jimenez Borja 1996: 171). The African population in Peru rose steeply during the sixteenth century as the Spaniards attempted to compensate for the declining indigenous populations by importing slaves to work on the coastal plantations and as servants of the Criolle elite. The African population spread throughout coastal and highland Peru within a century of the Conquest, and freed slaves came to constitute a large part of the population of Lima during late Colonial times.

The depiction of individuals with African features is a common theme in Colonial Peruvian drinking cups. The reason for portraying Africans on drinking vessels is unknown, but it may relate to the exoticism of these new arrivals and the fascination with slavery, a status that did not exist in the Central Andes prior to the arrival of the Europeans. These vessels may also be linked to the numerous masked dances, such as the Danza de los Morenos and the Danza de los Negritos, that these outsiders inspired and that became a common component in public festivals (Jimenez Borja 1996: 171–78).

187

Cat. No. 188
Miniature Jar with Conical Base
Cat. No. YPM 194266
Colonial Peru, 16th century
Sacsahuaman, Cuzco
Height 3.3 in. (8.3 cm)
Rim Diameter: 1.3 in. (3.0 cm)
Max. Diameter: 2.8 in. (7.0 cm)

The tradition of miniature vessels continued following the Spanish Conquest
in the Central Andes. It is likely that
this miniature conical jar, recovered
during excavations on the terraces of
Sacsahuaman, belongs to the period
immediately following the Inca defeat.
This miniature represents a broad
chambered jar with a straight-sided flaring neck and conical base. The form
and unusual ribbon-like asymmetric
handle do not conform to any of the traditional Inca shapes, and there are
patches of glaze on its irregularly finished surface. The parallel horizontal
surface markings on the neck raise the
possibility that the piece may have been
made on a potter's wheel.

Cat. No. YPM 16969
Miniature Jar with Vertical Handle
Colonial Peru, 16th century
Machu Picchu
Height: 3.9 in. (9.8 cm)
Rim Diameter 1.8 in. (4.6 cm)
Max. Diameter: 2.2 in. (5.5 cm)

In Colonial times, following Machu Picchu's abandonment by the Inca court,
there continued to be occasional occupants and visitors. Bingham and more recent investigators have encountered
traces of this post-Conquest presence.
The only complete Colonial vessel recovered by the 1912 expedition was this
miniature jar. Its unusual form is reminiscent of a European pitcher or flower-
pot (*florero*), with its long thick neck,
side flaring rim, single handle extending
from rim to shoulder, and flat bottom.
Traces of transparent greenish

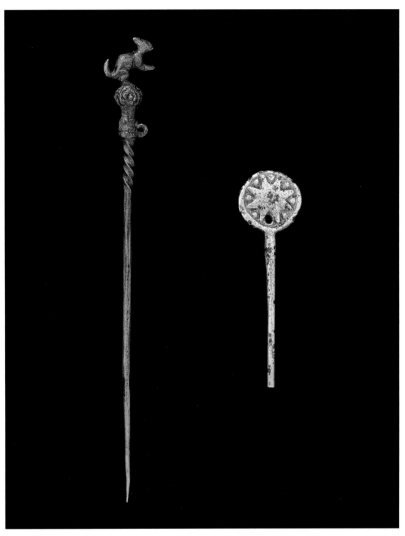

189

glaze appear to be present on the lower
portion of the unevenly finished chamber. The painted decoration consists of
solid red bands around the lip and lower
neck and a line of solid red circles
around the widest section of the jar's
mid-section.

Colonial Shawl Pins, or Tupus

Cat. No. 189
Cat. No. YPM 22060 *(left)*
Bronze Shawl Pin with Viscacha
Colonial Peru, late 16th century (?)
Machu Picchu
Height: 4.8 in. (12.2 cm)

Width: 0.5 in. (1.4 cm)

This bronze *tupu* has finely cast decoration of a profile rabbit-like Andean *viscacha* raised on its haunches with an
upturned tail. The animal is sitting atop
a rosette, and the upper section of the
tupu's tapering pin below is adorned
with a raised spiral pattern. A loop ap-
pended to the base of the pin-head
would have allowed it to be secured by
cordage. The decorative elements, particularly the rosette and spiral and the
style of the casting, all point to a post-
Conquest date for this piece. It is one of
the few Colonial items Bingham recovered at Machu Picchu.

Cat. No. YPM 17836 (*right*)
Bronze Shawl Pin with Celestial Motif
Colonial Peru, late 16th century (?)
Machu Picchu
Height: 2.3 in. (5.8 cm)
Width: 0.7 in. (1.7 cm)
Publication: Rutledge 1984: appendix

This small shawl pin is missing its tip. It
has a golden tone because of the high
tin content (12.5 percent). The *tupu's*
circular head has a distinctive bas-relief
decoration made by casting. On one
face is an eight-pointed motif, probably
representing the sun, surrounded by
eight dots, possibly representing stars.
On the other side is a crescent, probably representing the crescent moon,
surrounded by many dots. Decoration
contrasting the sun and moon was common in Colonial times, and the raised
band running along the edge of both
sides of the tupu head resembles Colonial coinage. A hole that interrupts the
decoration was perforated in the bottom
of the pin head to allow a cord to be
passed through it.

190

Colonial Wooden Drinking Vessels, or Qeros

The wooden drinking vessels, a characteristic feature of Inca culture in
Cuzco, continued to be produced and
utilized during the centuries following
the Spanish Conquest. In fact, the most
elaborate qeros are Colonial in date.
While often emulating the form of Inca
qeros, Colonial qeros display a rich tradition of figurative representations that
developed during the sixteenth, seventeenth, and eighteenth centuries. These
depictions constitute a key source for
tracing indigenous highland myths and
traditions following the Inca defeat.
Some scholars have viewed the continued production of qeros as an act of resistance against Spanish hegemony,
while others have emphasized the way
in which these vessels reflect the meld-

ing and transformation of these two distinct cultural traditions (Cummins
2002; Flores Ochoa et al. 1998; Rowe
1961). In Colonial times, as in Inca
times, qeros were used for the consumption of corn beer (*chicha*) during
public ceremonies and religious rituals,
and this practice continues today in
parts of southern Peru and Bolivia.

Cat. No. 190
Feline-Head Qero
Cat. No. YPM 30205
Colonial Peru, 18th century
Height: 9.8 in. (25.0 cm)
Rim Diameter: 3.1 in. (8.0 cm)
Max. Diameter: 8.7 in. (22.0 cm)
Related objects: Flores Ochoa et al.
1998: 56, 57; Morris and von Hagen
1993: 230.

As the cultural and economic integra-
tion of the tropical forest and the Peruvian highlands diminished in Colonial
times, the mythic importance of the
"savage" inhabitants of these lands
grew, as did the memories of the Inca's
largely unsuccessful attempts to subju-
gate these lowland peoples. Stories of
these jungle peoples — known as *inti* or
chunchu — flourished, and costumed
dances featuring chunchos became a
fixture in post-Conquest highland religious festivals (Jimenez Borja 1996).
The enduring fascination with the conflict between the Inca and the jungle
peoples was also expressed in ceremonial drinking vessels like the one shown
here.
    This large wooden qero is carved in
the form of a feline head. The pelage

markings indicate that it represents a tropical forest feline rather than the highland puma, since the latter lacks markings on its pelt. Judging from the form of the face, particularly the snout, this beaker-like drinking vessel may represent an ocelot (*Felis pardalis*) rather than the larger jaguar. Here the feline is shown with almond-shaped black eyes, a narrow wedge-shaped nose or snout without explicit nostrils, prominent pointed upright ears, and a massive open mouth with a set of painted triangular teeth and carved fangs, one of which broke off during the vessel's use. The pelage markings of the feline are shown as vertically oriented lenticular forms that alternate in color between red and cream; in the center of some of these are white spots with central red dots. Two rows of these pelage markings extend around the back of the head of the feline. The animal's neck is adorned with two horizontal rows of triangles with central spots flanking a row of diamond-shaped motifs.

The back of the *qero* is covered with a scene depicting a battle between Inca troops and tropical forest warriors. The six Inca soldiers wear tunics and are armed with slings and lances. The six chunchos wear feather headdresses and loose-fitting robes, or *cushmas*, decorated with pelage-like spots. Each of them is shown with a drawn bow and arrow, a weapon characteristic of the Amazonian drainage during prehispanic times. The two opposing groups are shown facing each other in active combat, and the prone body of a felled tropical forest warrior makes explicit the bellicose character of the confrontation. Judging from similar vessels in Cuzco and Arequipa, the representation of this battle scene is commonly shown on those qeros with a feline form (Flores Ochoa et al. 1998: 57, 181).

Cat. No. 191
Qero with Seated Chancas

191

Cat. No. YPM 30207
Colonial Peru, 18th century
Cuzco
Height: 7.9 in. (20.0 cm)
Rim Diameter: 4.4 in. (11.1 cm)
Max. Diameter: 4.4 in. (11.1 cm)
Related objects: Flores Ochoa et al. 1998: 159

Colonial wooden *qeros* represented a limited number of themes, many of which were of special importance in Inca history and mythology. One popular subject was the Inca defeat of their rivals and enemies, the Chancas (Flores Ochoa et al. 1998: 156–60). This vic-

tory, which established Pachacuti as the leader of the Incas, began the process of military conquest that eventually resulted in the Inca empire. According to Jorge Flores Ochoa et al. (1998: 159), qeros like the one shown here commemorate the Inca subjugation of the Chancas. The form of this qero is unusual, consisting of a relatively small shallow circular drinking receptacle supported by two large human figures sitting atop a solid circular base. The two adult males, depicted in white tunics, represent the defeated Chancas, who are reduced to supporting the wooden vessel from which the corn

192

193

194

beer (*chicha*) will be consumed. The two captives are shown with contrasting faces, one with a bearded narrow face, the other with a clean-shaven rounded visage; the lower bodies of the captives are shown unclothed as a symbol of defeat.

The base, a rounded mound-like form, is painted on the sides with geometric *tocapu* motifs punctuated with projecting depictions of Inca masonry walls. The structures represented may correspond to the famous towers at Sacsahuaman, which the Spaniards dismantled because of their effectiveness as a military feature.

The drinking receptacle is covered with colorful resin painting. The flattened lip of the cup, for example, is painted with repeating cantu flowers and concentric diamonds. The most complex painting appears on the sides of the cup, which shows a narrative scene that can be interpreted as an Inca emperor and his general, both shown frontally in elaborate costume. The Inca is identifiable because he wears a tunic covered with tocapu designs and is the largest figure. The general, shown on a slightly smaller scale, pulls three prisoners on a rope. Unlike the Inca and his assistant, the prisoners are

shown in profile; they wear plain tunics and lack elaborate headdresses. On the other side of the Inca, three other prisoners appear to have their arms raised in obeisance to the conquering Inca king. The remainder of the scene is devoted to a landscape featuring a cream-colored building with dome-shaped thatching, similar to Guaman Poma's drawings of Inca storehouses (Guaman Poma 1980: 309). It sits on a grassy knoll and is flanked by upright standards and large, leafy trees filled with birds. The painting on the drinking receptacle can be interpreted as depicting the Inca king and his advisor reviewing the captive Chanca prisoners in an idyllic and peaceful setting, perhaps lands in Cuzco. Painted and carved at least two centuries after the defeat of the Inca by the Spaniards, this qero reflects the longing for an idealized past by the descendants of the Incas.

Cat. No. 192
Wooden Qero in the Form of an Alpaca Head
The Field Museum
Cat. No. 4055
Neg. #A114208d, Photographer John Weinstein
Colonial Peru, 17th century

Height: 8.9 in. (22.5 cm)
Max. Width: 5.8 in. (14.7 cm)
Related objects: Flores Ochoa et al. 1998: 26

The carving of wooden cups in the form of naturalistic three-dimensional heads was less common than decorating them with incised *tocapu*-like geometric motifs or two-dimensional narrative scenes. Apparently, only three subjects were viewed as appropriate for the wooden portrait cups: tropical forest Indians (*chunchos*), felines, and alpacas. Given the potential universe, this selection of only three subjects is probably significant.

The depiction of the alpaca on this remarkable *qero* may be a function of the central role these animals played in the Inca economy as a source of fine wool and meat. Given the use of qeros in religious rituals, the portrayal of these animals may also relate to the use of alpacas by the Incas as sacrificial offerings during religious traditional rituals; this practice existed at Machu Picchu and has lasted to the present time (Miller 2003). The large-scale herding of alpacas was and is limited to high elevations, owing to the physiology of the animals and the availability of pasture.

These animals would have been familiar to the Colonial highland people who produced and utilized qeros such as this one. The carved upright ears, relatively short snout, and thickened wool above the eyes and below the head results in a representation more realistic than those found in most Inca and Colonial Inca art. The texture of the thick wool of the alpaca is further evoked through incision and painting. A similar piece, perhaps its matching pair, exists in the collection of the Museo Inka in Cuzco (Flores Ochoa et al. 1998: 196). In Inca times, the domesticated camelids (alpacas and llamas) were commonly portrayed on hammered silver and gold figurines, carved stone ritual receptacle (*illas* or *conopas*), and painted and modeled ceramics; this qero represents a continuation of that tradition.

195

Cat. No. 193
Colonial Wooden Drinking Vessel with Floral Decoration
Cat. No. YAG ILE 1939.192
Yale University Art Gallery
Colonial Peru, late 16th century
Height: 9.6 in. (24.5 cm)
Diameter: 8.0 in. (20.2 cm)

This large *qero* corresponds to the stylistic transition between Inca and the late Colonial wooden drinking vessels. It has straight sides, a flat base, and a rounded rim. Like most Inca qeros, it is decorated primarily by carving the exterior with geometric designs. The broad upper register is crosshatched and depicts a horizontal zigzag band, a patterning almost identical to that found on another Inca qero shown in this book (YAG 1940.601). The rest of the exterior is divided into a series of ten horizontal bands. Narrow and medium-width bands incised with parallel vertical lines alternate with each other. The narrow bands and the zigzag band are adorned with polychrome lacquer

painting, a technique typical of Colonial times. Multicolored flowers, perhaps the highland cantu, are shown on most of the narrow bands, while a central green line adorns the zigzag band. Although the presence of this lacquer painting points to a production date after the Spanish conquest, the continued dominance of carving as the main decorative technique suggests that this is an early Colonial piece produced before the Inca tradition of incised adornment was largely abandoned. This particular qero is unusual in its overall patterning, and few examples of comparable pieces have been published.

Cat. No. 194
Colonial Wooden Drinking Vessel in the Form of a Human Head
Cat. No. YAG ILE 1939.193
Colonial Peru, 18th century
Height 8.9 in. (22.5 cm)
Diameter 6.1 in. (15.5 cm)

Related objects: Flores Ochoa et al. 1998: 67, 108, 238

One of the most common types of Colonial *qeros* are vessels in the form of a modeled human head. These head cups almost invariably represent a male with a decorated horizontal head-band, elaborately painted face, prominent straight nose, and modeled ears. These features suggest that the visage is of a non-Inca individual, probably that of a tropical forest native (*chuncho*). The absence of ear ornaments reinforces the conclusion that someone from a non-Inca ethnic group is being represented. The depiction of parrots in profile on the head-band and other elements of the polychrome lacquer painting reinforce the "jungle" theme of this Colonial corn beer (*chicha*) vessel. The back of the qero represents a painted scene from the Inca court.

Wooden Royal Seat, or Tiana
Cat. No. 195
The Field Museum
Cat. No. 2832
Neg. #A114206d, Photographer John Weinstein
Colonial Peru, late 16th century
Height: 11.4 in. (29.0 cm)
Length: 15.9 in. (40.5 cm)
Publication: Niles 1992: 348, fig. 2

Tianas were wooden seats or stools whose use was limited to individuals of special authority. Like many classes of Inca objects, tianas continued to be produced after the Spanish Conquest. On Colonial *qeros* the Inca leader is often shown sitting on a tiana. Few tianas have survived from Colonial times, and this specimen from Chicago's Field Museum is one of the finest known. It has a pair of sculpted felines facing in opposing directions supporting the concave seat. The pelage markings on these creatures suggest that they represent jaguars or some lowland feline rather than highland pumas, whose coats are a uniform gray-brown. The use of painted and lacquered wood for this rare Colonial tiana was a post-Conquest innovation, paralleling the surface treatment of painted and lacquered Colonial qeros. In Inca times tianas were reserved for high officials to whom the privilege had been granted by the emperor (Rowe 1946: 224). In some Spanish chronicles, Inca tianas are described as being carved out of a single block of wood and having the shape of an animal with short legs and a raised tail. Colonial tianas, such as this specimen, along with Colonial *tocapu* tunics, Colonial qeros, and oil paintings of Inca rulers, were utilized by individuals of royal descent to assert their special rights and identity under the early Colonial Spanish administration.

198

Four Colonial Paintings of Inca Kings

Cat. No. 196
Capac Yupanqui
Peru
1995.29.5, The Brooklyn Museum of Art
Unknown artist, mid-18th century
23.5 x 21.8 in. (59.7 x 55.4 cm)

Cat. No. 197
Inca Roca
Peru
1995.29.6, The Brooklyn Museum of Art
Unknown artist, mid-18th century
23.1 x 21.5 in. (58.7 x 54.6 cm)

Cat. No. 198
Pachacuti, Oil on Canvas
Peru
1995.29.10 The Brooklyn Museum of Art
Unknown artist, mid-18th century
23.6 x 21.6 in. (60.0 x 54.9 cm)

Cat. No. 199
Huascar, Oil on Canvas
Peru
1995.29.13, The Brooklyn Museum of Art
Unknown artist, mid-18th century
23.5 x 21.5 in. (59.7 x 54.6 cm)
Related objects: See Fane 1996: 240–41, Nos. 94–96, for four other paintings in this series

199

In Colonial times, the indigenous elites displayed portraits of Inca kings as evidence of their noble descent and illustrious history. After the unsuccessful indigenous uprising led by Jose Gabriel Condorcanqui Tupac Amaru in 1780, the display of paintings of the Inca kings such as these were forbidden, along with other expressions of Inca identity. The four oil paintings exhibited were selected from a series of fourteen portraits painted in the mid-eighteenth century. These paintings were based on a 1615 engraving by Antonio de Herrera, which in turn was said to have been modeled on an earlier prototype (Fane 1996: 239). The idea of Inca portraits did not begin with the Spanish. According to the chroniclers, historical portraits of the Inca emperors were kept at the Temple of the Sun. A set of painted panels depicting the Incas was sent by Viceroy Toledo to the King of Spain in 1572, but none of these have survived. Inca portraits such as these four oil paintings reflect the European artistic tradition as it was absorbed and transformed by Peruvian artists.

Works Cited

Aguilar, Victor, L. Hinojosa, and C. Milla, with W. Nordt. 1992. Turismo y Desarrollo. *Posibilidades en la Región Inka.* Cuzco: CARTUC y CERA.

Alcina Franch, Jose. 1979. *Die Kunst des Alten Amerika.* Freiburg: Herder.

Aldunate del Solar, Carlos and Luis Cornejo. 2001. *Tras la Huella del Inka en Chile.* Santiago: Museo Chileno de Arte Peruano.

Allen, Catherine J. 2000. When Pebbles Move Mountains: Iconicity and Symbolism in Quechua Ritual. In *Creating Context in Andean Cultures,* edited by Rosaleen Howard-Malverde, pp. 73–84. Oxford: Oxford University Press.

Anders, Ferdinand. 1984. *Peru durch die Jahrtausende, Kunst und Kultur im Lande der Inka.* Recklinhauser, Austria: Verlag Aurel Bongers.

Año International de las Montañas. 2001. *PERU.* Grupo Nacional de Trabajo sobre Ecosistemas de Montañas. Documento de Conceptos. Lima.

Anton, Ferdinand. 1962. *Alt-Peru und Seine Kunst.* Leipzig: Veb. E. A. Seeman Verlag.

Ascher, Marcia and Robert Ascher. 1981. *Code of the Quipu.* Ann Arbor: University of Michigan Press.

Astete, Fernando. 2001. Aportes e Investigaciones en Machu Picchu (1994–2000). In *90 Años del Descubrimiento Científico de Machu Picchu 1911–2001,* edited by Ernesto Vargas, pp. 103–6. Cusco: Instituto Nacional de Cultura.

Aveni, Anthony. 1981. Horizon Astronomy in Incaic Cuzco. In *Archaeoastronomy in the Americas,* edited by R. A. Williamson, pp. 305–18. Los Altos, Calif.: Ballena Press.

Azoy, Mary L. 1985. *Peruvian Antiquities: A Manual for United States Customs.* Washington, D.C.: Organization of American States.

Barthel, Thomas. 1971. Viracochas prunkewand. Tocapu Studien 1. *Tribus* 20: 63–124.

Bauer, Brian S. 1991. Pacariqtambo and the Mythical Origins of the Inca. *Latin American Antiquity* 2 (1): 7–26.

———. 1999. The Early Ceramics of the Inca Heartland. *Fieldiana. Anthropology.* New Series, no. 31.

Bauer, Brian S., and David S. P. Dearborn. 1995. *Astronomy and Empire in the Ancient Andes.* Austin: University of Texas Press.

Benson, Elizabeth. 1963. *Handbook of the Robert Woods Bliss Collection of Pre-Columbian Art.* Washington, D.C.: Dumbarton Oaks.

Berrin, Kathleen (editor). 1997. *The Spirit of Ancient Peru. Treasures from the Museo Arqueológico Rafael Larco Herrera.* London: Thames and Hudson Ltd.

Betanzos, Juan de. 1987 [1557]. *Suma y narración de los Incas,* Maria del Carmen Rubio, ed. Madrid, Spain: Ediciones Atlas.

———. 1996 [1551–57]. *Narrative of the Incas,* translated and edited by Roland Hamilton and Dana Buchanan. Austin: University of Texas Press.

Bingham, Alfred. 1989. *Portrait of an Explorer: Hiram Bing-*

ham, *Discoverer of Machu Picchu*. Ames: Iowa State University Press.

Bingham, Hiram. 1909. *The Journal of an Expedition Across Venezuela and Colombia, 1906–1907: An Exploration of the Route of Bolivar's Celebrated March of 1819 and of the Battle-Fields of Boyaca and Carabobo*. New Haven: Yale Publishing Association.

——. 1912. Vitcos, the Last Inca Capital. *Proceedings of the American Antiquarian Society* 22 (April): 135–96.

——. 1913a. The Discovery of Machu Picchu. *Harper's Magazine* vol. 127, pp. 709–19.

——. 1913b. In the Wonderland of Peru. *National Geographic* vol. 24, pp. 387–573.

——. 1915a. The Inca Peoples and Their Culture. *Proceedings of the Nineteenth International Congress of Americanists*. Washington, D.C.

——. 1915b. The Story of Machu Picchu. *National Geographic* vol. 27, pp. 172–217.

——. 1915c. Types of Machu Picchu Pottery. *American Anthropologist* 17(April–June): 257–71.

——. 1916a. Evidence of Symbolism in the Land of the Incas. *The Builder* 2(12): 361–66.

——. 1916b. Further Explorations in the Land of the Incas. *National Geographic* vol. 29, pp. 431–73.

——. 1917. The Inca Peoples and Their Culture. *Proceedings Second Pan American Scientific Congress*, pp. 160–67. Washington. D.C.

——. 1922. *Inca Land: Explorations in the Highlands of Peru.* 2d edition. Boston: Houghton Mifflin.

——. 1930. *Machu Picchu, a Citadel of the Incas.* New Haven: Yale University Press.

——. 1948. *Lost City of the Incas: The Story of Machu Picchu and Its Builders.* New York: Hawthorne Books.

Bliss, Robert Woods. 1957. *Pre-Columbian Art: The Robert Woods Bliss Collection*. London: Phaidon Press.

Boone, Elizabeth, ed. 1996. *Andean Art at Dumbarton Oaks.* Washington, D.C.: Dumbarton Oaks.

Bouchard, J. F. 1987. La Métallurgie. In *Ancien Pérou: Vie, Porvoir et Mort*, edited by Marie-France Fauvet and Danielle Lavallée, pp. 127–36. Paris: Editions Fernand Nathan.

Bray, Tamara. 2000. Inca iconography: the art of empire. *Res* 38: 168–78.

Bridges, Barbara A. 1984. *Lithic Artifacts from Machu Picchu, Peru: A Discussion of Their Form, Function, and Forerunners.* Unpublished M.A. thesis, Archaeological Studies, Yale University.

Burger, Richard L. 1992. *Chavín and the Origins of Andean Civilization.* London: Thames and Hudson Ltd.

Burger, Richard L., and Frank Asaro. 1979. Análisis de rasgos significativos en la obsidiana de los Andes Centrales. *Revista del Museo Nacional* 43: 281–325.

Burger, Richard L., Frank Asaro, Guido Salas, and Fred Stross. 1998a. The Chivay Obsidian Source and the Geological Origin of Titicaca Basin Type Obsidian Artifacts. *Andean Past* 5: 208–23.

Burger, Richard L., Frank Asaro, Paul Trawick, and Fred Stross. 1998b. The Alca Obsidian Source: The Origin of Raw Material for Cuzco Type Obsidian Artifacts. *Andean Past* 5: 185–202.

Burger, Richard L., and Michael Glascock. 2000. Locating the Quispisisa Obsidian Source in the Department of Ayacucho, Peru. *Latin American Antiquity* 11(3): 258–69.

Burger, Richard L., Julia Lee-Thorp, and Nikolaas Van der Merwe. 2003. Rite and Crop Revisited: An Isotopic Perspective from Machu Picchu and Beyond. In *The 1912 Yale Peruvian Scientific Expedition Collections from Machu Picchu: Human and Animal Remains*, edited by Richard L. Burger and Lucy C. Salazar, pp. 119–37. New Haven: Yale University Publications in Anthropology 85.

Burger, Richard L., Karen L. Mohr Chavez, and Sergio J. Chavez. 2000. Through the Glass Darkly: Prehispanic Obsidian Procurement and Exchange in Southern Peru and Northern Bolivia. *Journal of World Prehistory* 14(3): 267–362.

Burger, Richard L., and Lucy Salazar-Burger. 1993. Machu Picchu Rediscovered: The Royal Estate in the Cloud Forest. *Discovery* 24(2): 20–25.

Burger, Richard L., Katharina Schreiber, Michael D. Glascock, and José Ccencho. 1998c. The Jampatilla Obsidian Source: Identifying the Geological Source of Pampas Type Obsidian Artifacts from Southern Peru. *Andean Past* 5: 225–39.

Burger, Richard L., and Nikolaas Van der Merwe. 1990. Maize and the Origin of Highland Chavin Civilization: An Isotopic Approach. *American Anthropologist* 92(1): 85–95.

Buse, Hermann. 1978. *Machu Picchu*. Lima: Librería Studium.

Carrión Cachot, Rebecca. 1955. El culto de agua en el antiguo Perú. La paccha, elemento cultural panandino. *Revista del Museo Nacional* 2(2): 50–140.

Cieza de León, Pedro. 1976 [1554]. *Crónica del Perú. Primera y Segunda Parte*, edited by Franklin Pease. Lima: Universidad Católica del Perú.

Cobo, Bernabé. 1964 [1653]. *Historia del Nuevo Mundo*. In *Obras del P. Bernabé Cobo de la Compañia de Jesus*. P. Francisco Mateos. Biblioteca de Autores Españoles, vols. 91 and 92. Madrid: Ediciones Atlas.

——. 1979 [1653]. *History of the Inca Empire*. Translated and edited by Roland B. Hamilton. Austin: University of Texas Press.

——. 1987 [1653]. *Historia del Nuevo Mundo*. Biblioteca de Auotores Españoles. Tomos 91–92. Madrid.

——. 1990 [1653]. *Inca Religion and Customs*. Translated and edited by Roland B. Hamilton. Austin: University of Texas Press.

Coe, Sophie. 1994. *America's First Cuisines*. Austin: University of Texas Press.

Cook, O. F. 1918. Peru as a Center of Domestication. *Journal of Heredity* 16(3): 95–110.

Cornejo, Luis E. 2001. Los Inka y sus aliados Diaguita en el extremo austral de Tawantinsuyu. In *Tras la Huella del Inka en Chile*, edited by Carlos Aldunate and Luis Cornejo, pp. 74–125. Santiago: Museo Chileno de Arte Peruano.

Cummins, Thomas. 2002. *Toasts with the Incas: Andean Abstraction and Colonial Images on Quero Vessels*. Ann Arbor: Univesity of Michigan.

Curatola, Marco. 2001. Adivinación, oráculos y civilización andina. In *Los Dioses del Antiguo Perú*, Tomo 2, edited by Krzysztof Makowski, pp. 223–47. Lima: Banco de Crédito.

D'Altroy, Terence N. 1992. *Provincial Power in the Inka Empire*. Washington, D.C.: Smithsonian Institution Press.

——. 2002. *The Incas*. London: Blackwell.

Dearborn, David, and Katharina Schreiber. 1986a. Here Comes the Sun: The Cuzco-Machu Picchu Connection. *Archaeoastronomy, Journal for the History of Astronomy* 9: 15–37.

——. 1986b. Houses of the Rising Sun. In *Time and Calendars in the Inca Empire*, edited by M. S. Ziollkowski and R. M. Sadowski, pp. 49–75. BAR International Series 454. Oxford: BAR.

Dearborn, David S. P., Katharina Schreiber, and Raymond White. 1987. Intimachay, a December Solstice Observatory. *American Antiquity* 52: 346–52.

Dearborn, David, and Raymond White. 1982. Archaeoastronomy at Machu Picchu. In *Ethnoastronomy and Archaeoastronomy in the American Tropics*, edited by Anthony Aveni and Gary Urton, pp. 249–59. *Annals of the New York Academy of Sciences*, vol. 285. New York: New York Academy of Sciences.

——. 1983. The "Torreón" at Machu Picchu as an Observatory. *Archaeoastronomy, Journal for the History of Astronomy* 5: S37–S49.

de Lavalle, José Antonio. 1988. *Chimu*. Colección Arte y Tesoros del Perú. Lima: Banco de Crédito en la Cultra.

de Lavalle, José, and Werner Lang. 1978. *Arte Precolombino. Segunda Parte. Escultura y Diseño*. Lima: Banco de Crédito del Perú.

DeNiro, M. J., and Christine Hastorf. 1985. Alteration of 13C/12C and 15N/14N Ratios of Plant Matter during the Initial Stages of Diagenesis: Studies Utilizing Archaeological Specimens from Peru. *Geochimica et Cosmochimica Acta* 49: 97–115.

Disselhoff, Hans-Dietrich. 1967. *Daily Life in Ancient Peru*. New York: McGraw-Hill.

Donnan, Christopher. 1992. *Ceramics of Ancient Peru*. Los Angeles: University of California, Fowler Museum of Cultural History.

Doyle, Mary E. 1988. The Ancestor Cult and Burial Ritual in Seventeenth- and Eighteenth-Century Central Peru. Ph.D. dissertation, University of California, Los Angeles. Ann Arbor, Mich.: University Microfilms.

Eaton, George. 1912. Notes on Yale Peruvian Expedition, Folders 14–26, Yale University Archives, Sterling Memorial Library, Yale University, New Haven.

——. 1916. *The Collection of Osteological Material from Machu Picchu: Memoirs of the Connecticut Academy of Arts and Sciences*, vol. 5. New Haven: Yale University Press.

Erdis, Ellwood. 1912. Unpublished Yale Peruvian Expedition Papers: Journal. Yale University Archives, Sterling Memorial Library, Yale University, New Haven.

Espinoza Soriano, Waldemar. 1978. Los Chachapoyas y Cañares de Chiara (Huamanga), aliados de España. *Historia, Problema y Promesa*, pp. 231–53. Lima: Pontificia Universidad Católica.

Fane, Diana. 1996. *Converging Cultures: Art and Identity in Spanish America*. New York: Brooklyn Museum with Harry N. Abrams.

Farrington, I. S. 1995. The Mummy Palace and Estate of Inka Huayna Capac at Quispeguanca. *Tawantinsuyu* 1: 55–65.

Fauvet-Berthelot, Marie-France, and Lavallée, Daniéle. 1987. *Ancien Pérou. Vie, Pourvenir et Mort*. Paris: Editions Fernand Nathan.

Flores Ochoa, Jorge. 1996. Buscando los espíritus del Ande: Turismo místico en el Qosqo. *La Tradición en Tiempos Modernos*. Senri Ethnological Reports 5: 9–29. Edited by Hiroyasu Tomoeda and Luis Millones. Osaka: National Museum of Ethnology.

——. 2000. En el principio fue el inka: El ciclo del Inti Raymi cuzqueño. *Desde Adentro y Desde Afuera*. Senri Etnological Reports 18: 123–47. Edited by Luis Millones and Hiroyasu Tomoeda. Osaka: National Museum of Ethnology.

Flores Ochoa, Jorge, Elibabeth Kuon Arce, and Roberto Samanez Argumedo. 1998. *Qeros. Arte Inka en Vasos Ceremoniales*. Lima: Banco de Crédito del Perú.

Foote, H. W., and W. H. Buell. 1912. The Composition, Structure and Hardness of Some Peruvian Bronze Axes. *American Journal of Science* 34: 128–32.

Galiano Sanchez, Washington. 2000. *Situación Ecológico-ambiental del Santuario Histórico de Machupiqcchu: Una Aproximación*. Cuzco: Programa Machu Picchu.

Garcilaso de la Vega, Inca. 1958 (1609). *Royal Commentaries of the Incas and General History of Peru.* Translated with an introduction by Harold V. Livermore. Austin: University of Texas Press.

Gasparini, Graziano, and Louise Margolies. 1980. *Inca Architecture,* translated by Patricia J. Lyon. Bloomington: Indiana University Press.

González Holguín, Diego. 1952. Vocabulario de la lengua general de todo el Peru llamada lengua qquichua o del inca [1608]. Edited by Raul Porras Barrenechea. Lima: Universidad Nacional Mayor de San Marcos.

Gordon, Robert B. 1984. Metallurgy of Bronze Tools from Machu Picchu. *Proceedings of the 24th International Archaeometry Symposium,* edited by J. S. Olin and J. J. Blackman, pp. 233–42. Smithsonian Institution, Washington, D.C.

———. 1985. Laboratory Evidence of the Use of Metal Tools at Machu Picchu (Peru) and Environs. *Journal of Archaeological Science* 12: 311–27.

———. 1986. Metallurgy of Bronze Tools from Machu Picchu. *Proceedings of the 24th International Archaeometry Symposium,* edited by J. S. Olin and M. J. Blackman, pp. 233–41. Washington, D.C.: Smithsonian Institution.

Gordon, Robert B., and John W. Rutledge. 1984. Bismuth Bronze from Machu Picchu, Peru. *Science* 223: 585–86.

Greenwood, David J. 1991. La cultura por kilos: Una perspectiva antropológica del turismo como una forma de mercaderización de la cultura. *Tinkuy: Antropología del Turismo* no. 11–20. Cuzco: CEAC.

Guaman Poma de Ayala, Felipe. 1980. *Primera Nueva Crónica y Buen Gobierno.* Mexico: Siglo Veintiuno Editores.

Hastorf, Christine. 1990. The effect of the Inka state on Sausa agricultural production and crop consumption. *American Antiquity* 55(2): 262–90.

Hastorf, Christine, and Sissel Johannessen. 1993. Pre-Hispanic Political Change and the Role of Maize in the Central Andes of Peru. *American Anthropology* 95: 115–38.

Helms, Mary W. 1998. *Access to Origins: Affines Ancestors and Aristocrats.* Austin: University of Texas Press.

Hemming, John. 1981. *Machu Picchu.* New York: Newsweek.

Heyerdahl, Thor, Daniel H. Sandweiss, and Alfredo Narvaez. 1995. *Pyramids of Tucume: The Quest for Perú's Forgotten City.* London: Thames and Hudson.

Horkheimer, Hans and Federico Kauffmann Doig. 1965. *La Cultura Incaica.* Lima: Imprenta Peruano Suizo.

Huaycochea Núñez de la Torre, Flor. 1994. *Qollqas. Bancos de Reserva Andinos.* Cuzco: Universidad Nacional de San Antonio Abad del Cuzco.

Idrovo, Jaime. 2000. *Tomebamba. Arqueología e Historia de una Ciudad Imperial.* Cuenca: Ediciones del Banco Central del Ecuador.

Isbell, Billie Jean. 1978. *To Defend Ourselves: Ecology and Ritual in an Andean Village.* Austin: University of Texas Press.

Jimenez Borja, Arturo. 1996. *Máscaras Peruanas.* Lima: Fundación Banco Continental.

Jones, Julie. 1964. *Art of Empire: The Inca of Peru.* New York: Museum of Primitive Art.

Joyce, Thomas A. 1912. *South American Archaeology.* New York: G. P. Putnam's Sons.

Julien, Catherine J. 1998. La metáfora de la montaña. *Qollana. Informe Especial* no. 6: 4–7. Cuzco.

———. 2000. *Reading Inca History.* Iowa City: University of Iowa Press.

Kendall, Ann. 1974. Architecture and Planning at the Inca Sites in the Cusichaca Area. *Baessler Archive Beiträge zur Völkerkunde,* n.s. 24: 41–159. Berlin.

———. 1985. *Aspects of Inca Architecture: Description, Function, and Chronology,* 2 vols. BAR International Series 242. Oxford: BAR.

King, Heidi. 2000. *Rain of the Moon: Silver in Ancient Peru.* New York: The Metropolitan Museum of Art.

Koloski, Daniel S. 1996. *Not Just the Knots: Decompressing the Data Held in Two Andean Quipu.* New Haven: Unpublished Senior Essay, Department of Anthropology, Yale College.

LaFarge, Henry, ed. 1981. *Museums of the Andes.* Tokyo: Kodansha, Ltd.

Laurencich, Laura, ed. 2000. *The Inca World: The Development of Pre-Columbian Peru, A.D. 1000–1534.* Norman: University of Oklahoma Press.

Lechtman, Heather. 1980. The Central Andes — Metallurgy without Iron. In *Coming of the Age of Iron,* edited by T. A. Wertime and J. D. Muhly, pp. 267–334. New Haven: Yale University Press.

———. 1993. Technologies of Power — The Andean Case. In *Configurations of Power in Complex Society,* edited by John Henderson and Patricia Netherly, pp. 244–80. Ithaca, N.Y.: Cornell University Press.

———. 1996a. El Bronze y el Horizonte Medio. *Boletín, Museo del Oro* 41: 2–25. Bogotá.

———. 1996b. Inca: Technical Analysis. In *Andean Art of Dumbarton Oaks,* edited by Elizabeth Boone, pp. 301–20. Washington, D.C.: Dumbarton Oaks.

———. 1997. El bronce arsenical y el Horizonte Medio. In *Arqueología, Antropología e Historia en los Andes: Homenaje a María Rostworowski,* edited by Rafael Varón y Javier Flores, pp. 153–86. Lima: Instituto de Estudios Peruanos.

LeVine, Terry Y., ed. 1992. *Inka Storage Systems.* Norman: University of Oklahoma Press.

Levenson, Jay A., ed. 1992. *Circa 1492: Art in the Age of Exploration.* New Haven: Yale University Press.

Levillier, Roberto. 1940. Informaciones de Toledo. In *Don Francisco de Toledo*, vol. 2. Buenos Aires: Espasa-Calpe.

Longato, Renato. 1991. Perú centro magnético. *Gnosis. Revista de Esoterismo Iniciativo* no. 5: 25, Qosqo.

Longhena, Maria, and Walter Alva. 1999. *The Incas and Other Andean Civilizations*. San Diego: Thunder Bay Press.

Lothrop, Samuel. 1938. Inca treasure as depicted by Spanish historians. *Publications of the Frederick Webb Hodge Anniversary Publication Fund* vol. 2, Los Angeles.

Lumbreras, Luis G. 1974. *The Peoples and Cultures of Ancient Peru*. Washington, D.C.: Smithsonian Institution Press.

———. 1975. *Guía de Arqueología Peruana*. Lima: Editorial Milla Batres.

Mackey, Carol. 1990. Comparación entre quipu inca y quipos modernos. In *Quipu y Yupana: Colección de escritos*, edited by Carol Mackey, pp. 135–56. Lima: Consejo Nacional de Ciencia y Tecnología.

———, ed. 1990. *Quipu y Yupana: Colección de escritos*. Lima: Consejo Nacional de Ciencia y Tecnología.

MacLean, Margaret G. 1986. *Sacred Land, Sacred Water: Inca Landscape Planning in the Cuzco Area*. Unpublished Ph.D. dissertation, Department of Anthropology, University of California, Berkeley. Ann Arbor: Michigan Microfilms International.

Mathewson, C. H. 1915. A Metallographic Description of Some Ancient Peruvian Bronzes from Machu Picchu. *American Journal of Science* 40: 525–616.

Matos, Ramiro. 2000. La Cerámica Inca. In *Los Incas: Arte y Símbolo*, pp. 109–67. Lima: Banco de Crédito.

Mayer, Eugen Friedrich. 1994. *Vorspanishe Metallwaffen und Werkzeuge in Boliven*. Bonn: AVA Materialien Band 53. Kommission für Allgemeinen und Vergleichende Archäologie des Deutschen Archäologischen Instituts.

McEwan, Colin, and Maarten Van de Guchte. 1992. Ancestral Time and Sacred Space in Inca State Rituals. In *The Ancient Americas: Art from Sacred Landscapes*, edited by Richard Townsend, pp. 359–71. Chicago: The Art Institute of Chicago.

Meddens, Frank. 1994. Mountains, Miniatures, Ancestors, and Fertility: The Meaning of a Late Horizon Offering in a Middle Horizon Structure in Peru. *Institute of Archaeology Bulletin* vol. 31, pp. 127–50.

Menzel, Dorothy. 1977. *The Archaeology of Ancient Peru and the Work of Max Uhle*. Berkeley: University of California.

Miller, George R. 2003. Food for the Dead, Tools for the Afterlife: Zooarchaeology at Machu Picchu. In *The 1912 Yale Peruvian Scientific Expedition Collections from Machu Picchu: Human and Animal Remains*, edited by Richard L. Burger and Lucy C. Salazar, pp. 1–63. Yale University Publications in Anthropology 85.

Miller, George R., and Richard L. Burger. 1995. Our Father the Cayman, Our Dinner the Llama: Animal Utilization at Chavín de Huántar, Peru. *American Antiquity* 60(3): 421–58.

Molina, Cristóbal de. 1916 [1573]. Relación de las Fábulas y Ritos de los Incas. *Colección de Libros y Documentos referentes a la Historia del Perú*. Tomo I, edited by Carlos Romero. Lima.

Morris, Craig. 1992. Signs of division, symbols of unity: Art in the Inka empire. In *Circa 1492: Art in the Age of Exploration*, edited by Jay A. Levenson, pp. 521–28. New Haven: Yale University Press.

Morris, Craig, and Adriana von Hagen. 1993. *The Inca Empire and Its Andean Origins*. New York: Abbeville Press.

Morris, Craig, and Donald E. Thompson. 1985. *Huánuco Pampa: An Inca City and Its Hinterland*. London: Thames and Hudson.

Mountain Institute, The. 1998. *Sacred Mountains and Environmental Conservation*. Franklin, West Virginia.

Muelle, Jorge. 1940. Espejos precolombinos del Perú. *Revista del Museo Nacional* 9(1): 5–12.

Murra, John. 1960. Rite and Crop in the Inca State. In *Culture in History*, edited by Stanley Diamond, pp. 393–407. New York: Columbia University Press.

———. 1962. Cloth and Its Function in the Inca State. *American Anthropologist* 64: 710–28.

———. 1990. Las etno-categorías de un Quipu regional. In *Quipu y Yupana: Colección de escritos*, edited by Carol Mackey, pp. 53–58. Lima: Consejo Nacional de Ciencias y Tecnología.

Niles, Susan A. 1987. *Callachaca: Style and Status in an Inca Community*. Iowa City: University of Iowa Press.

———. 1988. Looking for "Lost" Inca Palaces. *Expedition* 30(3): 56–64.

———. 1992. Inca Architecture and Sacred Landscape. In *The Ancient Americas: Art from Sacred Landscapes*, edited by Richard Townsend, pp. 347–57. Chicago: The Art Institute of Chicago.

———. 1999. *The Shape of Inca History: Narrative and Architecture in an Andean Empire*. Iowa City: University of Iowa Press.

———. 2001. Deception in Inca Architecture. Paper presented to the 41st Annual Meeting of the Institute of Andean Studies.

Niles, Susan A., and Robert N. Batson. 1999. Spud Huts and Bean Barns: New Views of Inca Storage. Paper presented to the 39th Annual Meeting of the Institute of Andean Studies.

Olsen, Dale A. 2002. *Music of El Dorado: The Ethnomusicology of Ancient South American Cultures*. Gainesville: University Press of Florida.

Owen, Bruce. 1986. The Role of Common Metal Objects in the Inka State. M.A. dissertation in Anthropology, University of California, Los Angeles.

Pardo, Luis. 1957. *Historia y Arqueología de Cuzco.* 2 vols. Lima: Imprenta Colegio Militar Leoncio Prado.

Pearsall, Deborah M. 1994. Issues in the Analysis and Interpretation of Archaeological Maize in South America. In *Corn and Culture in the Prehistoric New World*, edited by Sissel Johannsen and Christine Hastorf, pp. 245–72. Boulder, Colo.: Westview Press.

Pizarro, Pedro. 1978 [1571]. *Relación del Descubrimiento y Conquista del Perú*, edited by Guillermo Lohmann Villena. Lima: Pontifícia Universidad Católica del Perú.

Plowman, Timothy. 1986. Coca chewing and the botanical origins of coca (*Erythroxylum* spp.) in South America. In *Coca and Cocaine: Effects of People and Policy in Latin America*, edited by Deborah Pacini and Christine Franquemont, pp. 5–33. Cultural Survival Report 23. Cambridge, Mass.

Polo, de Ondegardo. 1916 [1571]. Informaciones acerca de la Religión y Gobierno de los Incas. *Colección de Libros y Documentos referentes a la Historia del Perú.* Tomo II, edited by Carlos Romero. Lima.

Protzen, Jean-Pierre. 1993. *Inca Architecture and Construction at Ollantaytambo.* New York: Oxford University Press.

Purin, Sergio. 1990. *Inca-Peru: 3000 Ans D'Histoire.* Belgium: Imschoot, uitgerers.

Quilter, Jeffrey, and Gary Urton, editors. 2002. *Narrative Threads: Accounting and Recounting in Andean Khipus.* Austin: University of Texas Press.

Ravines, Rogger, and Fernando Villiger. 1989. *La Cerámica Tradicional del Peru.* Lima: Editorial Los Pinos.

Reinhard, Johan. 1985. Sacred Mountains: An Ethnoarchaeological Study of High Andean Ruins. *Mountain Research and Development* 5(4): 299–317.

——. 1991. *Machu Picchu: The Sacred Center.* Lima: Nuevas Imágenes.

Reinhard, Johan, and Constanza Ceruti. 2000. *Investigaciones Arqueológicas en el Volcán Llullaillaco. Complejo Ceremonial Incaico de Alta Montaña.* Salta: Ediciones Universidad Católica de Salta.

Rostworowski, María. 1970. El repartimiento de Doña Beatriz Coya en el Valle de Yucay. *Historia y Cultura*, no. 4: 153–267. Lima

Rowe, Ann. 1977. Technical Features of Inca Tapestry Tunics. *Textile Museum Journal* vol. 17, pp. 5–28.

——. 1984. *Costumes and Featherwork of the Lords of Chimor. Textiles from Peru's North Coast.* Washington, D.C.: The Textile Museum.

Rowe, John Howland. 1944. *An Introduction to the Archaeology of Cuzco.* Papers of the Peabody Museum of American Archaeology and Ethnology, vol. 27, no. 2. Cambridge, Mass.: Harvard University.

——. 1946. *Inca Culture at the Time of the Spanish Conquest: Handbook of South American Indians*, edited by Julian Steward, vol. 2, pp. 183–330. Washington D.C.: U.S. Government Printing Office.

——. 1960. The Origin of Creator Worship Among the Incas. In *Culture in History: Essays in Honor of Paul Radin*, edited by Stanley Diamond, pp. 408–29. New York: Columbia University.

——. 1961. The Chronology of Inca Wooden Cups. In *Essays in Pre-Columbian Art History and Archaeology*, edited by Samuel Lothrop, pp. 317–41. Cambridge: Harvard University Press.

——. 1979. Standardization in Inca Tapestry Tunics. In *The Junius B. Bird Pre-Columbian Textile Conference*, edited by A. Rowe, E. Benson, and A. Shaffer, pp. 239–64. Washington, D.C.: Dumbarton Oaks, 1996.

——. 1982. Inca Policies and Institutions Relating to the Cultural Unification of the Empire. In *The Inca and Aztec States 1400–1800: Anthropology and History*, edited by George A. Collier, Renato I. Rosaldo, and John D. Wirth. New York: Academic Press.

——. 1987a. Machu Picchu a la luz de los documentos del siglo XVI. *Kuntur* no. 4, pp. 12–20. Lima.

——. 1987b. Pachacuti's Royal Estate of Machu Picchu. Lecture presented at the Annual Meeting of the Institute of Andean Studies.

——. 1990. Machu Picchu: A la luz de documentos del siglo XVI. *Histórica* 14(1): 139–54.

——. 1996. Inca. In *Andean Art at Dumbarton Oaks*, edited by Elizabeth Boone, pp. 301–20. Washington, D.C.: Dumbarton Oaks.

Rowe, John, and Ann Rowe. 1996. Inca Tunics. In *Andean Art at Dumbarton Oaks*, edited by Elizabeth Boone, vol. 2, pp. 453–65. Washington D.C.: Dumbarton Oaks.

Rutledge, John. 1984. *The Metal Artifacts from the Yale Peruvian Expedition of 1912, Catalogue and Commentary.* Unpublished Master Thesis. Yale University: Archaeological Studies Program.

Rutledge, John W., and Robert Gordon. 1987. The Work of Metallurgical Artificers at Machu Picchu, Peru. *American Antiquity* 52(3): 578–94.

Salazar, Diego, Carolina Jimenez, and Paulina Corrales. 2001. Minería y metalurgia: del cosmos a la tierra, de la tierra al Inka. In *Tras la Huella del Inka en Chile*, edited by Carlos Aldunate and Luis Cornejo, pp. 61–73. Santiago: Museo Chileno de Arte Precolombino.

Salazar, Lucy C. 1997a. Una revaluación de las Tumbas de Machu Picchu Excavadas por la Expedición Científica de la Universidad de Yale, 1912. Paper presented at the 49th Internacional Congress of Americanistes, Quito, Ecuador, July 1997.

——. 1997b. Machu Picchu's Silent Majority: A Consideration of the Inca Cemeteries. Paper presented at the symposium "Variations in the Expression of Inka Power," organized by Dumbarton Oaks Precolumbian Studies, Washington, D.C., October 1997.

——. 2000. Inca Religion and the Political Power of Sacred Space: Machu Picchu's Pachacuti Country Palace. Paper presented at the 50th Internacional Congress of Americanistes, Warsaw, Poland, July 2000.

——. 2001a. Inca Religion and Mortuary Ritual at Machu Picchu. In *Mortuary Practices & Ritual Associations: Shamanic Elements in Pre-Columbian Funerary Contexts in South America*, edited by Elizabeth J. Currie and John Staller, pp. 117–27. Oxford: BAR International Series, Archaeological and Historical Associates Limited.

——. 2001b. Ritual, Politics, Death and Power at Machu Picchu. Unpublished M.A. thesis, Archaeological Studies, Yale University.

Salazar, Lucy C., and Richard L. Burger. 2003. The Lifestyle of the Rich and Famous: Luxury and Daily Life in the Households of Machu Picchu's Elite. In *Ancient Palaces of the New World: Form, Function and Meaning*, edited by Susan Evans and Joan Pillsbury. Washington, D.C.: Dumbarton Oaks Research Library and Collection.

Salazar, Lucy C., and Vuka Roussakis. 2000. Tejidos y Tejedores del Tawantinsuyu. In *Los Incas: Arte y Símbolos*, pp. 269–303. Lima: Banco de Crédito.

Salomon, Frank. 1996. "The beautiful Grandparents": Andean Ancestor Shrines and Mortuary Ritual as Seen Through Colonial Records. In *Tombs for the Living: Andean Mortuary Practices*, edited by Tom D. Dillehay. Washington, D.C.: Dumbarton Oaks Research Library and Collection.

Sánchez Macedo, Marino Orlando. 1977. Estudios Arqueólogicos en uno de los centros cremoniales del sitio de Machu Picchu. Unpublished thesis. Licenciatura en Antropología, Dirección de los Programas Académicos de Ciencias Sociales. Cuzco: Universidad Nacional San Antonio Abad del Cusco.

Santillana, Julian I. 2000. Andenes, Canales y Paisaje. In *Los Incas: Arte y Símbolos*, pp. 61–107. Lima: Banco de Crédito.

Sarmiento de Gamboa, Pedro. 1943 [1572]. *Historia de los incas*, 2d edition, Buenos Aires: Emecé.

——. 1960 [1572]. *Historia índica*. Biblioteca de Autores Españoles, vol. 135, pp. 193–279. Madrid: Ediciones Atlas.

Sawyer, Alan. 1975. *Ancient Andean Arts in the Collection of the Krannert Art Museum*. Champaign-Urbana, Ill.: Krannert Art Museum.

Schindler, Helmut. 2000. *The Norbert Mayrock Art Collection from Ancient Peru*. Munich: Staatliches Museum fur Volkerkunde.

Schjellerup, Inge. 1985. *Chimu Pottery*. Herning: The National Museum of Denmark.

Schobinger, Juan, compiler (compilador). 2001. *El Santuario Incaico del Cerro Aconcagua*. Mendoza, Argentina: Editorial de la Universidad Nacional de Cuyo.

Stierlin, Henri. 1984. *Art of the Incas and Its Origins*. New York: AMS Press.

Stinson, Sara. 1990. Variation in Body Size and Shape among South American Indians. *American Journal of Biology* 2: 37–51.

Stone-Miller, Rebecca, ed. 1992. *To Weave for the Sun: Ancient Andean Textiles*. London: Thames and Hudson Ltd.

——. 2002. *Seeing with New Eyes: Highlights of the Michael C. Carlos Museum of Art of the Ancient Americas*. Emory, Atlanta: Michael C. Carlos Museum.

Thompson, L. G., E. Mosley-Thompson, W. Dansgaard, and P. M. Grootes. 1986. The Little Ice Age as Recorded in the Stratigraphy of the Tropical Quelccaya Ice Cap. *Science* 234(4774): 361–64.

Thompson, L. G., E. Mosley-Thompson, and B. M. Morales. 1988. One-half Millennia of Tropical Climate Variability as Recorded in the Stratigraphy of the Quelccaya Ice Cap, Peru. *Geophysics Monograph* 55: 15–31.

Topic, John R., and Theresa Lange Topic. 1997. *Arqueología, Antropología e Historia en los Andes. Homenaje a María Rostworowski*, edited by Rafael Varón and Javier Flores, pp. 567–90. Lima: Instituto de Estudio Peruanos.

Torres Della Pina, José, ed. 2000. *Plata. Transformación en el Arte Precolombino del Perú*. Lima: Patronato Plata del Perú.

Towle, Margaret. 1961. *The Ethnobotany of Pre-Columbian Peru*. Viking Fund Publications in Anthropology 30. New York: Wenner-Gren Foundation for Anthropological Research.

Townsend, Richard, ed. 1992. *The Ancient Americas: Art from Sacred Landscapes*. Chicago: The Art Institute of Chicago.

Uhle, Max. 1903. *Pachacamac*. Philadelphia: The Department of Archaeology of the University of Pennsylvania.

Urton, Gary. 1981. *At the Crossroads of the Earth and Sky*. Austin: University of Texas Press.

——. 1982. Report on Fieldwork in Pacariqtambo, Peru. *Archaeoastronomy* 5(4): 20–21.

——. 1990. *The History of a Myth: Pacariqtambo and the Origin of the Inkas*. Austin: University of Texas Press.

——. 1995. A New Twist in an Old Yarn: Variation in Knot Directionality in the Inca Khuipus. *Baesseler Archiv*, Neue Folge, Band XLII: 1–35.

Valencia Zegarra, Alfredo, and Arminda Gibaja. 1992. *Machu

Picchu: La Investigación y Conservación del Monumento Arqueológico después de Hiram Bingham. Cuzco: Municipalidad de Qosqo.

Verano, John. 2003. Human Skeletal Remains from Machu Picchu: A Reexamination of the Peabody Museum's Collections from the Peruvian Expedition of 1912. In *The 1912 Yale Peruvian Scientific Expedition Collections from Machu Picchu: Human and Animal Remains,* edited by Richard L. Burger and Lucy C. Salazar, pp. 65–117. Yale University Publications in Anthropology 85.

Villanueva Urteaga, Horacio. 1971. Documentos sobre Yucay en el siglo XVI. *Revista del Archivo Histórico del Cuzco* 13(1970): 1–148.

Wachtel, Nathan. 1982. The mitimas of the Cochabamba Valley: The colonization policy of Huayna Capac. In *The Inca and Aztec States 1400–1800,* edited by George Collier, Renato Rosaldo, and John Wirth, pp. 199–235. New York: Academic Press.

Willey, Gordon. 1974. *Das Alte America.* Berlin: Propylaen Verlag.

Wright, Kenneth R., C. Crowley, S. A. Marshall. 1999. *Archaeological Map of the Inca Trail on the East Flank of Machu Picchu.* Denver, Colo.: Wright Paleohydrological Institute.

Wright, Kenneth R., Jonathan M. Kelly, and Alfredo Valencia Zegarra. 1997c. Machu Picchu: Ancient Hydraulic Engineering. *Journal of Hydraulic Engineering* 123(10): 858–43.

Wright, Kenneth R., and Alfredo Valencia Zegarra. 2000. *Machu Picchu: A Civil Engineering Marvel.* Reston, Va.: ASCE Press.

Wright, Kenneth R., A. Valencia Zegarra, and C. Crowley. 2000. *Archaeological Exploration of the Inca Trail, East Flank of Machu Picchu and Palynology of Terraces.* Final Report, Instituto Nacional de Cultura. Denver, Colo.: Wright Paleohydrological Institute.

Wright, Kenneth R., Gary D. Witt, and Alfredo Valencia Zegarra. 1997b. Hydrogeology and Paleohydrology of Ancient Machu Picchu. *Ground Water* 35(4): 660–66.

Wright, Kenneth R., M. Wright, M. E. Jensen, and Alfredo Valencia Zegarra. 1997a. Machu Picchu: Ancient Agricultural Potential. *Applied Engineering in Agriculture* 13(1): 39–47.

Xérez, Francisco de. 1968 [1534]. Verdadera Relación de la Conquista del Perú y Provincia del Cuzco Llamada la Nueva Castilla. In *Biblioteca Peruana: El Perú a través de los siglos,* primera serie, 1, 191–272. Lima: Editores Técnicos Asociados.

Zapata Rodriguez, Mohemi Julinho. 1983. *Investigación arqueológica en Machu Picchu. Sector Militar.* Tesis de Licenciatura en Antropología, Departamento Académico de Antropología Social y Arqueología. Cusco: Universidad Nacional San Antonio Abad.

Zuidema, Tom. 1977. The Inca Calendar. In *Native American Astronomy,* edited by Anthony Aveni, pp. 215–59. Austin: University of Texas Press.

Index